Afterimage

Film, Trauma, and the Holocaust

In the series

Emerging Media: History, Theory, Narrative
edited by Daniel Bernardi

Afterimage

Film, Trauma, and the Holocaust

Joshua Hirsch

TEMPLE UNIVERSITY PRESS
Philadelphia

Temple University Press, Philadelphia 19122
Copyright © 2004 by Temple University
All rights reserved
Published 2004
Printed in the United States of America

⊗The paper used in this publication meets the requirements of the American National
Standard for Information Sciences—Permanence of Paper for Printed Library Materials,
ANSI Z39.48-1984

Library of Congress Cataloging-in-Publication Data

Hirsch, Joshua Francis, 1962–
    Afterimage : film, trauma, and the Holocaust / Joshua Hirsch.
        p.   cm. — (Emerging media: history, theory, narrative)
    Includes bibliographical references and index.
    ISBN 1-59213-208-1 (cloth : alk. paper) — ISBN 1-59213-209-X (pbk. : alk. paper)
    1. Holocaust, Jewish (1939–1945), in motion pictures.   2. War films—History and criti-
cism.   I. Title.   II. Series.

PN1995.9.H53H57 2004
791.43'658—dc21   2003053131

2   4   6   8   9   7   5   3   1

To Éva, Ferencz, Imre, and László Hirsch
and to Sophia and Isaac Horwitz-Hirsch

Contents

Preface

IF SCHOLARSHIP can never be wholly objective, writing about the Holocaust presents the historian with a limit case of scholarly implication. One of the effects of the trauma constituted by genocide and concentration camps is that it continues to thrust upon those who encounter it in the present the subjectivities assumed by or forced upon the participants in the events of the past. What reference to the Holocaust is not marked by an identification with the position of victim, perpetrator, collaborator, bystander, resister, or one of the many shades in between?

My own identification with the victim position must have begun earlier than I can remember. In 1944, at the age of sixteen, my father was deported with his family from Hungary to Auschwitz. When he was liberated at Buchenwald in 1945, only one cousin remained from his extended family. No photograph remains to show that my grandparents, my uncle, and all the rest had ever existed. Their images existed only in my father's decaying memory. In fact, it was a struggle for him just to call up an image of his mother's face, and even then it was often the image of a photograph of her that he carried through the selection line at Auschwitz, and that a guard finally knocked from his hand.

For me, these absent images received a substitution from *Night and Fog*, which I was shown at my synagogue as a child. The image from that film of a bulldozer pushing a pile of emaciated bodies into a mass grave became the most vivid icon with which I visualized the Holocaust. I pictured the corpses and thought, "Jews, what we are." Preparing a paper on *Night and Fog* for a graduate seminar, I watched the film again on videotape. When the bulldozer scene appeared, I watched it over and over, trying to repress my feelings of horror in order to record the details. In my memory of seeing the film as a child, the bulldozer was a weapon driven by a Nazi. Viewing the film again, I realized the scene was shot after the liberation, and the bulldozer was probably driven by an Allied soldier. In any case, the driver never appears in frame.

This book began not with a theory or argument about what might be called—but uncomfortably—"Holocaust films," but with a series of encounters with individual films that seemed to articulate in one way or another a paradox that felt familiar to me: the paradox of trying to visualize and narrate a trauma that could not be captured in an image; of trying to remember an absence; of trying to represent the unrepresentable. I suppose the process of trying to understand these films is, among other things, my attempt to work through a set of childhood experiences that might be profitably condensed as that first viewing of *Night and Fog*.

What was it, what is it, about these films that leads one to try to understand them better? In *Night and Fog*, it was not only the shock of bulldozed corpses—the shock of the visible—but also the vague sense of a present haunted by something invisible, something only suggested by a ceaselessly moving camera, or a man's voice speaking a language I did not understand, but with a tone that nevertheless conveyed not the kind of alienating authority one had come to expect from traditional historical documentaries, but instead what François Truffaut called a "terrifying gentleness."[1]

The melancholy moving camera of *Night and Fog* returns with a vengeance in *Shoah*, driven along seemingly endless tracks toward and around the sites of death camps and rail lines. The camera is constantly moving in István Szabó's *25 Fireman Street* as well, restlessly weaving its way through the characters' dreams of loss.

In other films it is the characters who cannot stop moving, while the camera follows: Marceline, who can only recount her memories while walking alone through the streets of Paris in the documentary *Chronicle of a Summer*; Sol, trapped by his memories, wandering all night through the streets of New York in *The Pawnbroker*; Anni, in Szabó's *Father*, speaking of the difficulty of a Hungarian Jewish identity after the Holocaust, while walking along the Danube in Budapest where Jews were shot in 1944.[2]

There are the trains: deportation trains in archival footage in *Night and Fog*; old trains trundling through Poland for what seems like hours of screen time in *Shoah*; a New York City subway in *The Pawnbroker* leading to a flashback of a fictional deportation train; indeed, the whole story of *Love Film* revolves around a train voyage that triggers the protagonist's memories.

Often there are faces, held in long close-ups, speaking or trying to speak, struggling to reconcile language and memory—faces like canvases where the traces of memory and forgetting collide. I will argue that these films and moments can lead us to a posttraumatic cinema, a cinema that not only represents traumatic historical events, but also attempts to embody and reproduce the trauma for the spectator through its form of narration. Behind this argument, however, lies a more basic concern with a question of Holocaust memory: that it is essential for Western societies—those that lived through the events and were directly affected by them—to encounter the Holocaust in the deepest possible sense, to attempt to admit the Holocaust into their historical consciousness, whatever that encounter or admission might mean or whatever meaning it might shatter.[3] This is less a concern with forgetting or revisionism than a concern that we never adequately admitted the Holocaust in the first place, that the initial encounter with concentration camps and genocide was characterized by a moment of shock, only to be followed by a long period of denial—denial not of the facts (though the facts have been denied often enough as well) but of their existential significance. In recent years, the subject of the Holocaust has become almost ubiquitous in both mass culture and scholarship. Whether this phenomenon represents a significant encounter with the Holocaust is another question, but insofar as a struggle between denial and admission has taken place since the war, these films, I argue, have been important participants in that struggle.

This book does not attempt to survey the totality of the relationship between the Holocaust and the cinema, to catalogue the variety of Holocaust narratives or images in film, or to analyze contemporary media debates about Holocaust films (hereupon without quotes). Rather, it focuses on a particular set of questions that can be traced back to the moment in history when the cinema confronted genocide. It asks what particular problems the Holocaust has posed for the cinematic representation of history, and what particular opportunities the cinema has afforded for the representation of the Holocaust. And it explores the way this confrontation played out in a small number of paradigmatic documentary and fiction films, films that straddled the boundary between avant-garde and mainstream cinema, and that used the cultural techniques of modernism as a way of provoking a posttraumatic historical consciousness of the Holocaust.

A different approach to historical films—one that has played a significant role in debates about Holocaust films, but will figure here only marginally—focuses on their historical content narrowly defined, rather than on the broader questions of form that concern me here. By historical content, I mean that aspect of form that concerns the historical events and themes represented in films, in isolation from questions of cinematic representation itself. Considerations of content have been significant in much writing on Holocaust films insofar as questions of historical accuracy, revisionism, and denial have assumed tremendous moral weight in the historical consciousness of the Holocaust. While such considerations are necessary, however, they are not sufficient to address the less obvious ways in which films mediate historical consciousness— what Hayden White has called "the content of the form."[4]

Any text that addresses "the Holocaust" assumes a definition of that term, and thus enters into the debates about that definition. The term was used by Jews after the war to refer to the distinct Nazi effort to exterminate them, at a time when the distinctiveness of that effort was not well understood by the public. Because of my own identity and knowledge, most of the films emphasized here focus on the Jewish experience—most important among them, Shoah, The Pawnbroker, and the three films by István Szabó. While I believe it is necessary to continue to struggle for a historical consciousness of the distinctive nature of "the Final Solution of the Jewish Question," however, I also think it is necessary to remember that Jews, Communists, Soviet POWs, Poles, resisters, Gypsies, gay men, the "disabled," criminals, Jehovah's Witnesses, and others were thrown together by the common trauma of the Nazi camps. For me, it is necessary to avoid either of two traps: the anti-Jewish trap of denying the specificity of "the Final Solution," and the trap of allowing the memory of "the Final Solution" to isolate Jews from non-Jews and their own traumatic histories.[5] Night and Fog—a film written by a non-Jewish resister, with a leftist rather than a Jewish point of view on the camps, but which was nonetheless crucial to the subsequent development not only of posttraumatic cinema in general but also of the Jewish cinematic consciousness of the Holocaust—demonstrates the inextricable linkage of historical subjectivities in this cinematic history. This linkage extends further in Hiroshima, mon amour, which binds two distinct traumatic histories within two "theaters" of a single war, and which, without touching on the Holocaust, was also crucial to the subsequent development of Holocaust films. In the final chapter, this notion of the linkage of historical subjectivities will be emphasized to an even greater degree, as I will conclude with a discussion of *History and Memory: For Akiko and Takashige*, which is not about the Holocaust, but rather the internment of Japanese Americans in the United States during the Second World War.

There are difficulties inherent in any attempt to do scholarship on the Holocaust. Is there not a terrible contradiction in using academic rhetoric to write about the genocidal death and brutalization of human beings? Should a scholarly work advocating posttraumatic narration not practice what it preaches, and attempt a posttraumatic form of scholarship? What would such a form of scholarship look like? I considered making such an attempt here, but gave up the idea, unsure that the answer to the above question is *yes*, and faced, at any rate, with the adequate challenge of writing a "normal" book on the dissonant relationship between the "magic" of the movies and the horror of history.

Acknowledgments

COUNTLESS UCLA faculty, students, and staff helped me move this project through the dissertation phase. Nick Browne patiently saw me through many intellectual and practical crises. Robert Rosen was my guardian angel. Without the generosity and insights of Gyula Gazdag, I could not have written the chapter on István Szabó. Jim Friedman gave advice and support during the search for a publisher. Chon Noriega, Peter Wollen, Janet Bergstrom, Teshome Gabriel, Marina Goldovskaya, and Saul Friedlander also gave intellectual and professional support, as did many of the staff at the Department of Film and Television and at the Arts Library.

For discussion and feedback, thanks to Micah Kleit, Janet Walker, Deborah Lefkowitz, Yael Danieli, Pier Marton, Anton Kaes, and Jennifer Moore. István Szabó graciously allowed me to interview him. Suzanne Regan of the *Journal of Film and Video* offered kind words, and published my article on Szabó. Larry Wilcox and Peter Rollins included an article containing parts of the first two chapters in *Film and History*, and E. Ann Kaplan and Ban Wang are reprinting it in their forthcoming volume, *Trauma, Memory, and Modernity: Histories in Trans-National Media*. Bill Nichols and Sonja de Leeuw encouraged me to test out some ideas at the sixth Visible Evidence Conference in San Francisco in 1998. The students in my course on Film and the Holocaust at the University of California, Riverside provided excellent questions and ideas that helped me to clarify some of my arguments.

The UCLA Film and Television Archive, the Simon Wiesenthal Center, the National Center for Jewish Film, and the Hungarian Film Archive gave me access to films. Thanks to Zoe Burman, who shared her knowledge of archival footage of the Holocaust; Steve Varady, who kindly gave me access to his amazing collection of Hungarian tapes; and Bruce Cathcart, who gave generously of his time, knowledge, and equipment to produce stills for the book.

xv

Numerous people have gotten me through this project by giving love, companionship, discussion, child care, and money—and often just by listening: Elizabeth Hirsch, Frances Olan, Karen Wongking, Lillian Horwitz, Nathan Horwitz, Ann Horwitz, many family members and friends—and especially Ruth Horwitz, who has sustained me in the most profound sense, and sacrificed more than anyone.

Four individuals made special contributions that transcend the boundaries of the personal, the intellectual, and the professional. Daniel Bernardi's intellectual generosity and persistence made a tremendous difference in my original conception of the dissertation. His advice helped me through many a crisis, and he brought the book to Temple University Press. Lionel Joseph listened, read, shared his knowledge of trauma and his love of film, and fussed with great affection and humor. Zsuzsanna Ozsvath has been an ideal and compassionate mentor in my study of Hungarian history and culture. My father, James Hirsch, is on every page of this book. He is, in a sense, its co-author.

1 Introduction to Film, Trauma, and the Holocaust

OF THE mass murdering of more than ten million people in German concentration camps, extermination camps, POW camps, euthanasia centers, *Einsatzgruppe* actions, and Jewish ghettos during the Second World War, there is only one known piece of motion picture footage, lasting about two minutes.[1] It was shot in 1941 by Reinhard Wiener, a German naval sergeant and amateur cinematographer, stationed in Latvia, who had received permission from the navy to film in the area of the fleet. According to testimony given by Wiener in Israel in 1981, he had walked into the town of Liepaja one day in August of that year carrying his 8mm camera loaded with stock, as he did whenever possible, in case he saw something he wanted to film. He was walking in a wooded park near the beach when a soldier ran up to him and told him not to walk any farther, because something "awful, terrible" was happening there. Asked what it was, the man replied, "Well, they're killing Jews there."

At the time, there was a Jewish forced labor detachment assigned to the naval base, and Wiener had heard stories from some of these Jews about family members who had been rounded up and killed. In fact, Wiener had a Jew working for him personally, a technician who built him a "filming installation."

Told that Jews were being killed farther along the park, Wiener decided to go and see for himself. He came to a clearing where a group of German soldiers had gathered near a trench to watch the proceedings. When a truck arrived full of people wearing yellow patches on their chests and backs, he began filming. He recorded about two minutes of film, in which one can see people running into the pit and then being shot by a firing squad.

Wiener sent the undeveloped film to his family's farm in Germany, but it was inexplicably confiscated by German military police at the

Illustration 1.1. The Wiener film: of the mass murdering of more than ten million people by the Nazis, this is the only known piece of footage. Courtesy of Richard Trank, Executive Producer of Moriah Films, The Simon Wisenthal Center.

Latvian-Lithuanian border, and disappeared for four months. In the meantime, he was transferred to a submarine school in Germany, where he was able to get the film back. He then mailed the film to an Agfa plant, where it was processed and mailed back to him. It was about this time that Himmler outlawed the filming of any activities related to the extermination of Jews, which had begun in June with mobile killing actions by *Einsatzgruppe* units, such as the one seen in Wiener's film, and continued with gassing in special extermination camps starting in December.

Wiener testifies that he did not tell his family what he had witnessed. In 1942, however, in Germany, he did tell a few of his comrades in the navy. They did not believe him. Certain that the film would be confiscated if it was discovered at this time, he had six of his comrades swear an oath of silence, and then showed them the film. He describes their reaction. "They were depressed. I was observing their faces and saw how shocked they were. We had never seen or found out about anything like it in the navy. The same happened to me while I was filming, I was shivering all over, I was that agitated." Wiener again sent the film to the family farm, this time successfully. When the front reached the area in 1945 and his mother had to flee, she placed her son's films in a trunk and buried it in the pigsty, covering it with dung. After the war, Wiener returned to the farm and dug up the film. It was sent to the Yad Vashem Holocaust Memorial in Israel in 1974.[2]

Wiener's story and film will lead to a theory of cinema as both a transmitter of historical trauma and a form of posttraumatic historical memory. The subsequent chapters will examine a series of documentary and fiction films that made significant contributions to the development of a posttraumatic cinema of the Holocaust in Europe and the United States: primarily the documentaries, *Night and Fog* (France, 1955) and *Shoah* (France, 1985); the fiction film, *The Pawnbroker* (United States, 1965); and three autobiographical fiction films by the Hungarian filmmaker and Holocaust survivor, István Szabó—*Father* (1966), *Love Film* (1970), and *25 Fireman Street* (1973).[3] These films responded to the trauma of the Holocaust by rejecting the classical realist forms of film narration traditionally used to provide a sense of mastery over the past, and adopting instead modernist forms of narration that formally repeat the traumatic structure of the experience of witnessing the events themselves.

THE LIMITS OF HOLOCAUST CINEMA

There have been thousands of Holocaust films, and their variety has been virtually as wide as the variety of cinema itself. There have been, among other genres, compilation documentaries, cinéma vérité exposés, docudramas, melodramas, biographies, autobiographies, experimental films, Academy Award winners, slapstick comedies, horror films, and pornography. Accompanying these films have been debates in the media and academia about their historical accuracy, validity, and effects. Since the 1993 release of *Schindler's List*, the volume of production of Holocaust films, and of debates about them, has risen dramatically, at the same time that Steven Spielberg's Survivors of the Shoah Visual History Foundation has created a new cultural space of production, incorporating video, film, and digital forms.

Debates among philosophers and critics on the limits of Holocaust representation date most notably to 1949, when Theodor Adorno wrote his now famous dictum, "To write poetry after Auschwitz is barbaric."[4] The question of the limits of the cinematic representation of the Holocaust in particular was first catapulted into public discourse with the 1978 broadcast of the television miniseries *Holocaust* in the United States.[5] The series itself was instrumental in bringing the historical memory of the Jewish genocide into the mainstream of U.S. and Western European societies. It elicited much grandiose praise in the U.S. mass media, as well as in Germany, where it was considered to have caused a long overdue coming-to-terms with the nation's responsibility for the Holocaust. In an article in the *New York Times* entitled "Trivializing the Holocaust: Semi-Fact and Semi-Fiction," however, Elie Wiesel articulated what would become a paradigmatic critique of *Holocaust*, and of its classical realist and melodramatic conventions as a form of Holocaust representation. (The term *classical realism* began to be used by film theorists during the 1970s to describe the dominant form of fictional cinema that originated in Hollywood during the 1910s. The classical realist film employs an array of formal conventions in order to give the spectator the sense of experiencing not a particular narrative construction of reality but its authentic reproduction.)[6] Wiesel criticized *Holocaust*'s "indecent" tendency, as a classical realist historical film, to show what he argued should not, indeed cannot be shown; he criticized the contrivance of its attempt to show not just a particular story of the Holocaust but the whole story; and he criticized its misplaced epistemological confidence ("You may think you know now how the victims lived and died, but you do not"). He also criticized what he considered to be the "cheapness," emotional manipulation, and stereotyped characterizations of the series as a melodrama. He summarized his critique with these words: "People will tell me that filmmaking has its own laws and its own demands. After all, similar techniques are being used for war movies and historical re-creations. But the Holocaust is unique, not just another event."[7]

Wiesel's assertion that the Holocaust exceeds the representational means of the conventional historical film is an example of what Berel Lang has called "moral limits" of representation (should nots), the paradigm of which is Adorno's earlier argument.[8] Wiesel, however, goes further; he also argues, as some others have done, for the existence of what

I would call an *inherent* limit of representation: that the Holocaust is ultimately unrepresentable in any form. "The Holocaust?" Wiesel writes. "The ultimate event, the ultimate mystery, never to be comprehended or transmitted. Only those who were there know what it was; the others will never know."[9]

A paradigmatic defense of *Holocaust* against the kind of criticism leveled by Wiesel was articulated by the German scholar Andreas Huyssen in an article published in 1980.[10] Huyssen critiques the modernism championed by many of *Holocaust*'s critics as too intellectual for the cultural needs of the public, and defends conventional realism and melodrama as facilitating the emotional identification with individual Jewish characters that, he argues, is necessary in order for the public to have a significant engagement with the memory of the Holocaust.[11]

The historical debate between Wiesel's and Huyssen's arguments, however, has its own limits. Wiesel's dismissal of melodrama as a possible genre of Holocaust representation, and his assertion of the essential unrepresentability of the Holocaust by cultural means, are inconsistent with basic and compelling laws of representation promulgated within the field of semiotics. The assertion of absolute unrepresentability, while appealing as a response to the terrible sense of otherness that seems to characterize the Holocaust, implies both a rule of representational transparency to which the Holocaust is the exception, and an assertion of an essential truth of the Holocaust known only to witnesses. Following Hayden White and others, on the other hand, I would argue that no historical representation gives access to essential truth, not even the memories of witnesses. All historical representation is, rather, limited in at least three ways: by signification (the ontological difference between the reality and the sign, including the memory-sign), by documentation (limited documentation of the past), and by discourse (limited framing of documents by the conventions of discourse).

I agree with Huyssen that the dismissal of melodrama by critics like Wiesel seems to be motivated more by aesthetic prejudice—the supposed incompatibility of the Holocaust as a "high" theme and melodrama as a "low" genre—than by a serious consideration of representational modes and their limits. On the other hand, Huyssen's own view of emotional identification with the victims is itself reductive, and forestalls critical discussion of the nature and effects of such a response. Also reductive is his equation of the dichotomy modernism/realism with the dichotomy cognition/emotion. Some modernist works, as I will argue, have indeed engaged the emotions.

This book joins more recent writings that seek to reframe the concept of limits of Holocaust representation through an examination of the metapsychological structures and formal conventions of discourse, and attempts to systematize that understanding in relation to the cinema.

THE QUESTION OF TRAUMA

One of Wiesel's statements in his article on *Holocaust* seems to lead in a different direction. He writes, "The witness does not recognize himself in this film."[12] Indeed, as may be evident from my emphasis on the Wiener film, I hold that an investigation into the cinema's confrontation with the Holocaust begins with the question of witnessing. From the beginning of "the Final Solution," the question of witnessing was central. The genocidal program was to be kept secret from the Jews and thus, necessarily, from the general public, in order to minimize Jewish resistance during the processes of deportation, concentration, and extermination. Perpetrators were sworn to secrecy, bureaucrats were protected by euphemisms, and Jews who were allowed to witness extermination because they had been selected for slave labor were slated for eventual extermination themselves. There were to be, effectively, no witnesses.[13]

Although the Nazis were shockingly successful in their attempt to exterminate the Jews (they succeeded in killing approximately two-thirds of the Jews of Europe), technically speaking, of course, "the Final Solution" failed. Witnesses survived. From this survival, some questions have arisen. What are the effects of having witnessed such things? Can something of this witnessing be transmitted to the public?

A case can be made for the special significance of the cinema in this respect. In addition to being one of the most influential mass media in the West at the time of the Second World War and its aftermath (arguably, it was the most influential medium outside the home, while radio was most influential in the home), cinema was the medium most closely analogous to both perception and fantasy. On the one hand, through the indexical recording of images and sounds, film imitates the experience of witnessing real events.[14] Documentary films in particular allow spectators to witness events after a fashion, but even fiction films carry with them this indexical aura, which can be used to create a sense of witnessing history. On the other hand, as Christian Metz argued, "more than other arts, or in a more unique way, the cinema involves us in the imaginary."[15] Both formally and technologically (through the projection of giant images in the dark), film imitates and engages the experience of processing what has been witnessed through mental imagery, memory, fantasy, and dreams. In these two senses—which are both complementary and contradictory—the cinema constitutes a kind of witnessing to both the outer, physical reality of historical events and the inner, psychological reality of the effects of those events on people. Insofar as historical films—both documentary and fictional, though with different emphases—contain a tension between the witnessing of reality and the witnessing of fantasy, they both help construct historical consciousness and embody a contradiction within historical consciousness.[16]

What happened when the Holocaust and the cinema came into contact with one another—when the technological, industrial, and formal apparatus of the cinema confronted the Nazi apparatus of genocide and its abysmal effects? If the cinema presented a significant opportunity for the public witnessing of history, and the Holocaust presented a significant difficulty for the public witnessing of history, in what ways has the cinema succeeded and failed as a witness to the Holocaust? Was the cinema changed by its confrontation with the reality of the camps? How has our understanding of these events been affected by their representation or lack of representation in documentary and fiction films? What is at stake, what are the consequences for historical memory, when different kinds of cinematic representations of genocide are produced and viewed?

The model of witnessing I will use to address these questions derives from the psychological concept of trauma. Since the 1990s, during the same period of time in which Holocaust films have become more prominent, the concept of trauma has emerged from its former place as a specialty of physical and psychiatric medicine to become a cornerstone in the discourses of historical memory and social representation. The questions asked in this book, then, have to do specifically with the Holocaust as a traumatic rupture in the Western experience and understanding of history, and with the possibility that the cinema may have been able to engage that rupture at the level of cultural practice—to represent the Holocaust *as* a rupture, to embody that rupture for the audience, perhaps even to assist in mourning that rupture.

Trauma originally referred to a physical phenomenon: a violent disruption of the body's integrity. In the late nineteenth century, the concept began to be applied to psychological phenomena by pioneers like Sigmund Freud and Pierre Janet in their work on hysteria. Psychological trauma was defined as an experience that overwhelmed a person's normal means of mentally processing stimuli. The unprocessed memory of the experience remained embedded in the mind, resulting in pathologies of memory, emotion, and practical functioning. The therapist viewed these symptoms as clues to the nature of the trauma, and hoped to assist the subject in belatedly processing the memory.

From the beginning, there were two strands of thinking about trauma. Initially, the emphasis was on exogenous trauma—trauma caused by external events, such as child sexual abuse (what Freud called "seduction"), mining disasters, and train wrecks. Freud later began to emphasize endogenous over exogenous trauma—trauma caused by psychic events such as fantasies and instinctual excitations, with no external counterpart. A series of historical developments, however, repeatedly returned exogenous trauma to the attention of the psychiatric establishment: the two World Wars, the Vietnam War, and the modern women's movement, with its attention to rape and child sexual abuse. The treatment of what has come to be called posttraumatic stress disorder (PTSD) now constitutes a major focus of psychiatry, with a generation of clinicians trained to treat the victims of natural and technological disasters, wars, and violent crime.[17]

During the 1990s, the psychiatric discourse on trauma began to be applied to the study of culture in a systematic fashion. The intellectual historian Dominick LaCapra has analyzed a series of historical and theoretical texts—primarily texts dealing with the Holocaust—in terms of a group of categories derived from Freud's work: texts that deny trauma, texts that act out or unconsciously repeat trauma, and texts that work through trauma. The poststructuralist literary critic Cathy Caruth has focused not on texts that explicitly treat historical trauma, but on the ways in which the traumas of twentieth-century European experience, including the Holocaust, are implicitly or symptomatically inscribed as forms and figures of language in a series of theoretical and literary texts.[18] Theories of cultural trauma have also begun to be applied to film, with a collection of articles on the subject in a 2001 issue of *Screen*, several books forthcoming, and a number of articles on trauma in *Shoah*.[19]

As James Berger has suggested, and as I hope to demonstrate, the application of trauma theory to culture may offer at least one method of bridging the apparent gaps between a historical approach to culture and a textual approach; between a focus on the past signified by a historical text and a focus on the text's work of signification in the present; between documentary and fictional modes of representing history; and between individual and collective experiences of history.[20]

At the same time, cultural trauma theory has its own dilemmas. Analogous to the conflict between exogenous and endogenous models of trauma are the conflicts between exceptional and universal models, between empirical and theoretical models, and between a model that emphasizes the traumatic event itself and one that emphasizes its "deferred action."

Many who write about the trauma of natural and human-made disasters, including most writing on the Holocaust, have tended to view trauma as an exception to normal experience. Another tendency, often found in poststructuralist writing, tends to universalize trauma as inherent in history, language, or even experience itself.[21] The poststructuralist tendency has its counterpart in contemporary colloquial discourse: the use of the word *traumatic* to add emphasis to the representation of potentially any unpleasurable experience. Caruth argues convincingly, however, that trauma must be understood as neither an exceptional experience nor the rule of experience, but, rather, a possibility of experience.[22]

One of the problems with relatively universal models of trauma is that they ignore existing empirical criteria for and evidence of trauma. Theories of cultural trauma in relation to concrete historical experiences such as the Holocaust can begin from an empirical model of trauma, citing the symptoms of individual survivors. Theoretical work, then, moves from the level of psychology to the level of culture. Relatively universal models of trauma as inherent in history, language, or experience, on the other hand, begin and end in theory.

Eric Santner's valuable work on German films as a form of cultural memory of Nazism demonstrates the significance of this distinction. In his 1990 book, *Stranded Objects: Mourning, Memory, and Film in Post-war Germany*, Santner follows the German psychoanalysts Alexander and Margarete Mitscherlich in arguing that Germans collectively have had difficulty accepting responsibility for the Holocaust and mourning the victims because they have not yet worked through their own melancholic dilemmas: the loss of their idealized self-image in Hitler and the Third Reich. Santner's critique of classical realism as a potential form for this "working through" process makes explicit an argument that remains implicit in earlier critiques such as Wiesel's: that classical realism, with its need for conventional resolution, promotes avoidance of the dilemmas of the past, rather than a working through of those dilemmas. To realism, Santner opposes not modernism but postmodernism, exemplified in Hans Jürgen Syberberg's 1977 experimental production, *Hitler: A Film from Germany*, and Edgar Reitz's 1984 television series *Heimat*.

It is appropriate that Santner and others have discussed the German memory of Nazism in terms of mourning and melancholy, while those of us working on the memory of the Holocaust from the victims' point of view have more often focused on trauma. (Trauma implies issues of loss and mourning, but the reverse is not true. Many losses require mourning but are not traumatic.) The problem is that Santner and others have increasingly begun to use the word *trauma* to refer to the German loss of self-image.[23] While many Germans must certainly have been traumatized by specific experiences of Nazi terror, World War II combat, Allied bombing, and postwar migration, I know of no empirical evidence of Germans being traumatized by the loss of Hitler and the Third Reich as symbolic objects. This application of the concept of trauma is thus entirely theoretical, with no empirical foundation. There may be nothing wrong with nonempirical theorizing per se, but to deempiricize the concept of trauma and appropriate it from the victims on behalf of their victimizers may constitute a symbolic repetition of the original victimization.

Relevant to any discussion of cultural trauma is the distinction emphasized by Angelika Rauch between an approach that emphasizes the traumatic event itself and Freud's original emphasis on "deferred action" (*Nachträglichkeit*). According to Rauch, American psychoanalysts, in their focus on the traumatic event itself, have mistakenly dismissed Freud's theory of deferred action, according to which the trauma must be understood in relation to the subject's belated and repeated restructurings of the memory of the event as time passes and circumstances change.[24] While I resist the poststructuralist tendency to efface the significance of the event itself as an empirical cause of trauma, I acknowledge the value of Rauch's argument insofar as it suggests that the way a cultural work narrates a trauma is a function not only of the nature of the event and its initial impact on the victims, but also of the conditions of the work's production and reception. Films respond not only to the past but also to the present, with its own ideological conditions through which the trauma is reinterpreted. These ideological conditions determine to what extent a film denies trauma and to what extent it repeats trauma, and they direct that posttraumatic response—explicitly, implicitly, or symptomatically—toward political processes that may have little to do with the Holocaust itself. In the chapters that follow, I may stress the continuity of posttraumatic response in order to draw attention to a significant cinematic discourse, but I hope to be sensitive also to the ways in which this response is always conditioned by historical context.

I do want to qualify my own use of trauma theory, however, by stating that I regard the concept of trauma as necessary but not sufficient to explain the crisis of representation brought on by the Holocaust. I would identify at least five aspects of this crisis. First is the broad problem of representing the past, of reckoning with the absent and haunting dimension of the past. Second is another problem of a more general type: the deforming effects of pain on representation, which have been addressed by writers like Julia Kristeva and Elaine Scarry.[25] Third is that specific type of haunting by past pain known as trauma, where the pain is unassimilable, and therefore punches a hole in the temporal continuum of past and present. Fourth is that dimension of trauma that is specific to massive human-inflicted violence—to concentration camps, genocide, and nuclear bombing. All trauma involves shock, pain, and loss, but in these cases they attain the force and scope of annihilation. In the case of the Holocaust, what was lost is so massive—the millions of dead, the communities, the culture, the language—that it constitutes the very ground of Ashkenazik Jewish collective memory, so that all representation of prewar European Jewish life or the Holocaust itself comes up against its own impossibility. Finally there is what Maurice Blanchot has called "the annihilation of the annihilation," the Nazis' partly successful attempt to erase the traces of the genocide, so that the loss itself becomes lost.[26] In their most profound moments, I think, the films in question take up the formidable task of reckoning with all five aspects of this crisis, not only with the single aspect of trauma.

THE HOLOCAUST AS A TRAUMA

Central to our understanding of the Holocaust as a trauma is the fact of its having lain beyond the Western imaginative horizon. The ban on filming certainly had a strategic function, but Himmler's commitment to secrecy seems to have had another motive as well. This is suggested in a secret speech given in 1943 to his immediate subordinates in the SS, in which Himmler called "the Final Solution" "the most glorious page in our history, one not written and which shall never be written."[27] One interpretation of the curious appearance of the word *never* in Himmler's speech is that he knew "the Final Solution" was so unthinkable that even in a future victorious Germany, it could never be assimilated into any conceivable public historical narrative. The Third Reich had a cinema policy of unparalleled ambition, as exemplified by the structuring of the 1934 Nuremberg Party Congress *around* the filming of *Triumph of the Will*, rather than the reverse.[28] But, for Himmler, "the Final Solution" lay outside the historical purview of cinema. The traumatic potential of Wiener's film is thus partly attributable to its giving a view of something deemed so transgressive that it was to disappear from history.

Deception of the victims was crucial to the implementation of "the Final Solution." En route to the unthinkable, they were given explanations that were painful but bearable—bearable, because there was a precedent for "resettlement" in the Jewish collective memory. They would not actually see the killing process until the last minute. At Treblinka, for instance, victims were sent to the gas chamber via the *Himmelstrasse* (road to heaven): a path bordered on both sides by barbed wire fences into which pine branches had been woven by a Camouflage Squad to block the view.[29]

A key moment in the traumatization of the victims, then, was the moment of finally seeing the unthinkable. Describing his first day in Auschwitz, Elie Wiesel wrote:

> Not far from us, flames were leaping up from a ditch, gigantic flames. They were burning something. A lorry drew up at the pit and delivered its load—little children. Babies! Yes, I saw it—saw it with my own eyes . . . those children in the flames. . . . I pinched my face. Was I still alive? Was I awake? I could not believe it. How could it be possible for them to burn people, children, and for the world to keep silent? No, none of this could be true. It was a nightmare.[30]

This is as good an articulation as any of what Freud called "fright" (*Schreck*), which, he argued in *Beyond the Pleasure Principle*, is crucial to the experience of trauma. Fright, he wrote, is "the state a person gets into when he has run into danger without being prepared for it; it emphasizes the factor of surprise."[31] In the case of an event like the Holocaust, however, fright goes beyond Freud's rather understated notions of ill preparedness and surprise. Fright resulted not simply from the fact that one did not know that one was going to be deported to a camp and gassed, or that one was going to see babies burned. It resulted from the fact that such things were literally inconceivable, that they did not fit any imagined possible reality.

FILM AS VICARIOUS TRAUMA

I want to return now to the story of the Wiener film, and particularly to Wiener's description of its effect on him and the comrades to whom he showed it. ("They were depressed. I was observing their faces and saw how shocked they were. We had never seen or found out about anything like it in the navy. The same happened to me while I was filming, I was shivering all over, I was that agitated.")

Of course, Wiener's statements, like all statements, are subject to question. But putting aside for the purposes of this argument the complex questions surrounding the German memory of the Holocaust, I remain interested in Wiener's story insofar as it suggests the way in which the victims' experience of suddenly seeing the unthinkable was often repeated in a muted form in the experience of others who witnessed the events or their aftermath. Indeed, the diagnostic criteria for PTSD found in the most recent *Diagnostic and Statistical Manual of Mental Disorders* apply not only to the direct experience of trauma but also to the witnessing of it.[32] Some witnesses, like Wiener, however, not only experienced a shock themselves, but also took advantage of the rare opportunity to record what shocked them, or to continue recording even after the shock, making it possible for others to witness what they had witnessed—in effect, to violate Himmler's ban by keeping the shock in motion. Wiener's film functioned as a traumatic relay, transmitting a shock from a specific scene of victimization—the shock having been presumably experienced by the victims only a moment before death—to other scenes, scenes of remote and mediated witnessing by spectators who received the shock in the form of what I will refer to, following recent work in psychology, as *vicarious trauma*.[33] If photography—in its ability both to reproduce a moment of vision and to be itself mechanically reproduced and disseminated endlessly throughout society—shattered the traditional "aura" of art and replaced it with a new politics of the image, as Walter Benjamin argued, then one of the effects of this new politics is the potentially endless reproduction and dissemination of trauma.[34]

The cinematic relaying of trauma exemplified by the Wiener film was repeated on a massive scale in 1945 when military film crews accompanied Allied troops liberating the camps, filmed what they saw, and sent those films back to production offices where they were edited into newsreels and documentaries and widely distributed in movie theaters. I do not believe that historians have yet adequately understood the nature of the shock experienced by the West when it first encountered those images of emaciated bodies stacked, piled, and strewn over the ground; of gas chambers, ovens, and mass graves; of skeletal survivors staring back at the cameras with eyes that seemed to testify to unimaginable horrors. Nor have we been able to understand adequately the meaning of that shock for the Western understanding of both cinema and history—of what this tool we had built could show us of ourselves, and of what there was to be shown. I would certainly not be the first to characterize this moment as a major epistemological shift in modern Western history.[35]

Crucial to the traumatic potential of these films (like *The Death Camps*, which will be discussed in some detail in the following chapter) was the condition of the human bodies represented. Close-up shots of individuals showed bodies and faces apparently stripped of everything that the Western imagination associates with meaningful human existence: individuality, personality, reason, dignity. Long shots showed masses of bodies strewn, piled, stacked, or dumped on the earth—bodies converted into things ("stacked like cordwood," the reports said), bodies that no longer had anything to do with persons.

Also crucial to the traumatic potential of the concentration camp footage, to its ability to cause "fright," was the prior absence of such images. The public had previously been exposed to written reports of concentration camps and mass killings—which, however, had vastly underestimated the extent of the violence—but there had been no footage. Suddenly there was an inundation of images. The British government, in fact, heightened the traumatic potential of these images through its policy of censoring explicit combat footage during the war, and then forcing first-, second-, and third-run theaters to show widely advertised concentration camp films without an "X" certificate to prevent children from attending.[36]

Perhaps the clearest statement on the relaying of trauma to the public through photographic imagery is Susan Sontag's often quoted description of her initial reaction not to atrocity films, but to atrocity photographs:

> One's first encounter with the photographic inventory of ultimate horror is a kind of revelation, the prototypically modern revelation: a negative epiphany. For me, it was photographs of Bergen-Belsen and Dachau which I came across by chance in a bookstore in Santa Monica in July 1945. Nothing I have seen—in photographs or in real life—ever cut me as sharply, deeply, instantaneously. Indeed, it seems plausible to me to divide my life into two parts, before I saw those photographs (I was twelve) and after, though it was several years before I understood fully what they were about. . . . When I looked at those photographs, something broke. Some limit had been reached, and not only that of horror; I felt irrevocably grieved, wounded, but a part of my feelings started to tighten; something went dead; something is still crying.[37]

But I want to guard against a reductive conception of traumatic relay. It is not a process by which a thing called *trauma* is mechanically and wholly conveyed via an image from one person to another. Trauma, first of all, is not a thing, like a letter, that can be delivered. It is not even an event, not even a genocide, which cannot in itself be relayed, but which—perhaps this too is unthinkable—merely happens. Rather, trauma, even before being transmitted, is already utterly bound up with the realm of representation. It is, to be more precise, a crisis of representation. An extreme event is perceived as radically out of joint with one's mental representation of the world, which is itself partly derived from the set of representations of the world that one receives from one's family and culture. The mind goes into shock, becomes incapable of translating the impressions of the event into a coherent mental representation. The impressions remain in the mind, intact and unassimilated. Paradoxically, they neither submit to the normal processes of memory storage and recall, nor, returning uninvited, do they allow the event to be forgotten.[38]

There is no such thing as a traumatic image per se. But an image of atrocity may carry a traumatic potential, which, as it circulates among individuals and societies with common conceptual horizons, may be repeatedly realized in a variety of experiences of vicarious trauma.

I also want to guard against the notion that the exact force and characteristics of traumatic experience are retained as that experience is transmitted across positions: from victim to eyewitness to spectator. Some of the more poststructurally inflected work on trauma and culture, such as Shoshana Felman and Dori Laub's 1992 *Testimony: Crises of Witnessing in Literature, Psychoanalysis, and History* (including Felman's influential reading of *Shoah*), has been criticized, rightly I think, for erasing important distinctions between historical experiences in the process of describing trauma as a text-based contagion.[39] The critic, I would argue, is responsible to the historical specificity of traumatic experience—whether, for instance, it takes place in the context of a concentration camp or a movie theater.

While my definition of the Holocaust as a trauma does ultimately rest on empirical research on PTSD in survivors, my argument about vicarious trauma resulting from the viewing of atrocity films remains, at this point, hypothetical.[40] There are, however, two strands of related research that support such a hypothesis. First is a series of psychiatric studies carried out between 1962 and the present that have compared subject responses to a "traumatic" or "stress" film and a neutral film. The traumatic film most often used was *Subincision*, an anthropological documentary showing an Australian aboriginal puberty ritual, described as containing repeated scenes of "extensive penile surgery, bleeding wounds, and adolescents writhing and wincing with pain." Repeated studies have verified that subjects display significantly higher levels of stress following the traumatic film, where stress is signaled by physiological symptoms, mood changes, and intrusive thoughts and mental images. The psychiatrist Mardi Jon Horowitz has argued that the data support Freud's theory of a repetition compulsion following traumatic experiences. While these studies were not concerned with the specific characteristics of film-induced trauma (what another researcher called "analogue" trauma) as opposed to what might be called direct trauma, they do at least indicate that film viewing can lead to symptoms of posttraumatic stress.[41]

The second strand of research supporting a theory of vicarious film-induced trauma is the study of vicarious trauma in the therapists and family members of PTSD sufferers. Lisa MacCann and Laurie Anne Pearlman have found that such people, who come into contact with trauma victims over a prolonged period, can themselves come to suffer from PTSD.[42] According to one report, a therapist treating a Vietnam veteran experienced a posttraumatic flashback of one of her client's memories as if it was her own.[43] The question is whether, if vicarious trauma can result from prolonged contact with a traumatized person, it can also result from a single exposure to a filmed representation, which, as an indexical sign, affords an experience closer to eyewitnessing.

While a hypothesis of vicarious trauma resulting from the viewing of atrocity films might be better left to psychiatric experts, I would suggest that it is a response to a different form of unpleasurable excitation than is direct trauma, because a film would be perceived by the viewer, barring severe psychological disturbance, at a degree of existential remove from the self. The excitation would be easier to defend against, and the effects may not normally be as severe or long lasting as in direct trauma. But the effects may include a number of the symptoms of PTSD, such as shock, intrusive imagery, grief, depression, numbing, guilt feelings, and loss of faith in humanity.[44]

The passage from Sontag, in fact, provides a remarkably clear picture of vicarious film-induced trauma, which, we might say, Sontag has simply renamed a "negative epiphany." There is the lack of preparedness Freud discusses, Sontag having come across the photographs "by chance." Reminiscent of Freud's notion of traumatic excitation breaking through a stimulus barrier is Sontag's formulation, "Something broke. Some limit had been reached." There is the use of the word *cut* to describe the immediate effect of the photographs, which recalls the indebtedness of the notion of psychic trauma to an earlier notion of physical trauma. There are the senses of shock, of numbing, of being forever changed. There is a reference to belatedness ("it was several years before I understood fully what they were about"), that aspect of Freud's writing on trauma that has been so stressed by Cathy Caruth.

And there is the suggestion of the posttraumatic collapsing of time in the formulation, "something is still crying."

POSTTRAUMATIC DISCOURSE IN FILM

As this interpretation of the Sontag passage demonstrates, my interest in vicarious trauma ultimately lies less in the realm of empirical experience than in the realm of discourse. It is my contention that there exists a period of time in the life of a society that has suffered a massive blow—after the initial encounter with a traumatizing historical event but before its ultimate assimilation—in which there arises a discourse of trauma. In the case of the Holocaust, this discourse is made up of texts such as the above quotations from the survivor Elie Wiesel, the witness Reinhard Wiener, and the photographic spectator Susan Sontag. Its significance for the purpose of this argument transcends the literal referencing of any particular experience of trauma or vicarious trauma—of surviving atrocity, witnessing it, or seeing images of it—and lies, rather, in the staking out, in the languages of various media, of a discursive space pertinent to all these experiences. One may be traumatized by an encounter with the Holocaust, one may be unable to assimilate a memory or an image of atrocity, but the discourse of trauma—as one encounters it in conversation, in reading, in film—gives one a language with which to begin to represent the failure of representation that one has experienced.[45]

It is in the discourse of trauma that we can move from the notion of individual responses to traumatizing events toward the notion of collective responses. Indeed, Dominick LaCapra has suggested that it may be a misconception of the significance of psychoanalytic theory to think of it as applying primarily to individual psychology and only secondarily, and by analogy, to societies and texts. Perhaps trauma is, instead, a broad social phenomenon, exemplified in individual psychology and in public discourse alike.[46]

When photographic evidence of genocide first appears, it may need relatively little narrative support in order to cause vicarious trauma. It would be enough for the image to be presented by a reputable source (newspaper, magazine, newsreel), to be identified in historical context ("this is a liberated concentration camp"), and to be authenticated ("this is an actual photo taken by Allied photographers"). This initial phase does not last long, however. Public interest wanes, the images leave the broad public sphere and become a specialty interest. Some have discussed this turn of events in terms of collective numbing and psychic defense.

In the second phase, when relatively unsupported images are no longer effective, the film must, in a sense, work harder. It must overcome defensive numbing. Documentary images must be submitted to a narrative form whose purpose is, if not to literally traumatize the spectator, then to invoke a posttraumatic historical consciousness—a kind of textual compromise between the senselessness of the initial traumatic encounter and the sense-making apparatus of a fully integrated historical narrative, similar to LaCapra's notion of "muted trauma."[47] The resulting cinema, exemplified by *Night and Fog*, attempts to produce in the spectator a traumatic afterimage, an image that formally repeats the shock of the original encounters with atrocity—both the original eye-witnessing of the atrocities themselves, and the subsequent cinematic encounter with the images of atrocity. This is less a cinema of vicarious trauma than a posttraumatic cinema.

While this second phase may have begun in a relatively direct fashion, through the reframing of atrocity footage within a posttraumatic narrative discourse, it did not always continue to rely on atrocity footage. Less direct but, I would argue, not less significant forms of posttraumatic cinema have included documentaries that, like *Shoah*, omit atrocity footage altogether, and fiction films that visualize atrocity through fictional construction (e.g., Szabó's *Love Film*), or refer to the Holocaust without visualizing it directly at all (e.g., Szabó's *Father*).

As trauma is less a particular experiential content than a form of experience, so posttraumatic cinema is defined less by a particular image content—a documentary image of atrocity, a fictional image of atrocity, or the absence of an image of atrocity—than by the attempt to discover a form for presenting that content that mimics some aspects of posttraumatic consciousness itself, the attempt to formally reproduce for the spectator an experience of suddenly seeing the unthinkable. And insofar as what is historically thinkable is partly constituted by the conventions of the historical film genre, the instigation of a posttraumatic cinema becomes a question of upsetting the spectator's expectations not only of history in general, but also of the historical film in particular.

The notion of a discourse of trauma can lead to a reframing of the question of the limits or impossibility of representation. Insofar as trauma deforms and throws into crisis a witness's mental representation of an event, it can be said to impose inherent limits of representation— limits of intelligibility and narratability. These inherent limits of representation, however, are different from those asserted by Wiesel. Wiesel's limits rely on an essentialist notion of representation: the distinction between an essentially transparent representation and an essentially oblique one. The limits imposed on representation by trauma, on the other hand, rely on a more historical notion of representation: the distinction between conventional representation and unconventional representation. The discourse of trauma, then, transforms the inherent limit of the witness's private memory into a moral limit of public memory; it transforms an involuntary psychological symptom into a voluntary aesthetic.

TRAUMA AND NARRATION: REALISM AND MODERNISM

The conventional historical film at the time of the Second World War was (and in many ways remains) a subgenre of the classical realist film. The classical realist historical film claims to make the past masterable by making it visible. The original, fictional variant can be traced back to films like *The Birth of a Nation* (1915) and forward to films like *Titanic* (1997) (both films represent traumatic historical events).[48] The documentary variant coalesced in a more piecemeal fashion, and arguably it was the Second World War itself that provided the impetus for its coalescence in films like the *Why We Fight* series (1942–45).

In discussing the narration of trauma in the following chapters, I will borrow the method of analyzing literary narration that Gerard Genette elaborated in his book *Narrative Discourse*.[49] Adapting this model to the historical film, I propose that *tense* regulates the relations between the temporality of the film text (screen time) and the temporality of the historical events represented by the film (as well as, in the case of documentary, the temporality of the filmic evidence, e.g., concentration camp footage). *Mood* regulates the point of view of the film on the images and events represented. And *voice* regulates the film's self-consciousness of its own act of narration.

In the realist historical film, tense works to provide the spectator with a sense of mastery over time, a sense of power to travel back in time to see the past, or to make the past visible to the present on command. Usually, this narration of the past assumes the form of a linear chronology; when flashbacks occur, they are contained within narrow formal boundaries. Realism assumes the omniscient point of view of one who is outside history epistemologically, emotionally, and morally—one who is free to enter into history through the image and assume a variety of embedded points of view, to see and feel history vicariously, on the condition of being free to return again unscathed to that exterior position from which one can know and judge the past without being personally implicated in it. And realism presents the past unself-consciously, drawing attention to the events represented, and away from the film's own act of presentation.

Realism abhors a vacuum; it converts the absence of the past into a visible presence. And yet, visually, the Holocaust is characterized by absence; of the killing of millions of people, there are only two minutes of film. Realism, then, must replace the missing image of death, and put the spectator in the position of being an eyewitness. Thus, Elie Wiesel says of *Holocaust*, "The witness does not recognize himself in this film." In other words, the realist Holocaust film positions the spectator as a false witness, one who can slip in and out of the witnessing position at will without having to experience the existential consequences of this act, one who can master the Holocaust as a spectacle.

Realist narration—mastery over time, omniscience and flexibility of point of view, and unself-conscious voice—renders a highly secondarized representation of the past, one that is masterable in the way that the French psychiatrist Pierre Janet argued in 1889 that normal, "narrative memories," as opposed to posttraumatic (then called hysterical) ones, are masterable.[50] In the "tense" of narrative memory, one can call up an image of the past at will, make it present to consciousness, and insert it into the proper chronology. Narrative memory is characterized by flexibility and mastery of point of view. One's point of view on the memory changes depending on the social conditions pertaining to a specific instance of remembering. One can become like an outsider, narrating one's own memory as if in the third person. And narrative memory is unself-conscious; one is not overly concerned with how one remembers the past.[51]

In posttraumatic memory, on the other hand, linear chronology collapses. Time is experienced as fragmented and uncontrollable. The past becomes either too remote or too immediate. It remains inaccessibly in the past (amnesia), or presents itself uninvited, seizing consciousness (hypermnesia).[52] Psychiatrist Henry Krystal describes the case of a concentration camp survivor who immigrated to the United States and was serving in the army, who experienced "mental confusion as to the past and present."

> For instance, on the anniversary of the day on which the patient had seen a fellow concentration-camp inmate hanged, he had become uncertain as to where he was and unsure that he was not still in Auschwitz in danger of further persecutions—despite the fact that he was in the uniform of an American soldier. Among the very typical symptoms for concentration-camp survivors which this patient displayed was a hypermnesia for certain events, along with memory defects regarding other events of the period of persecution. Because of the above findings, and because of massive distortions caused by continuing guilt and denial, the reconstruction of the persecution period is a slow, laborious, and painful procedure for both patient and examiner.[53]

Posttraumatic memory maintains the fixed and inflexible point of view of the witness to past events. As Janet argued, and as contemporary trauma research verifies, traumatic memories are not integrated into the mind as normal memories are, but rather become lodged in the mind where they can remain indefinitely, dissociated, or split off, from normal consciousness, returning in pathological forms. Whereas normal memories change over time as the rememberer and the conditions of remembering change, traumatic memories remain as literal recordings of past traumatic perceptions. Another way of putting it is that, in normal memory, the "I" that remembers in the present is different from the "I" that experienced the event in the past. The point of view has changed. In posttraumatic memory, on the other hand, the present "I" is invaded by the memory of the past "I." The point of view remains that of the witness.[54] The case of the therapist mentioned earlier, who experienced a flashback of her client's traumatic memory, demonstrates that this witness's point of view can even be transferred to a nonwitness through vicarious traumatization.

Posttraumatic memory may not be self-conscious per se. But insofar as posttraumatic memory is a kind of failure of memory, its therapeutic treatment requires a degree of self-consciousness that is uncharacteristic of narrative memory. The failure of memory in PTSD has been described in two ways. Cognitive psychologists have identified it as a failure of information encoding, a reversion from the third and most mature form of encoding—linguistic—to the less mature forms: sensorimotor and iconic. Bessel van der Kolk and Onno van der Hart write, "When people are exposed to trauma . . . they experience 'speechless terror.' The experience cannot be organized on a linguistic level, and this failure to arrange the memory in words and symbols leaves it to be organized on a somatosensory or iconic level: as somatic sensations, behavioral re-enactments, nightmares, and flashbacks."[55]

Many therapists who have treated Holocaust survivors describe the failure of memory in more existential terms. "I have frequently seen survivors just sit in my office and cry—they are very puzzled—it doesn't make any sense to them—they can't make any sense out of their experience."[56] "Many survivors refrain from speech because, perhaps, they no longer believe in words. . . . When it becomes necessary for them to express themselves, for instance, during the medical psychiatric evaluation and appraisal toward their compensation claim, they cannot go through with it. They remain silent."[57]

The trauma victim in treatment does not have the luxury of an unselfconscious memory. One is faced with troubling questions about memory itself: Why do I have this kind of memory? How can I live with this kind of memory? What role will the traumatic experience have in my life if it becomes a "normal" memory?

Insofar as posttraumatic narration is a kind of failure of narration—a collapse of mastery over time and point of view—it too tends toward a self-conscious voice, toward a consideration of its own failure to master the past.[58]

Around the turn of the century, a form of literary narration did in fact arise that adopted disorienting time shifts, hypersubjective points of view, and narrative self-consciousness. We call it modernism, and Walter Benjamin argued, citing *Beyond the Pleasure Principle*, that it originated as a response to the traumas of urbanization and industrialization that characterized modern capitalism.[59] Subsequently, modernism arose in the cinema, following, not surprisingly, the First World War. One can find instances of posttraumatic narration in some early modernist films, especially those of the French impressionist film movement. *Menilmontant* (1925), for example, uses a fragmented form of narration to represent the protagonist's experiences of shock both upon discovering her parents' murder and upon moving from the country to the city.[60] *La Maternelle* (1932) represents a girl's memories of abuse using a flashback sequence that anticipates the posttraumatic flashbacks of *Hiroshima, mon amour* (1959) and *The Pawnbroker*.

However, it was not until *Night and Fog* that a coherent discourse of historical trauma appeared in cinema.[61] In fact, *Night and Fog* constitutes a key link between the genre of Holocaust films, the development of post–World War II modernist film, and the appearance of posttraumatic cinema. The question, of course, is what were the precise relations among these three phenomena?

How large a role did the Holocaust play in the development of posttraumatic cinema? On the one hand, the Holocaust did not solely engender posttraumatic cinema. Alain Resnais, for example, was a key figure in the development of posttraumatic cinema, but he has made films about not only the Nazi concentration camps, but also the bombings of Guernica (*Guernica*, 1950) and Hiroshima (*Hiroshima, mon amour*), as well as the Algerian war (*Muriel ou le temps d'un retour*, 1963).[62] On the other hand, as I hope to demonstrate in the following chapters, neither was the Holocaust an indifferent referent of posttraumatic cinema. Rather, the Holocaust was a crucial but not the sole determining factor in the development of posttraumatic cinema.

Is all modernist art posttraumatic? One can argue, following Benjamin, that this is the case, but only in the relatively loose sense of a broadly dispersed culture of shock being a response to a broad set of social shocks beginning in the nineteenth century. Post–World War II posttraumatic cinema constituted a discourse, however, rather than a more vaguely defined response, insofar as it inhered in the relations between a specific set of referents (Auschwitz, Hiroshima, etc.), a specific set of signifiers (narrative techniques), and a specific signified (trauma).[63]

Once again, I want to guard against a reductive argument—in this case, against a reductive understanding of modernism as a vehicle of posttraumatic cinema. The point is not simply to classify certain films as modernist and posttraumatic as opposed to realist. The notion of posttraumatic cinema is ultimately less useful as a category of films than as the name given to a discourse that was disseminated across categories, appearing in many films that blended realist and modernist tendencies. As I will argue in the following chapter, even *Night and Fog*, which I see as a founding text of posttraumatic cinema, contains significant realist tendencies, as do *Shoah*, *The Pawnbroker*, and *Father*. These films did not abandon realism, but rather staged a collision between realism and modernism. It was from the collision between realism's discourse of omnipotent representation and modernism's discourse of the impossibility of representation that these films derived their formal and thereby their historical shock effects.

Of course, not all films about the Holocaust and other historical catastrophes attempt to invoke a posttraumatic historical consciousness. There are a variety of reasons to produce a Holocaust film—pedagogical, ideological, economic—many of which are inconsistent with the project of invoking trauma. Some films present images with traumatic potential only to counteract that potential by retaining a conventional form of historical narrative. Eric Santner has called this textual strategy "narrative fetishism," which he describes as "consciously or unconsciously designed to expunge the traces of the trauma or loss that called that narrative into being in the first place."[64] This narrative fetishism may be the price (unconsciously) paid for employing a film language capable of efficiently communicating a set of historical facts to a mass audience.

Moreover, it must be remembered that PTSD is not a universal response to catastrophe. Survivors of even the most potentially traumatizing experiences of genocide and concentration camps, while suffering a variety of psychological wounds, did not in every case develop PTSD.[65] On what basis, then, can one argue that this particular psychological response should be transformed into a cultural discourse? Why did certain texts adopt this traumatic response as a model of historical narration? And why do critics like myself explicitly or implicitly support this tendency?

First, it was logical for those who felt that a conventional form of narration was inadequate to represent historical catastrophe to turn to modernism as an already existing alternative to and revolt against conventional narration. Furthermore, modernist narration had an already existing affinity with posttraumatic consciousness. Artists may have thus indirectly and unconsciously learned from modernism to represent the Holocaust as a trauma.

Second, a collective posttraumatic consciousness seems to provide a form of resistance to the tendencies of avoidance and denial of a historical catastrophe that, I argue, Western societies should and must confront. This consciousness fulfills Nietzsche's criterion for the most effective form of collective memory: "If something is to stay in the memory it must be burned in: only that which never ceases to *hurt* stays in the memory."[66]

Not even all scholars who discuss the Holocaust as a collective trauma, however, agree on how that trauma should be represented. La-Capra has criticized *Shoah* for acting out rather than working through trauma. Geoffrey Hartman worries about the numbing effects of regular exposure to media representations of trauma, and prefers pure testimony as a form of Holocaust representation that downplays the repetition of trauma.[67] Felman and Laub, on the other hand, seem to promote a boundariless contagion of trauma that erases the distinctions between specific historical experiences. My position is closer to those of Saul Friedlander and Cathy Caruth: that in order to encounter historical trauma on the level of the Holocaust, one must be open to experiencing a textually mediated form of trauma.[68] As opposed to the discourses of narrative fetishism and efficiency, the discourse of trauma works toward a form of narration that can speak from the collective space of traumatic historical experience. It is, as Cathy Caruth has written, "a voice that cries out from the wound."[69]

Each of the subsequent chapters takes up a different aspect of posttraumatic cinema. Chapter 2 focuses on *Night and Fog*'s origination of posttraumatic narration, and its break from the classical realist forms of tense, mood, and voice in historical documentary, exemplified by the French newsreel *The Death Camps* (1945) and the Swedish compilation film *Mein Kampf* (1960). Chapter 3 continues to focus on the aspects of posttraumatic cinema that are specific to documentary, exploring the changes in historical documentary form brought about by cinéma vérité, with its privileging of the image of the present over the image of the past. The chapter also continues to focus on developments in France, examining the appearance of posttraumatic testimony in *Chronicle of a Summer* (1960), before proceeding to a detailed analysis of *Shoah*.

Chapter 4 turns to the appearance of a fictional posttraumatic cinema, tracing the history of the flashback as a technique of historical representation, and focusing on *Hiroshima, mon amour* as a breakthrough in both the splitting off of posttraumatic fiction from documentary and the development of the posttraumatic flashback. The chapter concludes with a close look at *The Pawnbroker* as a logical application to the Holocaust of Resnais's posttraumatic flashback technique, which is contrasted with the realist flashback technique exemplified in *Sophie's Choice* (1982). Chapter 5 explores autobiography as a form of fictional posttraumatic cinema, focusing on three early films by the Hungarian filmmaker István Szabó. The chapter examines the problematic relations among three discourses of posttraumatic memory—personal, national, and Jewish—that appear in the informal trilogy, as well as the way these discourses center productively on the figure of Szabó as autobiographer.

The final chapter considers the fate of posttraumatic cinema as modernism is increasingly displaced by postmodernism. The chapter compares two very different works—*Schindler's List* (1993) and *History and Memory* (1991)—in order to trace recent transformations in posttraumatic cinema across differences of fiction/documentary, center/margins, film/video, and European/U.S. history.

2   *Night and Fog* and the Origins of Posttraumatic Cinema

In FILM history, myths of origins have been correctly viewed with suspicion, both because of their inherently repressive tendencies, and because of the problem of lost and neglected films. I would argue, however, that there is good evidence supporting the recognition of *Night and Fog* as the most important, if not the sole, originator of posttraumatic cinema, not only because of its subject matter and formal innovation, but also because of its extremely wide distribution and profound international impact on both the broad public and intellectuals.

Before focusing on *Night and Fog*'s formal innovation of posttraumatic cinema, however, I want to attend to a problematic aspect of the film's content. At this level, the film not only worked to combat the repression of the memory of the camps in France; it also, paradoxically, contributed to the repression of the memory of the Jewish genocide. Attention to this repression of content, however, should not eclipse our attention to the film's contribution, ultimately of greater historical significance, to posttraumatic cinema, a cinema that influenced the memory of the Jewish genocide as well.

THE REPRESSION OF HOLOCAUST MEMORY IN FRANCE

About 115,000 non-Jews were deported from France to German concentration camps during the Occupation because of their opposition to German rule; about 40,000 survived, or 35 percent.[1] In addition, about 80,000 Jews were deported from special French camps for Jews, with a significant degree of cooperation from the French authorities and public. About 3,500 returned, or 4 percent.[2] Both the treatment of these two groups in the camps and their survival rates were different. The German policy toward political deportees was one of terrible, murderous punishment, which the majority did not survive. The policy toward Jews was annihilation.

After the war, the deportations became the object of a massive symbolic repression in France, as elsewhere. *Resistancialisme* is the name given by the historian Henry Rousso to the myth of a united French resistance to the German Occupation, a myth that dominated the French memory of the war from 1945 until the 1970s, and that tended to repress the memory of the deportations. Rousso writes, "Spectators at the earliest French parades had glimpsed the striped pajamas worn by deportees, but these were soon banished from official commemorations. The return of victims from the Nazi concentration camps was the event most quickly effaced from memory."[3]

Initially, knowledge about the deportation and the camps entered French society through a series of publications, films, and radio broadcasts between 1945 and 1948. About 100 testimonial books and pamphlets on the deportation were published immediately after the war, a number characterized by Annette Wieviorka as "voluminous." However, she goes on to write that, whereas the French literature of the First World War had found a large readership over a period of thirteen years, the built-in readership for the French literature of the deportation was small, and the stream of publications dried up in 1948, after just three years, "indicating the indifference of public opinion once the initial shock had passed."[4]

"The victims are still a nuisance," Emmanuel Mounier commented ironically in 1945. "Why, some of them are even disfigured. Their complaints are tiresome for those whose only wish is to return as quickly as possible to peace and quiet."[5] Wieviorka considers as typical the return of deportee Pierre Francés-Rousseau, as narrated in his memoir, *Intact in the Eyes of the World*. "His sister comes to meet him at the Lutetia hotel, looks him over, questions him, quickly reassures herself. He is intact. She takes his arm: 'I'm so glad you're back. Finally I'll be able to talk to someone about my problems.'"[6] Even Jean Cayrol, who continually evoked in his writings the psychological world of the survivor, never got any closer to narrating his actual experiences in the camps than his resolutely impersonal commentary for Resnais's film.

If the general deportation was repressed in postwar French memory, the Jewish genocide was doubly repressed, since it was also repressed within what little discourse of the deportation did appear. In official commemorations of the deportation, Jews were not allowed to march separately.[7] Even the French Jewish community opposed the construction of a Memorial to the Unknown Jewish Martyr in Paris in 1956. Historian David Weinberg writes:

> Despite the revelations of atrocities, many French Jews, like Frenchmen in general, simply could not grasp the immensity of the tragedy. The few survivors who wrote about their ordeal upon returning to France, such as David Rousset, continually stressed the frustrations they felt over the Jewish community's total ignorance of the true nature of the Nazi camp system and its refusal to believe the horrifying reality of the Final Solution.[8]

Ignorance of the distinctiveness of the Jewish genocide continued to dominate public memory until the 1970s in Western Europe and the United States, and until the 1990s in Eastern Europe.

According to André Pierre Colombat, there are only three French films—all documentaries—known to have explicitly addressed the deportation prior to *Night and Fog*. Two were released in 1945: *The Death Camps* and Henri Cartier-Bresson's *The Return*, which showed the return of deportees to France.[9] According to Colombat, the third, *Buchenwald* (1954), showing a visit of French resister-survivors to three former camps, articulated a strictly communist point of view. For the most part, French cinema ignored the subject until the 1970s, preferring, in the immediate postwar period, the favored themes of resistance and combat.[10]

In 1954, Olga Wormser and Henri Michel, heads of the *Comité d'Histoire de la Deuxième Guerre Mondiale* (Second World War Historical Commission), completed a book, *Tragédie de la déportation 1940–1945: Témoignages de survivants des camps de concentration allemands* (*Testimonies of Survivors of German Concentration Camps*), and oversaw the mounting of a related exhibition. The following year, the Comité commissioned film producer Anatole Dauman to produce a documentary film on the deportation for the tenth anniversary of the liberation.

Dauman asked Alain Resnais to direct the film. Resnais had established a reputation as a first-rate documentary filmmaker, after having made a series of films on art: *Van Gogh* (1948), *Gaugin* (1950), *Guernica* (1950), and *Les Statues meurent aussi* (Statues Also Die, 1953). Resnais initially refused the project, on the grounds that only a deportee was qualified to make a film on the deportation. When Dauman asked Resnais a second time, he accepted on the condition that he be allowed to collaborate with Jean Cayrol, a poet-novelist who had been deported to Mauthausen for his role in the resistance. Dauman and the Comité agreed.

That same year, Resnais collected the archival material and wrote the shooting script, he and his crew shot original footage at Auschwitz, and the image track was edited. Subsequently Cayrol wrote the commentary, which was performed by the actor Michel Bouquet.[11] The film lasts approximately thirty minutes, and is composed of fouteen brief color segments showing Auschwitz in 1955, intercut with thirteen longer black-and-white segments of archival footage and photographs.

The black-and-white segments, taken separately, narrate—in a series of "chapters" modeled on the Wormser and Michel book—the rise of Nazism, the creation and characteristics of the camps, and their liberation. They do not, however, refer to the difference between the treatment of Jewish and non-Jewish deportees, or to the difference between the many concentration camps for deportees in general and the six special extermination camps for Jews. The word *juif* is mentioned only once, in passing. (Its translation, "Jew," does not appear in the English subtitles.) Several six-pointed stars can be seen on the clothing of deportees in the film, but their purpose—the identification of Jews for extermination—is not explained. A gas chamber is shown and discussed, but its specifically genocidal function is omitted. This referential fogginess meant that those spectators who already understood the genocidal aspect of the deportation might have taken the film to be addressing both the deportation in general and the genocide in particular. But for the majority, this was not the case.

The omission of genocide from the film is typical of not only a global and a French repression, but also a particular leftist, anticolonial ideology espoused by Resnais. Resnais intended the film to be not only an explicit condemnation of Nazism, but also an implicit condemnation of France's war against Algerian independence. Apparently, Resnais believed—mistakenly, I would argue—that to distinguish the Jewish genocide from the general atrocities would make the film less applicable to Algeria.[12]

Thus *Night and Fog* intervened into the French, and ultimately the global, discourse on the Holocaust in three ways. At the level of content, it both combated the repression of the memory of the camps and contributed to the repression of the memory of the Jewish genocide. But at the same time, it contributed to a new discourse of historical trauma through the content of its form.

NIGHT AND FOG IN THE CONTEXT
OF THE HOLOCAUST DOCUMENTARY

In a 1986 interview, Alain Resnais said of *Night and Fog,*

> Then there was another problem, which was the form of the film: how to treat such a subject? Myself, I was completely overwhelmed (I always am, in any case). And I said to myself: there have already been many films on the concentration camps. Everyone has said this is very good but it doesn't seem to have had a very striking effect on people. Then since I am a formalist, perhaps I must ignore my qualms and attempt in the film, despite its subject, a formal experiment.[13]

The attempt by Resnais and his collaborators to experiment with the form of historical documentary cinema in order to produce a more striking (*frappant*) effect—what I am calling a posttraumatic effect—must be contextualized in relation to the conventions of historical documentary at the time, those "very good" but, by 1955, no longer striking concentration camp films to which Resnais refers.

Two formal types of historical documentary were used to represent the Holocaust before *Night and Fog.* First was the newsreel-type documentary, examples of which were produced by several Allied nations at the end of the war. In these films, footage of the liberated camps is edited into a synchronically structured visual representation, accompanied by highly didactic voice-over commentary providing historical context and assigning blame to Germany. Of course, no notion of a shared Allied culpability in the Holocaust—through, for instance, strict refugee quotas or the refusal to bomb the rail lines to Auschwitz—appears in these films. The French production *The Death Camps* will be used below as an example of the newsreel-type Holocaust documentary in order to maximize continuity with the other French documentaries that will be discussed—not only *Night and Fog,* but also, in the following chapter, *Chronicle of a Summer, The Sorrow and the Pity,* and *Shoah.*

The second formal type of Holocaust documentary to appear was the compilation film, in which the previously used concentration camp footage was edited into diachronically structured narratives of Nazi crimes. A series of such compilation films appeared in conjunction with the war crimes trials of the immediate postwar period, and a second series in conjunction with the trial of Adolf Eichmann in 1961. Instead of using one of the earlier films as an example of compilation documentary form (which would make more sense from a chronological point of view), I will use a later film, the Swedish production *Mein Kampf,* because of its wider availability.

The *Death Camps* and *Mein Kampf* are both examples of what Julianne Burton and Bill Nichols have called the *expository* mode of documentary, which is characterized by mostly nonsynchronized sound (before the appearance of efficient synchronized sound technology in the late 1950s); voice-of-God-style commentary directly addressing the audience; rhetorical editing (continuity maintained primarily by rhetorical rather than spatial relations); and an attitude of self-confidence in the film's ability to present objective, persuasive, and sufficient answers to straightforward questions.[14]

NEWSREEL FORM: *THE DEATH CAMPS*

The Wiener film consists of raw film evidence, devoid of narrative framing. Its traumatic potential is neither supported nor opposed by narrative rhetoric. *The Death Camps,* on the other hand, demonstrates the use of narrative rhetoric to frame potentially traumatic images and thereby attempt to affect the spectator's reaction to them.

Produced in 1945 by Actualités Françaises, *The Death Camps/Les Camps de la mort* is an approximately fifteen-minute documentary with an image track consisting exclusively of footage of liberated camps.[15] It is close to the newsreel in form, and I consider it here as typical of the first wave of documentaries on the concentration camps. The film is structured as a kind of visual tour of seven camps, one after the other, with each visit preceded by a title giving the name of the camp. There is no music.

In terms of tense, *The Death Camps* presents a collection of recently shot footage as a suspended moment of historical time—the liberation of the camps—to be witnessed by the spectator as if in the present. While of course spectators know that the images they are seeing on the screen are not taking place in the present, three factors encourage them to disavow this literal past tense and to experience the footage as taking place in a figurative present tense. First is the sense of presence inherent in the cinematic image, the lack, in any single shot, of the kind of tense markers that can be used to make individual words denote the past. Second, the commentary encourages the figurative present tense with its own literal present tense, as in "Here is where the land of horror starts." When the commentary moves into the past tense for purposes of historical explanation ("In 1933, when the first anti-Nazis were sent here, the Nazis already foresaw a long and useful future for this camp"), the image track does not undergo a corresponding shift, but continues to show footage of the liberated camp (Dachau), thus reinforcing the figurative present tense by way of contrast with the sound track. Third, classical editing of the footage creates an ease of viewing that is conducive to a fantasy of presence.

The classical editing of *The Death Camps* also supports omniscience and flexibility of point of view. Effortless movement from site to site and across boundaries of barbed wire implies the power of authority looking from outside into the camps, rather than the powerlessness of the victims or the shock of the liberators. Footage of each camp is broken down analytically, moving from establishing long shots, to medium shots of groups of living or dead bodies, to close-ups of individual bodies and wounds. In one close-up of a corpse, an unidentified hand reaches into the frame and quickly peels back the clothing from the corpse's chest, revealing a bullet hole. The gaze of the spectator is thus positioned as forensic: objective, knowledgeable, authoritative.

Illustration 2.1. Classical editing in *The Death Camps*: long shot.

Illustration 2.2. *The Death Camps*: medium shot.

Along with this epistemological position comes a moral position. The commentary draws a firm boundary between the positive morality of the signifying text—a morality that remains external to the represented world of the camps—and the negative morality of the signified Nazis, who created and ruled the camps, and who are condemned by the text.

The voice of the film is relatively unself-conscious, within the limits of documentary (which is inherently more self-conscious than the classical fiction film). *The Death Camps* directs the spectator's attention toward the evidence of atrocity and the guilt of the Nazis, and away from the epistemological, moral, or psychological problematics of this act.

In its unself-conscious mastery over time and point of view, *The Death Camps* attempts to present the image of the liberated camps as a historical spectacle that poses little difficulty for the conventional cinematic, historical, and forensic discourses by which Western societies could attempt to comprehend and contain the past. There is ample evidence, however, that the atrocity footage that appeared in films like *The Death Camps* did vicariously traumatize some spectators, despite

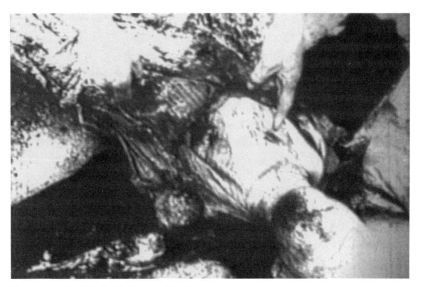

Illustration 2.3. *The Death Camps*: close shot.

the films' rhetorical efforts. This traumatization may have betrayed the ideological goals of the films' producers by setting in motion powerful emotional responses that could not be controlled by the rhetoric of, and the rhetoric surrounding, the films.

COMPILATION FORM: *MEIN KAMPF*

The historical compilation film is far more ambitious than the newsreel-type film in terms of the relationship between image and narrative.[16] It aims to combine the sensual and emotional power of cinematography with the explanatory power of the written historical narrative. Where *The Death Camps* attempts to give the spectator a glimpse of a historical moment by giving a tour of several historical sites, the compilation film promises a visual tour of history itself. Its figurative present tense is diachronic; history seems present not simply as a moment in time, but as a pageant unfolding before the spectator's eyes at a rate of speed attuned to the dramatic requirements of the narrative.

In *The Death Camps*, while the images carry the evidentiary and emotional burden, it is relatively obvious that in themselves they have little power of historical explanation, which inheres, rather, in the commentary. Images of brutalized bodies have profound effects, but it is only the verbal discourse of and surrounding the film that inserts those images and effects into a historical narrative, explaining the identity of the victims and perpetrators, the causes of the violence, and the prosecution of the guilty.

The division of labor in the compilation film is less obvious, but not generally different. Historical explanation inheres in the commentary and in the selection of images, rather than in the images themselves. But here the attempt is made to present a range of footage capable of illustrating a full-scale historical narrative. As each step in the commentary's explanation is illustrated by an image, the explanation can appear to inhere in the images themselves. The visible becomes the true. The compilation film not only adopts certain techniques of tense and mood from the newsreel—the apparent presence of the image, the classical editing, the moral binarism—but adds to these techniques this diachronic, seemingly self-explanatory, visual narrative in order to promote an even more powerful sense of mastery over time and point of view.

Written and directed by the German Jewish refugee Erwin Leiser under Swedish auspices in 1960, the almost two-hour-long *Mein Kampf* treats the history and crimes of the Third Reich, moving more or less chronologically from the purported roots of Nazism in the First World War to the Nuremberg trials. Like other compilation films, its visual track presents mostly archival footage, plus photographs and documents. Its sound track consists of a voice-of-God commentary, source sound accompanying the relatively few archival shots that have it (mainly German newsreels showing speeches by Nazi leaders), sound effects added to silent footage (gunfire, marching bands, etc.), and a musical score.

While neither concentration camps nor genocide are the main subject of the film, they receive specific attention in three distinct segments: an eight-minute segment on the Warsaw ghetto; a five-minute segment on concentration camps and gassing; and the final, three-minute segment of the film, on the death toll of the Nazi crimes, illustrated by footage of liberated camps, of mountains of suitcases, eyeglasses, dentures, hair, and so on.

I will use the middle segment, on concentration camps and gassing, as an example of the problem of tense in the Holocaust compilation film. The following are excerpts from the segment.

1. Commentary: "In Eastern Europe, Himmler sets up huge concentration camps. They swallow up hundreds of thousands of people. The healthy become slave workers in branches of German factories. The others are doomed." Image: period footage of deportees on train ramps. Postliberation aerial footage of camp barracks.

2. Commentary: "Cross-examined after the war, Höss stated that, in Auschwitz alone, approximately two-and-a-half million people were liquidated, mostly Poles, Russians, Gypsies, and Jews."[17] Image: postliberation footage of barbed wire and towers at a camp.

3. Commentary: "It was Höss' idea to use the cyanide compound Zyklon B for the mass extermination of humans." Image: postliberation close-up shot of a Zyklon B can.

4. Commentary: "The condemned were led into gas chambers that were built to look like ordinary shower baths. First came the women and children." Image: photo showing a line of naked women and children.

5. Commentary: "The doors were locked and the gas introduced through ventilators. After twenty minutes at the most, all were dead." Image: postliberation footage of an empty gas chamber.

6. Commentary: "The corpses were burned. Crematoria I and II in Auschwitz had a capacity of two thousand corpses a day." Image: postliberation footage of ovens filled with bones.

This segment illustrates the way the compilation film can combine commentary with visual documents originating from different times (before and after the liberation) and different sources (German and Allied) in order to give the impression of a seamless visual narrative. But whereas the figurative present tense of *The Death Camps* actually allows the spectator to witness the liberation of the camps in some limited way, the figurative present tense of *Mein Kampf* smoothes over and covers up a tremendous gap in the photographic record of the Holocaust: the absolute lack of a photographic image of the gassing of millions of people. This gap—the missing image of what was for Himmler unfilmable and for the victims unthinkable, the image that disappeared forever with the victims—this gap, rather than being preserved *as a gap*, or amnesia, in the image track of the film, disappears into an apparently seamless chain of shots. Thus in *Mein Kampf* there are no rhetorical limits placed on the spectator's ability to witness the genocide as a steadily unfolding and self-explanatory scenario, no temporal gaps or blockages of per-spective. The spectator is positioned as having visually accompanied the victims to their extermination, emerging from the gas chamber to continue watching even as the victims are burned in the crematorium.

The segment also illustrates the tendency of compilation films to sub-stitute available images for missing images in a misleading fashion. According to Yad Vashem, the photo of naked women and children, presented as an illustration of gassing, actually shows a mobile killing action in Misocz, Ukraine, in October 1942, before gassing had even begun.[18]

Voice in the film is generally unself-conscious. However, there are ex-ceptions, one of which occurs at the beginning of the Warsaw ghetto seg-ment. The commentator says, "Goebbels' own cameramen have taken these pictures, which show how an ordinary quarter of a town is trans-formed into a living hell. It was his intention to use them as propaganda, but he gave up the idea for fear that people would feel sympathy for the victims." The footage shows emaciated corpses lying on the sidewalk, then taken away by Jewish workers as ghetto inhabitants walk by in the foreground, looking straight ahead. Why in this instance does the film become self-conscious about the origin of the footage it is presenting? What is the difference between this footage and the footage of corpses in the liberated camps, inspected by Eisenhower, that appears at the end of the film without comment on its origins?

The difference lies in the gaze of the witnesses who appear in the footage. Eisenhower's presence not only authenticates the evidence, but, since he is a moral outsider to the Nazi world, viewing evidence of crimes that he himself has already helped to stop, his presence also provides for the spectator an identificatory position characterized by the mastering distance of pity. In the ghetto scene, on the other hand, we know that we are seeing not the aftermath of the crimes but the crimes themselves, in the process of being committed. We know this not only explicitly from the accompanying commentary and the placement of the footage within the film's chronology, but also implicitly from the averted gaze of the onscreen witnesses, who walk past the corpses of their fellow Jews without looking.

How to read the averted gaze of these witnesses who are also victims? Were they ordered not to look, so as to present to the audience an image of Jews as inherently uncivilized?[19] Were ghetto inhabitants generally forbidden from responding to the presence of corpses in public? Or was it that surviving the ghettos and camps required an attitude, or at least a posture, of numbed indifference to the death of others?

In any case, while Eisenhower's detached gaze offers spectators their own detached viewing position, the disturbing aversion of the witnesses' gaze in the ghetto segment implicates the footage and the camera operator in the negative moral world of the Nazis, positioning the spectator as complicit in the very crimes being documented.[20] A gap is thus opened up in the realm of mood—a gap between the outsider's point of view of the film as a whole, and the morally implicated, insider's view of the ghetto footage. This gap in the realm of mood must then be closed in the realm of voice, through the explanation of the origins of the footage. This departure from the unself-conscious voice

Illustration 2.4. Nazi footage of the Warsaw ghetto in *Mein Kampf*: how to read the averted gaze of these witnesses who are also victims?

constitutes not a questioning of the content or the form of the narration, but rather a reestablishment of the moral authority of the text. Using the diachronic figurative present tense to close the visual gap in the historical record, and with minor adjustments in the realm of mood and voice, *Mein Kampf* was able to extend the synchronic realism of *The Death Camps* into the form of a full-scale historical narrative. The film's occasional deviations into a morally implicated point of view and resulting self-conscious voice demonstrate the strain inherent in that extension. The traumas of concentration camps and genocide were thus contained and assimilated into the master narratives of the Third Reich and the Second World War.

Posttraumatic Form: *Night and Fog*

Night and Fog / Nuit et brouillard is significant in a number of ways. Not only is it a founding text of posttraumatic cinema, it is also an important precursor of the French New Wave; it is one of the most highly regarded Holocaust films; it has been shown to large numbers of students in mainstream and Jewish schools and universities, having been, until *Schindler's List*, the film most commonly used to teach the Holocaust in several countries, including the United States; and it was one of the first and most influential modernist historical documentaries, especially in its revolutionary use of the image of the present to signify the past. As such, it is also an important precursor of what Burton and Nichols call the *reflexive* mode of documentary, which, they propose, did not come into its own until the 1970s.[21] As a reflexive film, *Night and Fog* does not simply turn away from the realism of the expository compilation film, however. Rather, it engages the techniques of the compilation film, and then uses a series of other techniques—reflexive, modernist, poetic— to effect a radical break with the traditional documentary discourse of atrocity. It is in this radical break that I locate *Night and Fog*'s engagement with a posttraumatic historical consciousness.

The contribution of *Night and Fog* to posttraumatic cinema cannot be understood outside the context of Resnais's films as a whole.[22] A consummate modernist, Resnais rejected classical realist epistemology— the drive, going back to the nineteenth-century realist novel, to present the work as a transparent window onto a plausible world—striving instead for a hyper-realistic representation of consciousness, of the way the world is perceived, distorted, and given meaning by the mind. The modernism of Resnais's *Night and Fog* and *Hiroshima, mon amour*, in particular, constituted a rejection of classical realism as a form for representing the new forms of collective trauma introduced during the Second World War—the baffling, technologically advanced annihilations of the Nazi concentration camps and the bombing of Hiroshima. For Resnais, the overwhelming historical traumas of the recent past rendered classical historical narrative ineffective; they demanded narratives constructed on the subjectively fragmented terrain of memory.

Night and Fog's break with the realist tradition of documentary, and its contribution to a modernist countertradition, are constituted by a number of formal characteristics, in addition to its use of tense, mood, and voice, to which I will turn below. The commentary, for example, repeatedly breaks away from the traditional chronicling and explanation of historical events, and enters into poetic meditations on the difficulties of historical memory. This, of course, resulted partly from Resnais's decision to hire the poet Jean Cayrol, who had no prior experience in film or historiography, to write the commentary. Resnais also obtained a rigorously modernist score for the film by hiring the German composer Hanns Eisler, who was an important figure in modernist music, having worked with such figures as Arnold Schoenberg, Bertolt Brecht, and Theodor Adorno.

But it was primarily Resnais himself who effected a break with the traditional historical documentary in his overall construction of *Night and Fog*. The film is constructed with a degree of formal rigor uncharacteristic of historical documentaries. In this sense, the film not only invites the spectator to attend to the past by presenting artifacts in the form of historical footage and photographs, it also invites the spectator to attend to the film's presence as both a historical and an artistic artifact.

One aspect of Resnais's overall construction of *Night and Fog* in which we can see this break from the traditional historical documentary is in the relations between the image track, the commentary track, and the music track. Realist historical films rely upon a specific hierarchy in these relations. First and foremost, they ask spectators to believe their eyes; they place the photographic image in the dominant position in the hierarchy, invoking an empirical discourse of visual evidence. In the second position in the hierarchy, the commentary places the image into historical context, giving it historical meaning. In the third position, the music provides emotional cues in an attempt to weld the historical narrative to preexisting historical genres—epic, tragic, comic, and the like.[23]

Consistent with the theories of Bertolt Brecht, which he had encountered in 1947, Resnais sought throughout his career to break apart this hierarchy, and to replace it with more egalitarian relations between the tracks, through which formal and discursive tensions could be staged.[24] First, he sought to demote the image track from its elevated position of epistemological irrefutability to a lower position, where it would have to exist in dialogue with, and sometimes in conflict with, the words on the sound track. Second, he sought to free the use of verbal language from cinematic convention, opening it up to other, competing conventions—novelistic, poetic, or operatic.[25] It is for this reason that Resnais neither worked with established screenwriters nor wrote his own screenplays, instead collaborating with accomplished novelists and poets, such as Cayrol, Marguerite Duras, Alain Robbe-Grillet, and Jorge Semprun, none of whom had prior screenwriting experience. Thus traditional cinematic forms of knowledge, including the cinematic modernism Resnais inherited from figures like Sergei Eisenstein, Louis Delluc, and Orson Welles, were demoted by Resnais and placed into collision with literary forms of knowledge, in particular with the literary modernism of the French New Novel.

The epistemological tension between image and language tends to be heightened when Resnais directly encounters historical trauma in his films. In the prologue sequence of *Hiroshima, mon amour*, the disembodied voices of a woman and a man wrestle with the memory of the bombing of Hiroshima, in a kind of operatic duet, while the image track juxtaposes photographic documents of the bombing with fictional reconstructions. In *Muriel*, we hear a French veteran reciting a fragmented narrative of rape, torture, and execution in Algeria, while the image track presents a soldier's amateur film showing the banality of daily life behind the lines. And while the black-and-white segments of *Night and Fog* display a relatively traditional hierarchy of image and commentary tracks, the color segments problematize that hierarchy, showing images of Auschwitz in the present while the commentary considers those aspects of the past that no image can represent.

Tense

Night and Fog's single most significant contribution to posttraumatic cinema is its experimentation with tense. As such, it draws from a variety of modernist traditions that have in common the rejection of the classical linear chronologies that dominated historical, literary, and cinematic narratives, in favor of hypersubjective and fragmented inscriptions of time.

Classical linear chronology in historiography, which arose in conjunction with the Enlightenment, allowed the historian to use documentary evidence to rhetorically transport the reader to the past, and then forward through a narrative of significant events. A series of critics, however, have called this kind of temporal rhetoric into question, and attempted to deconstruct the classical historical sense of the past by attending to the present-tense context of historical writing. An early example was Nietzsche's *The Use and Abuse of History* (1874). Closer to Resnais was the French historian Marc Bloch, who wrote in 1944 that the historian must "understand the past by means of the present." Employing a cinematic metaphor, he wrote that in order to undertake this historiographic project, one had to "unwind the spool in reverse."[26] *Night and Fog* represented the first major attempt to practice this new historiography in documentary film.

The most direct influences on Resnais's experiments with tense, however, were affiliated with cultural modernism, rather than with a new historiography. These two tendencies had in common the rejection of the idea of the signifier as a transparent window onto reality, and a concern to attend to the effects of the signifier itself on the construction of reality. In this sense, both are indebted to Ferdinand de Saussure, the founder of European semiotics.

In terms of literary modernism, the primary influence was Marcel Proust's cycle of novels, *Remembrance of Things Past* (1913–27). Proust rejected the classical bracketing off of the past as a containable source of story information and character motivation in favor of a more complex interpenetration of past and present, in which questions of memory provided both the form and the central theme of the work. Proust, in turn, had studied with the philosopher Henri Bergson, who had explored the distinction between voluntary and involuntary memory.

A second literary influence on Resnais's experiments with time was the French New Novel, exemplified by Cayrol, Duras, and Robbe-Grillet. In 1946, after his return from Mauthausen, Cayrol published a volume of poetry, *Poèmes de la nuit et du brouillard*. The volume took its name from Hitler's Night and Fog Decree of 1941, and gave its name to Resnais's film. The decree was designed to destroy resistance to German rule in the occupied territories through the arrest of resisters and their deportation to German concentration camps, and especially through the withholding of all information about their fates. Under the decree, several thousand French resisters were arrested without warning in the middle of the night. They effectively vanished without a trace. Cayrol was one of these.

In a pair of essays published in 1950, Cayrol presented a "lazarean" theory of the novel based on a prototypical figure who had physically returned from the land of the dead, while remaining psychologically bound to traumatic memory. "The Lazarus-type character," Cayrol has said, "is one who has been shocked—figuratively speaking—by some explosive force and who has remained dazed."[27]

The past never appears directly in Cayrol's writing, but always haunts the present, displaced onto a problem of writing. "I belong to silence, to the shadow of my voice," he wrote in 1944, immediately after his return from Mauthausen.[28] He seemed to be building a new literary practice from the posttraumatic space that Wiesel described when he wrote, "So heavy was my anguish that I made a vow: not to speak, not to touch upon the essential for at least ten years. . . . Long enough to regain possession of my memory. Long enough to unite the language of man with the silence of the dead."[29]

In Cayrol's early novels, such as the trilogy, *Je vivrai l'amour des autres* (*I Lived the Love of Others*, 1947–50), the memories are specifically of deportation. In later works, like *Foreign Bodies* (1959), the problem loses its historical specificity. The narrator, writing his fragmented life story, complains:

> Every minute contradicts the next. Like a broken necklace whose beads are running at my feet. How to put it back together? How to string the memories in order of size? There's always one in the corner; I never can dig it out in time. There's always one missing, and none of it will be true anymore. . . . There are memories the dead have taken with them, others that are beyond my grasp, strangely hidden in someone who merely passed through.[30]

Marguerite Duras also worked consistently with questions of memory in her writing. Her autobiographical book *The War: A Memoir* (1985) represents her memories of the return of her husband from a German concentration camp, and her confrontation with his memories. According to Herman Rapaport, her 1979 pair of films, *Aurelia Steiner, dite Aurelia Melbourne* and *Aurelia Steiner, dite Aurelia Vancouver*, obliquely deal with memories of the Holocaust.[31] An early treatment of *Hiroshima, mon amour* even had the female protagonist's mother as a hidden Jew in Occupied France.[32]

Resnais also collaborated on two films with the Spanish novelist Jorge Semprun after reading Semprun's autobiographical novel *The Long Voyage* (1963). The novel takes place on a deportation train, where the protagonist, a Spanish leftist being deported to Auschwitz, remembers his life in a series of fragmented flashbacks.

What these works have in common is the stripping away of the literary representation of the past per se, and the pursuit in its place of writing as a form of struggle with memories that can be neither escaped nor possessed. Resnais has been seen by many critics as having pursued a kind of cinematic equivalent of the New Novel, attempting in several of his films to inscribe a problem of memory as a problem of narration. French film critic René Prédal sees Resnais as creating a more specifically lazarean cinema, in which everyone resembles a concentration camp survivor.[33]

While there had been no major experiments with retrospective temporal structures in historical documentary before Resnais, he was influenced by experiments with time in a series of modernist fiction films. There were the French impressionist films of the 1920s by Abel Gance, Louis Delluc, Marcel L'Herbier, and Jean Epstein.[34] Carné and Prévert's *Le Jour se leve/Daybreak* (1939) created a highly elegiac tone with its ultraslow dissolves alternating between the present and the past. Welles's *Citizen Kane* (1941) and Kurosawa's *Rashomon* (1950) experimented with multiperspective flashbacks, and Cocteau's *Orphée* (1950) contained disorienting time shifts, lacking clear temporal markers.

Almost all of Resnais's films foreground questions of time and memory in one way or another. Four of his films—*Guernica* (1950), *Night and Fog*, *Hiroshima, mon amour*, and *Muriel*—focus on the memory of historical trauma in particular. The documentary *Guernica* uses Picasso's drawings and paintings, rather than archival footage or photographs, as visual references to the atrocious bombing of that town by fascist forces during the Spanish civil war. *Hiroshima, mon amour* begins with a collage of forms of collective memory of the atomic bombing of that city—photos, film clips (both documentary and fictional), models, artifacts, ruins—which are then juxtaposed with flashbacks of a French woman's memories of loss, ostracism, and madness during the German

Occupation of France. Similarly, *Muriel* juxtaposes a woman's memory of lost love with her son's memory of atrocity in the Algerian war.

In comparing these four films, a number of things become apparent. We can see how Resnais's concern with posttraumatic memory spans the distinction between personal and collective trauma. We can notice the variety of memory catalysts that are presented in the films: a painting (*Guernica*), a ruin (*Night and Fog*), a lover's hand (*Hiroshima, mon amour*), a film (*Muriel*).

Common to all four films is what might be called an archeological theory of cinematic historiography. Each film transcribes the temporal dimensions of history, which cinema represents with relative awkwardness, into more easily represented spatial dimensions. Thus *Guernica* transcribes the past bombing of that village into the present space of a canvas; *Night and Fog* transcribes the past atrocities of the Holocaust into the dimensions of present-day Auschwitz; and *Hiroshima, mon amour* may be thought of as a film about the conversion of Hiroshima from a ruin into a memorial.

A variety of types of visual relationships between the present and the past appear in these four films. In *Hiroshima, mon amour*, the woman's memories appear in the present via mimetic representation, in the form of flashbacks. In *Guernica*, Picasso's painting constructs an imaginary but powerful image of the past. On the other hand, attempts to visualize the bombing in *Hiroshima, mon amour* and torture in *Muriel* are presented as failures.

The relations between image, tense, and trauma become apparent in the first shot of *Night and Fog*: a high-angle view of an empty field, accompanied by a hollow drumbeat droning on the sound track.[35] Contradicting the traditional hierarchy of registers in historical documentary, this image shows us virtually nothing: a simple field containing no sign of the past. But the drumbeat suggests a state of suspension, perhaps even apprehension, anxiety. What are we waiting for?

As the shot continues, the camera proceeds to answer our question, craning slowly and smoothly down to reveal a barbed wire fence in the foreground. This revealing gesture is repeated in the second and third shots. In the second, the camera tracks backward—like Bloch's spool unwinding in reverse—to reveal the fence. In the third, the track is lateral. Perhaps by now the spectator can recognize this particular barbed wire fence, its state of ruin, a particular curl at the top of a concrete post.

Illustration 2.5. The opening sequence of *Night and Fog*: an apparently harmless present.

Guard towers appear in the background; perhaps their historical significance, too, is recognized. The accompanying commentary is as follows:
"Even a peaceful landscape; even a field with crows flying over; even a
road with cars, peasants, and couples passing by; even a holiday village
with a fair and a steeple can lead the way to a concentration camp."[36]

The field, which can still be seen beyond the fence, is now revealed to
be no ordinary field, the fence no ordinary fence. We are at the border—
between the present and the past, between the outside world and the
inner world of the concentration camp. More precisely, the camera, and
we, are inside Auschwitz, looking out.

This film about the past begins in the present, with footage whose
very form—in color and tracking—distinguishes it from the whole body
of footage conventionally associated with history: black-and-white footage that, if it moves at all, pans gracelessly or is handheld. While *Night
and Fog* proceeds to image the past directly through such traditional
archival footage, that footage is always framed within the image of the
present. Thus, we are dealing here not simply with the past, but with

Illustration 2.6. *Night and Fog*: the camera tracks backward to reveal a sign of the past.

the relation between the present and the past—in other words, with memory.

More specifically, the relationship between the present and the past is characterized by the image track in these three opening shots as one of entrapment. In whichever direction one travels—downward, backward, laterally—one is pulled from an apparently harmless present, as if by an irresistible gravitational force, into the black hole of some terrible memory, embodied in the wire that one encounters wherever one turns. This gravitational relationship between the field and the wire can be seen as a metaphor for posttraumatic memory, in which the present is indeed a field of anxiety and hypervigilance, in which any encountered object may trigger a terrifying memory of events from which time provides no escape, of a wound that time alone does not heal.

At the end of this first color segment is the earliest example of which I am aware of what might be called a documentary flashback. This flashback—the transition from a color shot tracking alongside the Auschwitz fence in 1955 to a black-and-white shot taken from *Triumph of the Will* showing German soldiers marching in formation at the Nuremberg Nazi Party Congress in 1934—is presented formally as a shock. Almost every conceivable stylistic element of the two joined shots undergoes a total reversal at the edit point. Color turns to black and white; clean footage to aged; an eye-level camera position to one on the ground; a moving shot to a stationary one, and simultaneously a stationary mise-en-scène (fence) to a moving one (marching soldiers); slow, smooth movement (tracking) to fast, jagged movement (soldiers); the incantory voice-over of the first segment to the staccato, "1933"; a drum roll that is soft, slow, sustained, low-pitched, and hollow-timbred to one that is loud, fast, brief, high-pitched, and using a snare. Thus, the film's movement from the present to the past is not characterized by the ease of mastery, but by the shock of trauma; one is jolted into the past, or, alternately, the past intrudes violently on the present.

And yet, while the past in *Night and Fog* is characterized as too insistent, it is simultaneously characterized as too remote. This sense of remoteness becomes apparent in comparing the temporal framing of archival footage in *Night and Fog* and *Mein Kampf*. In *Mein Kampf*, the

Illustration 2.7. A documentary flashback in *Night and Fog*: the present.

Illustration 2.8 A documentary flashback in *Night and Fog*: the past.

literal past tense of the archival footage—its obviously having been recorded decades before the production of the documentary—is disavowed by the figurative present tense of the film's narrative rhetoric. In *Night and Fog*, on the other hand, while the tense of the black-and-white segments taken by themselves may resemble the figurative present of *Mein Kampf*, that figurative present is repeatedly disavowed by the color segments, which wrest the present tense away from the black-and-white segments, reframing them by bringing to the fore once again their literal pastness. *Night and Fog* thus repeatedly enacts a double movement in time: the intrusion of the past into the present with each flashback, followed by its flight into the remoteness of memory with each return to the present.

This sense of the remoteness of the past also becomes apparent in comparing the temporal framing of footage of the gas chamber in *Night and Fog* and *Mein Kampf*. In *Mein Kampf*, as I have described, the actual lack of footage of gassing is disavowed when a postliberation shot of an empty gas chamber is used—in the figurative present tense—to illustrate the commentary's description of gassing before the liberation.

A postliberation shot of a gas chamber appears in *Night and Fog* as well. But the present tense of this shot—a color shot moving slowly and smoothly through the chamber—is literal. It accompanies the words, "The only sign—but you have to know—is this ceiling ripped by fingernails. Even the concrete was torn." In this case, no attempt is made to substitute the gas chamber shot for the missing image of the gassing itself. *Night and Fog* thus suggests that the spectator understand the image of gassing precisely as missing, something that can only be confronted through the image of its ruins.

In addition, *Night and Fog* characterizes the past as remote by diminishing the present tense effect of the compilation segments it does contain. This is done first by lowering the proportion of film clips and raising the proportion of still photographs in comparison with a film like *Mein Kampf*—photographs having a more past-tense effect; and second by including none of the source or added sound accompanying archival footage that contributes to the present-tense effect of *Mein Kampf*. The sound track of *Night and Fog* contains only commentary, music, and silence.

At times, *Night and Fog* represents the past as not only remote, but unknowable. The film's commentary repeatedly reminds the spectator of the failure of its images to be able to capture the reality of the past. These words, for example, accompany a color shot tracking through an empty barrack:

> The reality of the camps, despised by those who made them, inconceivable to those who suffered in them—in vain do we try to discover its remnants. These wooden barracks, these shelves where three slept, these burrows where one hid, where one concealed food, where sleep itself was a menace—no description, no image can restore their true dimension, that of un-interrupted fear.

The implication is that not even the archival image, for all its shocking realism, is adequate to represent what took place in the camps.

In its use of crosscutting to establish a set of relations between the present and the past, *Night and Fog* could be said to apply an Eisensteinian theory of cinema to the representation of posttraumatic historical consciousness. Eisenstein, one of the first great film modernists, rejected the view (later theorized by André Bazin and Sigfried Kracauer) of the shot as a window onto reality, in favor of a different kind of realism. For Eisenstein, reality inhered not in the ontology of the photographic image but in the structural relations between images. Similarly, in *Night and Fog* Resnais rejects both the notion of the archival image as a window onto history and the notion of the image of the present as a window onto memory. He constructs a cinematic theory of historical consciousness from the montage relations between the image of the present and the image of the past.

Like this montage form of historical consciousness, trauma is defined neither by the past event nor by the present vicissitudes of memory but by the relations between the two, the event's overwhelming of narrative memory, and memory's struggles to belatedly master the event. In addition, posttraumatic memory is characterized by montage-like relations of intrusiveness and remoteness, of vision and blindness, of remembering and forgetting. PTSD is characterized by a dialectic of hypermnesia and amnesia; memories are not mastered, but rather are experienced as involuntary, hallucinatory repetitions, or, alternately, are blocked. Accordingly, the black-and-white segments of *Night and Fog* are like hypermnesic or hallucinatory episodes; we see too much. The image of the past repeats with a shocking literality, intruding on the present. The image track takes the lead, the commentary at times registering its own inability to make sense of the images, as when a series of shots of brutalized corpses discovered in the liberated camps is accompanied by the words, "Nothing left to say." The images continue in silence; the spectator must watch helplessly.

With the return of color footage, the image of the past is blocked by the image of the present; we don't see enough. With the failure of visual memory, the commentary must take the lead, attempting to describe what no image exists to show, or simply pointing out the failure. One such instance follows a segment of archival footage showing the departure of a deportation train. Classical realist editing would call here for a cut to an image of the train's arrival at the camp. But no such footage exists. Resnais cuts to a color tracking shot along the rail line leading into Auschwitz. The commentary says, "Today on the same track, the sun shines. Go slowly along it, looking for what? Traces of the bodies that fell to the ground? Or the footmark of those first arrivals gun-bullied to the camp, while the dogs barked and the searchlights wheeled and the incinerator flamed."

Another aspect of the film's montage theory of memory is its treatment of artifacts as catalysts of memory. At times, these artifacts succeed

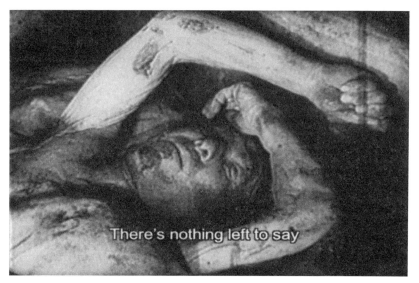

Illustration 2.9. *Night and Fog*: the shocking literalness of the flashback renders the commentary self-consciously mute.

in triggering visual memories, as Proust's madeleine triggers visual memories of his childhood. Cayrol has said of this kind of triggering:

> One day in the Gusen concentration camp I found a broken egg shell on the floor between two slabs of stone. At first, I did not understand how this egg shell could have gotten there and then, suddenly, my sensibilities were awakened: I grabbed the remains of the egg shell, as though it were a valuable object. Symbolically speaking, it represented the world for me; and I was moved to tears by it. I tried to create my universe starting from this egg shell.[37]

But in *Night and Fog*, artifactual memory—for example, the initial revealing of the barbed wire—leads not out of the camp but into it.

At other times, artifacts appearing in the frame seem to confront us with nothing but their mute materiality, devoid of memory. The wooden blocks whose past no image can restore suggest the threatening "in-itself" of the material world in the writings of Sartre, or Robbe-Grillet's resolutely antisubjective *chosisme* (thingism). The material present in

Night and Fog thus functions as a double-edged sword, both triggering and blocking memory.

But Cathy Caruth argues for a second, and more subtle, dialectic of memory and forgetting in PTSD: that the failure of traumatic memory to submit to the normal forgetting process—its pathologically literal repetition—stems from an earlier forgetting inherent in the experience of the original traumatic event; that it is precisely this original forgetting of the event as it happens, the mind's failure to register the event and place it into narrative memory, that gives rise to the later pathological repetitions of memory.[38] Accordingly, the massive influx of visual data constituted by the filming of the liberated camps and the original dissemination of the footage in 1945 so overwhelmed the historical consciousness of the spectating public that the images failed to register in some sense; through its montage structure, *Night and Fog* stages the dialectic of forgetting and repetition engendered by this original failure.

Mood

The modernist rejection of classical omniscient narration and the turn to a more restricted narrational subjectivity is pointed out by Erich Auerbach when, at the end of his survey of the history of realism in Western literature, *Mimesis*, he concludes with a discussion of Virginia Woolf's *To the Lighthouse* (1927).

> The writer as narrator of objective facts has almost completely vanished. . . . We are not given the objective information which Virginia Woolf possesses regarding these objects of her creative imagination but what Mrs. Ramsaye thinks or feels about them at a particular moment. . . . This goes so far that there actually seems to be no viewpoint at all outside the novel from which the people and events within it are observed, any more than there seems to be an objective reality apart from what is in the consciousness of the characters. . . . This attitude differs entirely from that of authors who interpret the actions, situations, and characters of their personages with objective assurance, as was the general practice in earlier times. Goethe or Keller, Dickens or Meredith, Balzac or Zola told us out of their certain knowledge what their characters did, what they felt and thought while doing it, and how their actions and thoughts were to be interpreted.[39]

Hayden White has cited Auerbach's discussion of Woolf as an effective description of a new form of writing that was "an effort to represent a historical reality for which the older, classical realist modes of

representation were inadequate, based as they were on different experiences of history or, rather, on experiences of a different 'history.' "[40] It
was to this literary countertradition that Resnais turned when, making
Night and Fog, he asked himself, "how to treat such a subject?"

Night and Fog's regulation of point of view, like its regulation of tense,
is characterized not by a complete rejection of realism, but by the montage of opposed forms of narration in the monochrome and color segments. In representing the camps, Resnais could hardly dispense with
"objective reality" altogether. In fact, the narration of the compilation
segments is relatively conventional in its omniscience. The commentary
of the first compilation segment begins in the most classically objective
manner: "1933."

It is the color segments that problematize this classical form of narration. The sense of entrapment evoked by the opening shots of the film
applies not only to time—entrapment in the past—but also to point of
view. The rigid categories into which Nazism forced its subjects did not
disappear with its defeat, but continue to exert a pressure upon historical consciousness in the present. *Night and Fog* takes up this pressure,
and applies it to the spectator, not in order to repeat the oppression of
Nazism, but in order to recognize and begin to work through the lingering effects of the past.

The possibilities for the construction of a visual point of view using compilation footage are relatively limited, given the constraints on
available material and the necessity for combining that material into a
coherent historical narrative. One of the effects of Resnais's decision to
shoot new footage at Auschwitz, then, was a tremendous increase in his
control over the image track, and a concomitant expansion of the formal
vocabulary with which he could construct a point of view.[41]

Of the footage Resnais produced at Auschwitz, one cinematographic
trope dominates: the tracking shot—moving at a slow and constant
speed, smooth, eye level, approaching and passing alongside ruins and
artifacts, occasionally adjusting its direction or angle for a different
view. This is not the point of view of a military, forensic, or historical authority—powerful, flexible, teleological, omniscient. It is the existential point of view of the anguished individual walking through
the camp, confronting the ruins of the past. Like the Sartrean antihero,
the wandering consciousness of Resnais's anthropomorphic camera is
a lone presence, thrown into the world, devoid of predetermined mean-

ing. It confronts the threatening muteness of inanimate objects. It confronts human evil: the retreat from individual responsibility into the mass passivity of fascism, the objectification of the human. Finally, it confronts its own responsibility to others, its freedom to act on their behalf.[42]

The point of view of this existential consciousness does not exist in a historical vacuum; it may not be *pre*determined, but it is determined in the present by its confrontation with the past. It exists in the shadow of the Holocaust, inheriting the historical subject positions enforced by the atrocities. This confrontation, this inheritance, begins in the opening shots described above, in the subject's entrapment behind the wire. It continues after the camera assumes a position firmly imprisoned in the world of the camp, where no suturing edit provides an escape from the camera's melancholy, walking stare at the remnants of atrocity.

This is the point of view, first and foremost, of the traumatized witness. As such, it may be thought of as conflating two positions: the position of the firsthand witness—the survivor who, like Cayrol, returns to the scene of the trauma, who sees, alternately, hallucinations of the past and the ruins covering over the past, and who testifies; and the position of the secondhand witness, the liberator or documentor—the outsider, like Resnais, whose attention to the other's memories places him or her in danger of vicarious traumatization, and whose decision to relay the witnessing experience keeps the trauma moving.

Paradoxically, the move to a more subjective point of view is accompanied not by a gain in epistemological confidence but by a loss. Alain Robbe-Grillet has summarized the loss of epistemological confidence that characterizes modernist writing: "During the nineteenth century, an author who knows a story relates it to a public who does not know it yet. . . . In the twentieth century, the situation has developed that gave rise to the Nouveau Roman: that of an author who does not know a story recounting it to a public who does not know it either."[43]

The epistemological position of the traumatized witness is, in fact, highly conflicted. A tremendous emotional investment in the past, and an unshakable certainty about the reality of certain events and facts, are countered by a crippling sense of failure—the failure to be able to resolve the past by narrativizing it conclusively and assigning meaning to it, as well as painful failures of knowledge, such as of the fates of lost loved ones. In *Night and Fog*, the gain in emotional investment in the past is accompanied by this loss of mastery, as the commentary repeatedly points out the limits and failures of knowledge.

Along with the rejection of the omniscient epistemological point of view of the realist documentary comes a rejection of its external moral point of view. *Night and Fog* is at some pains, particularly in its conclusion, to implicate the spectator in the question of responsibility for crimes against humanity: "There are those of us who look at these ruins today as though the monster were dead and buried beneath the ruins, who take hope again as the image fades, as though there were a cure for the scourge of these camps, those of us who pretend to believe this only happened at a certain time and in a certain place, and who refuse to look around us, and who refuse to hear the endless cry."[44]

Voice

In his 1953 book, *Writing Degree Zero*, French literary critic Roland Barthes distinguishes between a classical mode of writing that claimed the status of a window on universal truth, and a newer mode, beginning in the second half of the nineteenth century—what others have called a modernist mode—in which mimesis began to give way to *écriture*: writing as the self-conscious unfolding of language, writing as a consideration of its own materiality.

In this, Barthes's first book, he was attempting to theorize the emerging French New Novel, and give it an ancestry. After referring to Albert Camus, Maurice Blanchot, and Jean Cayrol as practitioners of the new French *écriture*, Barthes observes that this mode of writing, "not without an additional tragic implication, binds the writer to his society."[45] What I want to point out, even if this may not be what Barthes meant, is that one of the tragedies of the new French writing lay in its relationship to what happened in France during the German Occupation. Each of the three writers Barthes refers to attempted at one time or another to write his way through the impasse of the Occupation and the Holocaust— Camus as a resister (*The Plague*), Blanchot as a one-time anti-Jew (*The Writing of the Disaster*), and Cayrol as a survivor.[46] *Night and Fog* makes Resnais one of these tragic figures as well, insofar as it demonstrates his attempt to work out a new relationship between a film form—a kind of cinematic *écriture* equivalent to that of the New Novel—and the atrocities of the war.

Of course, Resnais's self-consciousness is not of the abstract type championed by art critic Clement Greenberg, in which the work achieves its highest form by shedding any reference to a reality outside the work itself and its own materials. The realist impulse in cinema seems to have been so strong that, even in modernist films, pure abstraction has constituted only a minor tendency. Of all film genres, documentary has, of course, traditionally been the most insistent on film's referencing of the real, and perhaps therefore one of the more resistant to modernist self-consciousness. One of Resnais's most important achievements, then, is his attempt to work out a form of cinema in which the distinction between historical reference and artistic self-consciousness breaks down. The central motif of his oeuvre is the interrogation of cinema as an analogue for the way the mind constructs knowledge of the world through visualization, narration, and thought. Insofar as he is concerned with a kind of cinematic self-interrogation, then, Resnais is a paradigmatic modernist. Insofar as this self-interrogation concerns our knowledge of Guernica, Auschwitz, and Hiroshima, Resnais's modernism functions in a way that becomes relevant to the representation of historical trauma. When history exceeds the mind's accustomed habits of visualization, narration, and thought, *Night and Fog* asks, in effect, what must happen to the accustomed habits of the historical documentary? As these habits begin to collapse in response to the crisis, the film turns in on itself, asking, like Resnais, "how to treat such a subject?"

There are two types of self-consciousness in *Night and Fog* with which I am concerned here: formal and historical. By formal self-consciousness, I mean the film's efforts to draw attention to its own form. *Night and Fog*, unlike some of Resnais's other films, contains no explicit visual references to the cinema, nothing like the scenes of filmmaking in *Hiroshima, mon amour*. But there is a degree of self-consciousness implicit in the film's rigorous experiments with documentary form. The crosscutting between monochrome and color footage (particularly the initial cut to black and white discussed above, with its shocking stylistic reversals) and the highly controlled, extended tracking shots—these devices draw attention to themselves by virtue of their excessiveness, their rigor, and their deviation from documentary convention. The film thus presents itself as something not simply to be looked through, but also to be looked at.

The commentary, on the other hand, becomes explicitly self-referential at times during the color segments. "The blood has clotted, the voices have died, the barracks are abandoned by all but the camera. . . . There is no longer any footstep but our own." The reference to a footstep may even be more surprising than it first seems. For it is less the filmmaker who leaves footsteps in this narrative than the abstract, anthropomorphic, enunciating presence of the narrator itself. Through this analogy between the camera and the body, the film proposes the cinema—and itself—as an analogue of witnessing.

The commentary at times assumes an enunciatory self-consciousness reminiscent of the title of Cayrol's first novel, *On vous parle* (*Someone Speaks to You*).[47] "As I speak to you now, the icy water of the ponds and ruins fills the hollows of the charnel house." "Useless to describe what went on in these cells." "Nothing left to say."

Finally, there is a reference to the film as a projected image: "There are those of us who . . . take hope again as the image fades."

It is as if the narration of *Night and Fog*, confronted with a traumatizing subject, faltered, and in that faltering suddenly became aware of itself, of the entire apparatus supporting its activity—the camera, the narrator, the commentary, the projector—became aware, that is, of its body in crisis, like someone suddenly frightened, whose attention shifts from her external surroundings inward to her pounding heart, her struggle for breath, or her burning eyes.

By historical self-consciousness, on the other hand, I mean the film's interrogation of itself as a representation of history. The problem of historical representation is even implicit in its title, which, unlike *The Death Camps*, fails to make a clear historical reference, naming instead the very crisis of historical representation engendered by the Holocaust—the night and fog that intervenes between us and a history of annihilation.

At times, the film's historical self-consciousness takes the form of a questioning of the truth-value of artifacts. Whereas, in realist historical documentary, onscreen artifacts are presented unself-consciously as evidence of historical truths, *Night and Fog* problematizes the artifacts it surveys in the color segments, as mentioned above: "The reality of the camps . . . In vain do we try to discover its remnants. These wooden barracks, these shelves where three slept . . . No description, no image can restore their true dimension."

In the final, color segment, the film's project seems to shift from confronting artifacts to sifting through ruins. At times, the ruins surveyed by the camera are not even identifiable: the brown surface of the ground littered with stones, broken pieces of wood, and weeds; the metal shell of something vaguely resembling a chair used by a doctor or a torturer; broken slabs of concrete with metal rods twisting out; the buckled remains of a bombed crematorium. Meanwhile, the commentary characterizes the past as a threat of horror lying beneath the decay: "As I speak to you now, the icy water of the ponds and ruins lies in the hollows of the charnel house. A water as cold and opaque as our own bad memories. . . . Faithful as ever, grass grows once again on the Appelplatz, around the barracks, an abandoned village still full of menace. . . . Nine million dead haunt this landscape."

On other occasions, the commentary points out those aspects of the past for which there are no artifacts, not even ruins. "Go slowly along [the track], looking for what? Traces of the bodies that fell to the ground?" But, of course, on the image track, there are no traces. In another instance, the commentary refers to a "black transport that leaves at night, and about which no one will know anything."

Through consideration of its own form, its own limitations, its own failures, *Night and Fog* draws attention not just to the past but to the traumatic effects of the past on us—its deformation of historical memory—and the necessity of working through those effects.

The Death Camps, Mein Kampf, and *Night and Fog* present some of the same atrocity footage, but narrativize that footage differently. In *The Death Camps,* fifteen uninterrupted minutes of atrocity footage tend to overwhelm the narration's efforts to master its traumatic potential, resulting occasionally in actual vicarious trauma, or more frequently in a numbing effect, a denial of trauma, and a desire to forget. Fifteen years later, *Mein Kampf* provided a more successful mastery over the atrocity footage, assimilating it into a classical cinematic narrative of the rise and defeat of evil.

Night and Fog attempted a new cinematic response to atrocity footage, one that sought to have spectators open themselves up to the traumatizing potential of the images without having to resort to the defenses of numbing, denial, or premature mastery. The color segments functioned both as a buffer against the atrocity footage and as the ground of its return as a form of posttraumatic memory. The film worked out a modernist form of historical documentary narration in order to engage a dialectic of memory and forgetting, of vision and blindness, of the necessity and the impossibility of representing historical trauma. Questioning both history and film, *Night and Fog* suggested that cinematic knowledge of a traumatic past might not lead to the containment of that past, but rather to its continued disturbance of the present.

It is important not to forget that *Night and Fog* repressed the memory of the Jewish genocide. At the same time, it originated a posttraumatic form of narration that did not disappear after 1955, but, with the film's wide distribution as both an educational film and a documentary classic, spread to a variety of cinematic practices, and became available for the representation of the genocidal dimension of the Holocaust in ways that I will trace in the subsequent chapters. This form of narration consisted of the fragmentation of temporality, the restriction of point of view to the subjectivity of the witness, and formal and historical self-consciousness. Some of its more influential stylistic tropes were the use of the image of the present as a signifier of the past (used later in *Shoah, Hiroshima, mon amour, Father,* and *History and Memory*), the experimental flashback (*Hiroshima, mon amour, The Pawnbroker, Love Film*), the extended tracking shot (*Chronicle of a Summer, Shoah, Father, 25 Fireman Street*), and the self-conscious critique of historical filmmaking (*Hiroshima, mon amour, Father, History and Memory*). This new posttraumatic discourse in film spread to other regions (the United States, Eastern Europe) and other genres (fiction), influencing other modes of narration (realist and postmodern), and becoming available for the representation of other traumas (the Vietnam War, rape, the internment of Japanese Americans) in a world that has become increasingly conscious of trauma as a historical experience and a form of historical knowledge.

3 *Shoah* and the Posttraumatic Documentary after Cinéma Vérité

WHILE NEWSREEL-TYPE films like *The Death Camps* traumatized the public by constructing their image tracks exclusively from atrocity footage, they failed to distinguish the genocidal aspect of the concentration camps. Claude Lanzmann's *Shoah*, released forty years later, focuses exclusively on the genocide, but constructs its posttraumatic discourse without a single frame of atrocity footage. What had happened in the intervening years to transform so starkly the relations between a historical trauma, the filmic evidence of that trauma, and its documentary representation?

Shoah has most often been seen by critics as an exemplary representation of the Holocaust. It has also been seen by some scholars as exemplary of a recent transformation in the documentary representation of history—a transformation that has been variously identified as postmodern, reflexive, or posttraumatic. Linda Williams, Bill Nichols, Paula Rabinowitz, and Janet Walker have separately identified *Shoah* as crucial to the development of what Williams has termed "the new documentary."[1] I agree with both of these differing contextualizations of the film—one in terms of a specific historical event, and one in terms of the more general question of the documentary representation of history. However, I would also like to suggest that neither context makes sense without the other. *Shoah*'s significance as an intervention into the documentary representation of history cannot be separated from its confrontation with the difficult historiography of a specific limit case of historical representation. This chapter will continue to explore the development of a meta-historical discourse in documentary film: the relations between a historical trauma and the forms of documentary used to represent it. The chapter will look at the changes in this discourse brought about by the revolution in documentary form known as cinéma vérité, and the possibilities engendered by this revolution for the representation of the present—and in particular the representation of the witness—as an archive of the past.

CHRONICLE OF A SUMMER AND CINÉMA VÉRITÉ

The invention and dissemination of an efficient apparatus for synchronized sound recording on location in the late 1950s made possible the development of a new form of documentary.[2] The ability to film events on location with synchronized sound rendered the expository mode of documentary archaic. Rather than using a voice-of-God commentary to explain silent footage, the new form was able to present sound footage that seemed to explain itself, or at least to allow spectators to perform their own interpretations. The emphasis of the new form was thus not on the representation of the past, inhering in silent archival footage, but on the creation of a kind of archive of the present. However, *Chronicle of a Summer / Chronique d'un été*—one of the first of the new documentaries, and the film for which the term *cinéma vérité* was coined (*cinema truth*, the term itself being a translation of the name of Dziga Vertov's Soviet newsreel, *Kino-Pravda*, 1922–25)—demonstrated the new form's additional potential for extending *Night and Fog*'s innovations in the representation of historical memory.

The ninety-minute *Chronicle of a Summer*, directed by the anthropologist Jean Rouch and the sociologist Edgar Morin, was an attempt to reverse what Rouch had come to regard as the colonialist rhetoric of his previous anthropological films, by turning the camera back on the colonizing nation.[3] The film presented a kind of snapshot of French society in 1960, focusing on themes of happiness, work, leisure, class, alienation, race, colonialism, romance, the Algerian war, the generation gap, womanhood, and childhood (in the order presented by the film). Perhaps the fact that Morin is a Jew has something to do with the fact that memory of the Holocaust also entered into this snapshot. In one sense, this memory constitutes just another of *Chronicle*'s many themes; the film is known as a pioneer of cinéma vérité, not as a significant cinematic representation of the Holocaust. (It is not mentioned in any book on Holocaust films.) I would posit, however, two significant relationships between *Chronicle* and the Holocaust. First, the appearance of Holocaust memory in the film may reflect not just the presence of a Jew in the director's chair, but also the impossibility of presenting a snapshot of French society in 1960 without either confronting or repressing the unresolved collective memory of the deportations. Second, because the important technical/formal innovations of the film were, as I will show, inextricably linked to the memory of the Holocaust, it constituted a crucial moment in the development of a documentary discourse of historical trauma in Europe.

Chronicle features two main types of "characters": the filmmakers, Rouch and Morin, who are seen on camera interviewing people; and the subjects of the film, interviewees who talk about their lives and attitudes. There is one exceptional character, however, who crosses over— at times a subject interviewed by Rouch and Morin, and at other times a filmmaker, assisting Rouch and Morin by interviewing others. She is identified only as Marceline, and is characterized by the filmmakers at the beginning of the film as "the center of our experiment." In a scene in which Marceline speaks about a failed romance, the camera tilts down to reveal a tattooed number on her forearm. Ten minutes later there is scene in which Europeans and Africans discuss colonialism. During this discussion, Marceline compares African and Jewish experiences. Rouch then asks the Africans whether they know the meaning of Marceline's tattoo. They do not, and Marceline explains that she received it when she was deported to a concentration camp as a Jew during the war. There follows immediately a scene in which Marceline walks alone through the Place de la Concorde, and then Les Halles, talking to herself. We hear Marceline's voice mingled with traffic noise:

The Place de la Concorde is empty. Empty like it was twenty, fifteen years ago, I can't remember now. "You'll see. We'll go there, work in the factories. We'll see each other on Sundays," father said. And you used to answer me, "You're young, you'll come back. I'll never return." [Singing.] And here I am in the Place de la Concorde. I came back, you stayed. We'd been there six months before I saw you. We fell into each other's arms. Then that dirty SS officer hit me in front of you. You said, "She's my daughter." He made to hit you. You had an onion in your hand. You put it in mine and I fainted. [Singing.] When I saw you, you asked, "Mother and Michel?" You called me your little girl. I was almost happy to be deported, I loved you so much. I wish you were here now. When I came back, it was hard. I saw them all at the station, mother, everyone. They kissed me, my heart felt like a stone. It was Michel who softened it. I said, "Don't you know me?" He said, "Yes, I think so, I think you're Marceline."

Illustration 3.1. *Chronicle of a Summer*: an early example of posttraumatic testimony.

These are Marceline's words (subtitled) in their entirety. The scene lasts three-and-a-half minutes, and consists of three traveling long takes in which the camera follows Marceline. In the first, Marceline's entire body can be seen; the second is a close-up on her face; the third gradually travels out to an extreme long shot, in which Marceline becomes a distant silhouette.

This scene binds two anomalies in the film. It is both the only scene containing Holocaust testimony (indeed, the only scene containing historical testimony of any kind) and the only scene with this peculiar formal structure. Most scenes in the film show stationary people talking to an interviewer or to each other. In some other scenes, the camera follows a walking subject, but in these cases, the sound track consists of either a voice-over interview or background noise with no synchronized speech. The formal structure of Marceline's scene, then, displays the new synch sound technology in a unique fashion. The synchronization is visible (moving lips, footsteps) but its apparatus is invisible; we see no microphones or wires. Perhaps more important, the long camera distance in the first and third shots leaves no room for an offscreen space in which we can imagine the microphone to be located, as is the case in many other scenes. The effect is of a heightened realism; the spectator can hear Marceline's hushed monologue clearly even when her walking figure can be seen only in the distance. This is precisely the technique required to record testimony so painful that it cannot be spoken to any living person, but only to the dead father. The location noise prevents anyone in the vicinity from hearing the testimony as it is spoken, but the necktie microphone and hidden tape recorder hung over Marceline's shoulder record her testimony for an impersonal audience to hear at another time and place.[4] Paradoxically, however, the technological realism of the apparatus gives rise not to the realist discourse of objective history, but to a more poetic discourse of subjective memory. Marceline testifies to the effects of historical trauma only through a narrative whose form as well as whose content is defined by a sense of disarticulation.

Night and Fog's representation of memory relied on a split between the visual and sound tracks—between the image of the site of memory and the disembodied commentary. *Chronicle* demonstrated the potential for synchronizing the image and sound tracks in a representation of historical testimony. Here for the first time is a cinematic discourse of history without any archival image to anchor it. In this archive of the present, we discover the witness Marceline, and in the testimony of this witness, we discover an archive of the past. In *Chronicle*, the past inheres in the relationship between the speaking body situated in a space of memory and the audible and visible signs of memory emanating from and written on the body.

Not only does Marceline's testimony present a highly subjective point of view on historical events—marked by ellipses and interrupted by song—but the film's point of view on Marceline's testimony is also implicated in her subjectivity. The location of the monologue in the Place de la Concorde as a site of memory, Marceline's ceaseless walking, her speaking to herself rather than an interviewer or the audience, and the extreme variations in her distance from the camera—these stylistic devices situate the spectator inside the fragmented space of Marceline's subjectivity.

Contrast the modernist subjectivity of this representation of testimony with what has become the realist tradition of testimony in historical documentaries, exemplified in Steven Spielberg's Survivors of

the Shoah Visual History Foundation, and in the first documentary produced by the Foundation, *Survivors of the Holocaust* (United States, 1995).
In these films, the speaker is seated in a "safe" indoor location, and de-
livers a relatively coherent narrative to an offscreen interviewer, while
filmed in a static medium close-up. Thus, the traumatic potential of
what is being said is countered by an "objective" formal presentation.[5]

Chronicle's rejection of the rhetoric of objectivity characterizing the
traditional anthropological documentary is consistent with Nichols's
inclusion of the film within the *interactive* mode of documentary, which,
he writes, "introduces a sense of partialness, of *situated* presence and
local knowledge that derives from the actual encounter of filmmaker
and other."[6] The subjectivity of this encounter is pushed to the limit in
Marceline's transgression of the classical boundary between filmmaker
and subject. The tradition of documentary objectivity, in other words,
breaks down precisely on Marceline's performance of her traumatic
memories of the Holocaust.

Marceline's memories become subject to the same process of representational self-consciousness that characterizes the film as a whole. At
the end of the film, the interviewees sit in a screening room after having viewed the footage of their interviews, and discuss the question
of how the presence of the camera affected their ability to be truth-
ful (their vérité). Marceline says, "They were very personal, intimate
memories. Maybe when I was saying those words, I was reliving the
past." The relationship between psychological reliving and cinematic
self-consciousness would be taken further in *Shoah*.

What *Chronicle of a Summer* contributed to posttraumatic documentary was the representation of the witness as a bearer of traumatic memory. The presence of the survivor in the film helped to problematize the
rhetorical objectivity and unself-consciousness of classical documentary, stretched to the limit the new documentary technique of revealing the present, and necessitated the return of the past to rupture that
present.

HOLOCAUST MEMORY IN FRANCE, 1955–1985

Night and Fog was produced at a time when the French collective memory of the Holocaust was still largely repressed by the myth of *resistancialisme*; by the time Claude Lanzmann was making *Shoah* (1975–

85), that myth had been weakened and Holocaust memory had begun to surface. According to historian David Weinberg, French attitudes toward the Occupation, the deportation of French Jews, and the Holocaust in general began to change significantly around 1960, as the war generation began to age and a new generation—including a new generation of historians—began to emerge.[7] A series of novels dealing with the Holocaust by French Jewish writers began to appear: Elie Wiesel's *Night* in 1958, André Schwartz-Bart's *The Last of the Just* in 1959, and Jean-François Steiner's *Treblinka* in 1966.[8]

A series of war crimes trials helped propel the memory of the Holocaust into the French public sphere. The Eichmann trial in Israel in 1961 had a tremendous impact in France and internationally, while the efforts of the French Nazi hunters Serge and Beate Klarsfeld impacted French society in particular, especially their capture in 1983 of Klaus Barbie, who had been the German Gestapo chief in Lyons.[9]

A wave of anti-Judaism sweeping through France between 1967 and the early 1980s also contributed to this process. A series of Israeli-Arab wars triggered this tendency, as when, following the 1967 war, President de Gaulle called Jews "an elitist people, sure of itself and domineering."[10] In 1972, Jean-Marie Le Pen founded the fascist, anti-Jewish, and at times quite popular National Front Party. A wave of violence against Jews swept the country between 1978 and the early 1980s, most significantly the bombing of a Paris synagogue in 1980, killing four people.[11] Finally, Robert Faurisson emerged as a prominent French denier of the Holocaust in 1979.[12]

One film in particular played a key role in both the demolition of the myth of *resistancialisme* and the development of a new form of historical documentary: Marcel Ophuls's 1970 documentary *The Sorrow and the Pity/Le Chagrin et la pitié*. In order to attack the myth of *resistancialisme* and reveal the more complex interpenetration of resistance and collaboration that characterized the Occupation, Ophuls created a complex new form of historical documentary, which I term *historical vérité*. Much of the film consists of location interviews in the manner of *Chronicle of a Summer*, in which Ophuls himself, and his collaborator André Harris, can be heard, and sometimes seen, questioning witnesses, often digging beneath the facile testimonies initially presented to get at the sometimes shameful underlying complexities. These interviews are then intercut with period footage, often propaganda footage, to create ironic juxtapositions, revealing the manipulations, deceptions, and self-deceptions inhering in one artifact or the other. I do not regard *Sorrow* as a posttraumatic film; rather than employing a melancholic discourse of trauma to repeat the effects of the larger crimes of persecution and genocide, it uses a comic discourse of irony to expose the smaller crimes of complicity. On the other hand, *Sorrow* constituted a key link in the history of the documentary in Europe, one that was essential for Lanzmann's later work in *Shoah*. If *Chronicle of a Summer* marked the appearance of a cinéma vérité in which an anomalous representation of historical trauma ruptured the representation of the present, and if *The Sorrow and the Pity* marked the appearance of a full-fledged historical vérité, *Shoah* marked the appearance of a cinéma vérité fully invested with a posttraumatic historical consciousness.[13]

Shoah

Of course realism, as an evolving form, continued to dominate Holocaust documentary after *Night and Fog*, for example, in two compilation films called *Genocide*—one a 1974 British television production for *The World at War* series, the other a film produced by the Simon Wiesenthal Center in 1982. Meanwhile, the posttraumatic modernism of *Night and Fog* was inherited by, and transformed by, *Shoah*.

Shoah is a nine-and-a-half hour film on a single topic: the extermination of the Jews. It attempts to strip away a series of adjacent questions that, Lanzmann has argued, only distracted attention from the genocide and excused its repression from historical memory for many years—questions surrounding the traumas of the war in general and the suffering of the occupied nations; the historical causes and context of the Holocaust; the motives of the perpetrators; and the more "positive" aspects of the history, such as rescue, survival, and the "lessons" of the Holocaust. Through a near total avoidance of historical generalization and the substitution, in its place, of an obsessive attention to the physical and perceptual details of the killing process, *Shoah* attempts to sustain an investigation into the irredeemable fact of annihilation.

Shoah's posttraumatic discourse, as opposed to that of *Night and Fog* and *Chronicle of a Summer*, has already received a significant amount of attention—most important, in a 1991 article by Gertrud Koch and a 1997 article by Dominick LaCapra.[14] LaCapra, however, criticizes the film for, in terms borrowed from Freud, "acting out" the trauma of the Holocaust—repeating it in an impulsive, unconscious, and irresponsible manner—more than "working it through."[15] Some of LaCapra's observations about the film address questions of its content, or historical argument: the obsessiveness of its focus on extermination; its refusal to explain, contextualize, and compare events; and its alleged overemphasis on Polish anti-Judaism, and underemphasis on non-Jewish victims, survival, rescue, and the enforced collaboration of the Jewish Councils. Without disagreeing that these characteristics may in part constitute the film's posttraumatic discourse, I wish to follow up on some of LaCapra's other observations on the roles of repetition and transference in the film, relating them to the narrational procedures of tense and mood, and ultimately defending the film's posttraumatic discourse against LaCapra's criticism.

Tense

As *Mein Kampf* extended the use of archival footage in *The Death Camps* by making it diachronic, so *Shoah* continued the reduction of archival footage that *Night and Fog* had begun, replacing it entirely by images of the present: primarily images of witnesses (survivors, perpetrators, bystanders, etc.) and historical sites (extermination camps, rail lines, ghettos, former Jewish settlements, etc.). Given the deep roots of the tradition of archival footage in historical documentaries (even the vérité *The Sorrow and the Pity* has it), the absence of such footage from *Shoah* constitutes a stark refusal. This refusal has several possible motivations:

1. None of the existing archival footage that normally appears in Holocaust documentaries, with the exception of the Wiener film, actually shows the events on which *Shoah* is at some pains to focus: the physical destruction of the Jews. By excluding the existing footage of the preparations and the aftermath of the genocide, *Shoah* avoids creating the sense, as in films like *Mein Kampf*, that by seeing the film one has seen, and hence assimilated, the events themselves.

Related to this absence of images is the absence of traces and, finally, of the dead themselves. The absence of the photographic image of the past in the film literalizes these other absences that resulted from the Nazis' determination to erase both the Jews and their extermination from history. *Shoah* refuses to substitute the photographic images of a certain number of victims for the absent six million, visualizing Emil

Fackenheim's assertion that "the European Jews massacred are not just of the past, they are the presence of an absence."[16]

2. Archival footage is conventionally, and mistakenly, taken to be objective. As Lucy Dawidowicz has argued, footage taken by the Nazis, which has often been disseminated in documentaries as objective historical evidence, replicates their point of view—their ideology and propaganda aims—on the victims. It thus positions the spectator as a victimizer, potentially eliciting a voyeuristic or sadistic response. As James Young has suggested, even Allied footage of the liberated victims tends to objectify and revictimize them.[17]

3. Atrocity footage is both so shocking as to numb the audience and, paradoxically, not shocking enough to represent the extermination of millions of human beings.

4. The Holocaust was an ultimate evil, and remains a negative sublime, which, to adapt the Second Commandment banning the making of idols, must not be imaged.[18]

The concept of the Holocaust as a negative sublime can also be reframed by the discourse of trauma. The traumatic event remains lodged in the mind as a searing, watershed moment, an all-consuming focus of existence in which a tremendous amount of psychological energy is invested. As such, it becomes, ironically, sacred to the victim as the foundation of a new, traumatized identity, as dysfunctional as that identity may be. Such a sacred event, again adapting the Second Commandment, must be kept hidden away in a pure and unseen state.

Of course, for my purposes, *Shoah*'s exclusive visual focus on the present constitutes a development in the posttraumatic narration of time in documentary. Whereas realist historical documentary masters trauma by moving effortlessly through time, and *Night and Fog* repeats trauma by jerking from the present to the past and back again, *Shoah* repeats trauma differently—by creating a cinematic time in which the present and the past are collapsed into one another. The past in the film exists not as a separate time frame literally imaged in black and white, but as a dimension that pervades the present like a fog. Koch has called this collapsed time "a caesura": "It intrudes like a black box between the time before and the time after the traumatic event and it is experienced as a discontinuity. The black box assumes the form of a time-eradicating chamber. The complex organization of temporal and spatial dimensions in *Shoah* evokes this very immediate sense of being swallowed up in a black box."[19] *Shoah* traps the spectator in this haunted present, where signs of the catastrophic past appear whatever one does and wherever one turns. This past is indexed by physical remains, and denoted by words of testimony; but most powerful of all is the film's reenactment of the past: testimony that formally reenacts what it recalls, and shots of historical sites that formally reenact what took place there.

An example of testimony that reenacts what it recalls is the beginning of the interview with Jan Karski, former courier for the Polish underground, who met with two Jewish underground leaders in Warsaw in 1942, secretly toured the Warsaw ghetto, and reported on "the Final Solution" to Allied leaders. The interview begins with Karski sitting on a couch, staring intently at some point below the camera, apparently visualizing, or trying not to visualize, his memories of the ghetto. Finally, he begins to speak. "Now, now I go back thirty-five years." After a moment, he begins to shake his head and his hand. "No, I don't go back." He starts to cry. He begins to stand, then sits again. Again he stands and sits. Finally, he leaves the room, weeping. The camera begins to follow him as he leaves the room, but then reverses itself, and returns to the couch. We see the empty couch for a moment. In the following scene, Karski returns to the couch and gives his testimony.

In Karski's testimony, he describes his meeting with the two Jewish leaders, in which they testified to him about the extermination of the Jews, showed him the ghetto, and demanded that he testify to Allied leaders. Describing the end of his tour of the ghetto, Karski says, "Frankly, I couldn't take it anymore. Get me out of it. . . . I was sick. Even now I don't want . . . I understand your role. I am here. I don't go back in my memory. I couldn't take any more. . . . I never saw such things, I never . . . nobody wrote about this kind of reality. I never saw any theater, I never saw any movie . . . this was not the world."[20]

Karski's words suggest that his earlier flight from the interview couch was a reenactment of his original emotional reaction to witnessing the ghetto. "I couldn't take it anymore," "Get me out of it," "I was sick": these are descriptions of his emotional reactions at a time in the past when he could not freely act on those emotions. He was required to stay and witness. He testifies on more than one occasion that he has repressed these memories for thirty-five years. It seems, however, that the memories were there in his mind all the time, with their emotional content intact. Now Karski has the freedom to act on those feelings, since what is at stake in his testimony is no longer life and death, but memory. If he cannot take the memories anymore, if they make him sick, then he can actually get out of them. Time, for Karski, has collapsed. He is not merely testifying to the past, he is, like Marceline, reliving it.

And yet Karski's freedom to act out his thirty-five-year-old feelings by fleeing the couch does not stop him from finally testifying, from completing the chain of testimony begun in 1942. This chain extends from the two Jewish leaders to Karski to the Allied leaders (who failed, for the most part, to take responsibility for what they were told) and finally to Lanzmann and *Shoah*'s audience. Each step in the chain of testimony is potentially traumatizing. *Shoah* becomes a link in the traumatic chain of testimony, not only denoting this other reality, this other world, but also modeling its traumatic effects.[21]

At times, Lanzmann attempted to encourage his witnesses to re-enact their memories by re-creating the remembered environment. Jean Rouch seems to have tried this method in *Chronicle of a Summer* when, according to Ellen Freyer, he brought Marceline to the Place de la Concorde to film her testimony because he thought there would be German soldiers there, the sight of whom would stimulate her memories.[22] The most famous example from *Shoah* is the testimony of Abraham Bomba, a Polish Jewish barber who was deported to Treblinka and assigned to cut the hair of women who did not know that they were about to be gassed. By the time Bomba appeared in *Shoah*, he had retired from cutting hair. So Lanzmann rented a barbershop for the film, where he had Bomba cut hair while testifying. Perhaps Lanzmann got the desired result. One of the most frequently cited scenes in the film shows Bomba cutting hair:

Bomba: A friend of mine worked as a barber. He was a good barber in my hometown. When his wife and sister came into the gas chamber . . .

Lanzmann: Go on, Abe. You must go on. You have to.

Bomba: I can't. It's too horrible. Please.

Lanzmann: We have to do it. You know it.

Bomba: I won't be able to do it.

Lanzmann: You have to do it. I know it's very hard. I know and I apologize.

Bomba: Don't make me go on please.

Lanzmann: Please. We must go on.[23]

Finally, Bomba completes his testimony.

Koch hypothesizes that, in this method, Lanzmann was influenced by Sartre's existential psychoanalytic theory that "there is a physical materiality even prior to the symbolizing process of language. . . . Such materiality breaks through only when gestures, physical movements, are repeated."[24] One might perhaps as easily cite the theories of involuntary, associative memory propounded by Freud, Bergson, Proust, and others. At any rate, it is clear that Lanzmann is interested not only in what happened at Treblinka but also in how the memory of Treblinka is experienced, or how it is reexperienced, or how its transmission is interrupted in a way that recalls the descriptions by psychiatrists of their traumatized survivor patients for whom language fails.

Even when one shifts one's focus on testimony from the collapsed temporality of reenactment (how the witness testifies) to the relatively straightforward temporality of historical denotation (what the witness says), one discovers a significant refusal of linear chronology. While much of the film does follow a kind of logical, if not strictly chronological, order in tracing the process of extermination (e.g., deportation, arrival at the camps, gassing), it begins with a long segment on the Nazis' destruction of the traces of the genocide, a segment that does not fit into this order in any obvious way.[25] Richard Glazar recalls the burning of corpses in huge pyres at Treblinka in November 1942. Jan Piwonski testifies about the Nazis' dismantling of the death camp Sobibor, and their planting of pine trees to camouflage the site during the winter of 1943. Itzhak Dugin and Motke Zaidl recall digging up mass graves at Ponari, Lithuania, in January 1944, so that the corpses buried there could be burned.

Perhaps the most striking of these testimonies on the destruction of traces is the first—the testimony of Simon Srebnik, which is the first significant piece of testimony in the film. Srebnik is one of two survivors of the death camp Chelmno, in Poland, where between 152,000 and 400,000 Jews were gassed.[26] The scene begins as Srebnik walks silently for about ninety seconds along a dirt road surrounded by forest. The handheld camera travels backward, showing Srebnik's face in a single long take. Then Srebnik stops, gazes offscreen for several seconds, begins to nod, and says (in German, subtitled in English),

> It's hard to recognize, but it was here. They burned people here. A lot of people were burned here. Yes, this is the place. No one ever left here again. The gas vans came in here. There were two huge ovens, and afterward the bodies were thrown into these ovens, and the flames reached to the sky.
>
> Lanzmann: To the sky?
>
> Srebnik: Yes. It was terrible. No one can describe it. No one can re-create what happened here. Impossible.[27]

Meanwhile, there has been a cut away from Srebnik's face to the object of his gaze: a clearing in the forest, in which only some stone foundations remain.

Shoah begins by posing a history of genocide as a problem of memory. While the Nazis attempted to erase the memory of the dead at Chelmno by burning their corpses, grinding their bones to powder, dumping the powder in the Narew River, and finally exterminating the slave labor-

Illustration 3.2. *Shoah*: Srebnik recognizes the site of the erasure now made almost unrecognizable by its own erasure.

ers who had done the work, Srebnik—who survived his extermination, a gunshot to the head—begins to reverse the effects of this attempted erasure by remembering it, by rewitnessing it, by recognizing the site of the erasure now made almost unrecognizable by its own erasure.[28] The process of unerasing memory, in other words, begins with the memory of the erasure itself.[29]

This scene, too, with its focus on Srebnik's gaze, is as much about the processes of remembering, witnessing, and recognition as it is about the denoted cremation itself. And it is about the difference between Srebnik's past witnessing, which was slated for destruction, and his present witnessing, which is to be transmitted again and again with each audience's witnessing of the film. At its beginning, the film thus announces that what will follow will be not a simple representation of the past, but a desperate struggle in the realm of memory and forgetting.

The Chelmno forest returns later in the film, this time the subject of a reenactment by the camera. In a scene shot in front of the Chelmno village church, witnesses testify that Jews were imprisoned in the church, vans were backed up to the church doors, and the Jews were loaded into the vans, locked inside, and gassed to death using the vans' own exhaust while the vans drove out to the forest clearing, where the bodies were burned.[30] The scene ends with a shot of the church doors taken from the back of a truck, which then drives away, out of the village, to the forest. Lanzmann has said that sites of annihilation like the route of the Chelmno gas vans must be resuscitated not by archival footage but by an extraordinary act of the mind: "These disfigured places are what I call non-places of memory. At the same time it is nonetheless necessary that traces remain. I must hallucinate and think that nothing has changed."[31] Lanzmann's camera revives these historical sites, in other words, through posttraumatic hallucination.

Mood

Crucial to the regulation of point of view in *Shoah* is the visible and audible presence of Lanzmann himself. *Night and Fog* presents no such visible filmmaking figure, and even in *Chronicle of a Summer*, in which Rouch and Morin are frequently prominent, the scene of Holocaust testimony is presented without their obvious presence. What can be induced from *Shoah* about the point of view of the filmmaker on the historical evidence presented?

Shoah offers no outside of the genocide from which to view it. As past events are revived through testimony, so are the rigidly determined positions from which those events were originally perceived. True to the tradition of cinéma vérité, there is no voice-over commentary, only Lanzmann himself conducting interviews with witnesses, leading them not to speak as experts but, as Ora Avni put it, "to assume fully their position as subjects."[32] The narration of events proceeds through the juxtaposition of testimonies from different positions, which sometimes corroborate one another and sometimes conflict.

Lanzmann's interview techniques are strictly differentiated according to the position of the witness. Interviewing bystanders, he is a clever interrogator; with perpetrators, he is a spy; with survivors, he is a compassionate but exacting questioner. At the same time, he often seems like a hypnotist, bringing his subjects to reexperience their memories. In the case of witnesses like Jan Karski and Abraham Bomba, this means triggering the unbearable return of traumatic memories.

This does not mean, however, that Lanzmann has no point of view of his own. The scene in which he confronts the Chelmno survivor Simon Srebnik with a group of Chelmno villagers in front of the village church is a good example of the way Lanzmann creates a point of view by framing the points of view of others.

The scene relies on a remarkable coincidence: the villagers recognize Srebnik. This has been established at the very beginning of the film, in the moments before Srebnik's recognition of the clearing in the Chelmno forest where the victims were cremated. It is narrated, in titles, that Srebnik was known to the Chelmno villagers for his singing; as a slave laborer, he was regularly made to sing while rowing guards up the Narew River. The titles are followed by a scene in which Srebnik reenacts his singing on the river, and a villager comments offscreen, "When I heard him again . . . I really relived what happened."[33] Whereas in *Chronicle of a Summer* the role of reliving is only made explicit at the end of the film, here it is made explicit from the very beginning.

Later in the film, the villagers stand in front of the crowded church, with Srebnik placed conspicuously in the center, and the open church doors visible directly behind him. Lanzmann, off camera but audible, questions the villagers, through an interpreter, about the extermination of Jews in the village, which a number of those present seem to remember in detail. At first, they corroborate certain facts of the extermination, in particular that their own church, visible in the background of the shot, was used in the gassing of Jews. As the interview continues, however, their testimony changes. They testify that the reason the Jews were gassed was because they were rich, that their suitcases were full of gold, that they submitted to their deaths willingly to atone for the Jewish betrayal of Christ, that their extermination was "God's will."[34]

The testimony is interrupted in the middle by a procession celebrating the birth of the Virgin Mary, which exits the church doors in the background. The camera zooms in to show young girls dressed in white, casting flowers on the ground.

As the testimony begins, Srebnik is often seen smiling and nodding, seemingly in discomfort. By the end, he is still smiling, but now also smoking a cigarette and standing with his arms crossed over his chest. The scene ends with the cut to the shot of the church doors taken from the back of a truck.

In this scene, Lanzmann has staged a collision between two points of view on the same event. While Srebnik and the villagers agree that the church held Jews for gassing, the meanings assigned to this fact in

Illustration 3.3. *Shoah*: Lanzmann stages a reenactment of the unbridgeable gap between the points of view of the Catholic villagers and the Jewish Srebnik.

the two separate accounts miss one another by an unbridgeable gap. Srebnik sees the church from the point of view of the Jewish victims, from inside the genocide. The villagers see it from the point of view of their traditional religious mythology, as bystanders to the genocide. For Srebnik, the terrible events are incomprehensible; for the villagers, they are only too readily explained. For Srebnik, the church is a grave for innocent Jews; for the villagers, the church's past as a grave is canceled out by the guilt of the Jews, and the church remains the innocent birthplace of the Virgin.[35]

Lanzmann's apparently disinterested staging of this collision, however, has already been framed by hours of testimony about the extermination of the Jews. Lanzmann's role as disinterested interviewer serves his deeper and complete identification with the victims, which LaCapra has characterized as an unobstructed transference, and which is evident in Lanzmann's statement, "The idea that always has been the most painful for me is that all these people died alone. . . . A meaning for me that is simultaneously the most profound and the most incomprehensible in the film is in a certain way . . . to resuscitate these people, to kill them a second time, with me; by accompanying them."[36]

Lanzmann's identification with the victims becomes apparent in the reenactment by the camera of the gas van route, which concludes the church scene. Here he dispenses altogether with the secondhand witness position implicitly occupied by Resnais in relation to Cayrol's firsthand witnessing in *Night and Fog*. While Resnais's moving camera conflates both positions, Lanzmann's directly inhabits the point of view of the victims locked into the van. The camera hallucinates itself as a Jew gassed to death, but who can still see—and record for posterity—the route to the ovens.

Like *Night and Fog*, *Shoah* implicates the spectator not only epistemologically but also emotionally and morally, charging the spectator to continue the chain of traumatic witnessing begun during the genocide and relayed by the onscreen witnesses and the camera. This seems to have been a more or less conscious decision on Lanzmann's part, as evidenced by his statement, "I had the feeling that in suffering myself, a compassion would pass into the film, permitting perhaps the spectators as well to pass through a sort of suffering."[37]

Shoah's moral implication of the spectator is exemplified in the scene of Karski's flight from the couch. The camera could have simply continued to follow Karski's departure from the room, emphasizing a literal problem: the interview has been interrupted. The decision to return to the empty couch, however, moves from the literal to the symbolic. The couch's emptiness becomes an open symbol—for the myriad losses and absences of the past—as well as, perhaps, a symbolic mirror image of the spectator's own chair.[38] If part of what made Karski's witnessing of the Warsaw ghetto so traumatic was that it was unprecedented in his experience of the world—not only had he never seen such things in reality, but he had never even seen them, as he says, in a movie—then *Shoah* presents itself as a new kind of movie, one that can relay the trauma of witnessing this other reality to the audience, simultaneously making spectators wish to flee their seats, like Karski, and challenging them, also like Karski, ultimately to assume their responsibility as witnesses.

Voice

As cinéma vérité, *Shoah* displays a form of self-consciousness that is not found in *Night and Fog*. Much of *Night and Fog*'s historical self-consciousness originates in the split between the visible evidence of inanimate objects and the commentary's spoken discourse on that evidence, and on its limitations. In *Shoah*, on the other hand, the evidence speaks. Like *Chronicle of a Summer* and *The Sorrow and the Pity*, *Shoah* derives much of its self-consciousness from the form of its interviews—from the testimony itself and from the interaction between Lanzmann and his witnesses. In the realist form of the historical interview, the spectator's attention is directed toward what the witness or expert is saying, toward the historical content of the interview, and away from the form of the interview or the process by which the film constructs historical knowledge through the interview. *Chronicle of a Summer, The Sorrow and the Pity*, and *Shoah* exemplify the modernist tendency in cinéma vérité (as opposed to the realist tendency of American "direct cinema" documentaries like those of Leacock, Wiseman, and the Maysles brothers), where the spectator's attention is to be balanced between the content of the interview and its form, and where the film's process of constructing historical knowledge is relatively evident.

In *Night and Fog*, it is the commentary that says of the image, "Useless to describe what went on in these cells." *Shoah* presents the image of Srebnik himself telling the filmmaker, "No one can describe it. No one can re-create what happened here. Impossible. And no one can understand it." Srebnik is, in effect, telling Lanzmann that his testimony and the film itself are ultimately doomed to failure. They cannot do what historical documentaries are supposed to do: re-present the past, so that it may be better understood. Lanzmann, of course, does not contest Srebnik's assertion; he merely goes on filming. In a realist documentary, this assertion might have been edited out of the finished film, since it invites the spectator to question the film's mastery over the past. In *Shoah*, however, Srebnik's antitestimony is itself a form of testimony—to the failure of representation in the face of historical trauma.

The interrupted testimonies of Karski and Bomba function in a similar fashion. The flow of evidence comes to a halt, the testimony falls silent, the witness disappears from the screen. And yet the camera rolls on, recording what?—its own inability to surmount the obstacles of posttraumatic memory.[39]

Like *Night and Fog*, however, *Shoah* displays a range of self-conscious strategies that cannot be explained solely as a response to the collapse of mastery over time and point of view in posttraumatic memory.[40] In *Night and Fog*, I would argue, posttraumatic self-consciousness is part of a broader strategy of left/modernist self-consciousness: an interrogation of the hegemonic form of historical consciousness in documentary, with that interrogation embodied in the film as a formal conflict between the historical authority of the archival image and the refusal of that authority in the color segments.

Shoah's overall strategy of self-consciousness, on the other hand, is not embodied as a formal conflict in the film. If there is a dyad in *Shoah* corresponding to *Night and Fog*'s dyad of authority and refusal, it is the dyad of testimony as a representation of the past and testimony as a representation of the present, and of the failures and vicissitudes of memory. But the film does not place these two aspects of testimony in conflict. At the stylistic level, there is no corresponding conflict between monochrome and color, or image and voice. (This is why formal self-consciousness is less pronounced in *Shoah* than in *Night and Fog*.) Testimony to the past and testimony to the present are bound together formally in the film's representation of the witnessing body, and bound together historiographically as twin poles in the memory of genocide.

Self-consciousness in *Shoah* points, rather, to a conflict between the film and something other: the erasure of memory, "the annihilation of the annihilation" that characterized "the Final Solution," that necessitated the film, and which it is the primary goal of the film to reveal and hence reverse. I would call this a performative self-consciousness; it is the film's drawing attention to its own performative dimension as a weapon in the ongoing struggle against erasure. More important, it is the film's drawing attention to itself as a model for the continuation of that struggle, through vicarious witnessing, after the final and inevitable erasure: the death of the last witness.

The interruption of testimony that constitutes a part of *Shoah*'s self-consciousness, then, functions on two levels. At one level, it draws attention to the posttraumatic failure of "narrative memory" that characterizes the aftermath of the genocide. But the film then shunts this self-consciousness to another level; at this level, the interruption of testimony draws attention to the desperate struggle, dramatized by the film, between forgetting and memory; between the erasure of the genocide, and the responsibility—the witnesses', the film's, and the spectator's—to unerase the genocide. In traumas like the Holocaust, these two levels—the original victimization and the erasure of its memory—are closely related. Something similar applies to molested children who are told by their molesters that they (or, worse, their parents) will be killed if they tell anyone what happened, or who are told by their molesters that they have not in fact been molested. The attempt to erase the memory exacerbates the original trauma. The working through of the original trauma requires the consciousness, and hence the reversal, of this attempted erasure.

Conclusion

While one may choose to characterize some of Lanzmann's public behavior as acting out trauma (for instance, his statement that if he found footage of gassing he would destroy it), I contest LaCapra's critique of the film as a form of acting out.[41] And while *Shoah*, like, presumably, many other films, is certainly available to be used by spectators as a trigger for acting out trauma, this does not mean that the film preconditions, causes, or excuses such a use. I would argue, first, that the film's purported lack of historical balance must be put into the context of a long period of broad public denial of the specific, catastrophic aspects of the genocide, which arguably necessitated a strategic focus on the irredeemable fact of annihilation.

Second, as LaCapra acknowledges, the symbolic repetition of trauma is a necessary aspect of working it through.[42] That may be all we can ask of a film, and all that we should demand of *Shoah*: that it reverse the attempted erasure of the annihilation, overcome silence and denial, and transmit the traumatic memory to the public. The task of working through the trauma may be more appropriate either to a subsequent time or to a different context. Furthermore, perhaps a trauma, like the Holocaust, that was characterized by such silence—the silence of those who allowed it to take place, the silence of the dead, the silence of vanished traces, the silence of survivors whose testimony was not heard for many years—requires an extraordinary degree of repetition.

Third, even if we were to insist on making a distinction between films that act out trauma and films that work it through, I would argue that *Shoah* fulfills a key requirement of working through. Acting out trauma means repeating it as if one were still cut off from humanity by an act of victimization taking place in the present. It is, psychologically speaking, a solitary activity.[43] In working through, on the other hand, the sympathetic attention of the other combats the isolation associated with past trauma, and offers in its place the possibility of an awareness that the traumatic event is over, that there exists in the present a safe space within which the memory can be converted from unassimilated impressions into symbolic narrative and transmitted to a listener. As I have argued, *Shoah* is structured precisely as an attempt to relay the experience of traumatic witnessing from the victim to the public, and hence to undo the victim's enforced historical isolation. Indeed, it is precisely by formally collapsing time that the film works to enlist a present-day witness to past events. Though the witnesses in the film may themselves be acting out trauma (but how could we ascertain this?), the point is that they do it for Lanzmann, and, more important, for the camera, for the public, for history. Thus, through the film, the terrible burden of witnessing genocide may be relayed (but not removed) from the victims to a public who can lend to traumatic memory the degree of awareness, of consciousness, possible only to the outsider. The closer the film can bring the spectator to a confrontation with the incomprehensible nature of witnessing genocide, the more the trauma of incomprehension can be diluted, if never altogether erased.

4 *The Pawnbroker* and the Posttraumatic Flashback

I⤙ It is no accident that posttraumatic cinema originated in documentary. The indexical mode of representation that is the basis of documentary was necessary to the cinematic relaying of trauma by films like the Wiener footage and *The Death Camps. Night and Fog,* too, relayed trauma through indexical reference to atrocity, but did more: it originated a cinematic discourse of trauma through a form of narration that was not in itself bound to a documentary mode of representation. Posttraumatic narration then became available for adaptation by fiction films, in which the referencing of historical reality did not depend on indexical signification.

It was *The Pawnbroker* that most clearly demonstrated the possibilities for extending posttraumatic narration into the realm of the fiction film, through its contribution to the posttraumatic flashback. A U.S. independent production made in 1962 and released in 1965, the film is based on a novel by Edward Lewis Wallant, was directed by Sidney Lumet, and stars Rod Steiger as Sol Nazerman, a Jewish Holocaust survivor from Poland and the proprietor of a Harlem pawnshop.[1] The story takes place during the course of several days leading up to the twenty-fifth anniversary of the day Sol, his wife, his two young children, and the rest of his family were deported to a concentration camp. Only Sol and his sister survived. Having banished these memories from his mind, Sol has been living as a kind of walking corpse. But as the anniversary approaches, a series of events reminding him of his past triggers a series of involuntary memories, represented in nine flashback sequences.

In the sixth flashback sequence, which I take as a paradigm of the posttraumatic flashback, a prostitute (unnamed in the film, but named Mabel in the novel) comes to the pawnshop, leads Sol to the back of the shop, and propositions him. She bears her breasts and says, "Look."

The reverse shot shows him looking away. The next shot is a soundless flashback consisting of just four frames of film, lasting one-sixth of a second. The flashback is set in a concentration camp, and shows Sol, bald and wearing a prisoner's uniform, being addressed by an SS officer. There is a return to Sol in the present looking away, followed by another four-frame flashback showing Sol's wife, Ruth, sitting naked in a cell, a graphic match to the previous shot of Mabel. The shots continue as follows.

1. Mabel as before, saying again, "Look."
2. Sol turns to look at Mabel.
3. Flash: Ruth in the cell.
4. Sol looking at Mabel.
5. Mabel: "That's it."
6. Sol looking at Mabel.
7. Flash: Ruth again, with the sound of Mabel saying, "Look."
8. Sol looking at Mabel.
9. Flash: Ruth.
10. Mabel.
11. Sol looks away from Mabel.
12. Flash: SS officer addressing Sol.

There are several more of these alternations, during the course of which the flashbacks double in length to eight frames, and the sound of the flashbacks comes in: rain, and the officer saying to Sol, "Willst du was sehen?" ("Do you want to see?"). This sound continues over the subsequent inserted shots of Sol and Mabel in the present.

Then the alternations cease, and there is a more conventional extended flashback sequence. Sol, in the camp, watches a line of female prisoners in the distance being led into a barrack, followed by a line of soldiers. As he watches, the SS officer approaches him, asks, "Willst du was sehen?" several times, drags Sol to the barrack, smashes his head through a window, and forces him to look inside.

At this point, the alternations resume. Shots of Mabel telling Sol to look and shots of Sol looking away alternate with silent shots of Sol in the past looking into the barrack, and reverse shots showing Ruth in the cell, apparently about to be raped by a soldier. Finally the flashbacks cease, Sol covers Mabel and gives her money, and she leaves.

POSTTRAUMATIC DOCUMENTARY
AND POSTTRAUMATIC FICTION

The relationship between the posttraumatic documentary and the post-traumatic fiction film is demonstrated in the relationship between *Night and Fog* and *Hiroshima, mon amour*, and in Resnais's career in general, which can be divided neatly into two halves. Before 1959, he directed only documentaries; afterward, only fiction films. At the same time, he repeatedly deconstructed the difference between the two modes, often employing fictional techniques in his documentaries and documentary techniques in his fiction films. Among his documentaries, for instance, *Guernica* (like *Shoah*) contains no photographs of the bombed village, relying exclusively on Picasso's imaginative renderings; and *Night and Fog* adapts the fictional technique of the flashback to the documentary mode. Among Resnais's fiction films, on the other hand, *Muriel* contains actual amateur footage of the Algerian war; and *Mon oncle d'Amerique* (1980) intercuts its story with segments documenting the research of human behaviorist Henri Laborit, who "explains" the fictional events.

On the cusp between these two halves of Resnais's career is *Hiroshima, mon amour*. This film was conceived when the producers of *Night and Fog* asked Resnais to direct a feature-length documentary on the atomic bomb.

> For three or four months I researched the atomic problem, read a number of books, met with a few scientists; but, after three months, I had got nowhere, and I decided to give up the project and do some other job. . . . Such a film would have been like a remake of *Night and Fog*. Why do it all over again? It was while informing the producers of my decision that I said, almost jokingly, "Of course, if someone like Marguerite Duras would agree to work with me on such a project, we could consider the problem from another angle."[2]

The transformation of *Hiroshima* from documentary to fiction is repeated in the film's own structure, as if Resnais and Duras were determined to retain the film's documentary origins as a remnant within the fictional work (or as if Resnais had already shot the film's thirteen-minute prologue sequence before deciding to make it a fiction). The visual track of this sequence consists almost exclusively of documentary material relating to Hiroshima and its bombing. At the same time, placed side by side with horrific archival footage of ruined bodies and cityscapes, are quite artificial-looking clips from Japanese fiction film dramatizations of the bombing. *Hiroshima*'s questioning of the relationship between documentary and fiction thus repeats within the documentary sequence itself. Over these images, the sound track presents the voices of the film's female and male protagonists speaking in a poetic dialogue about the possibilities and impossibilities of representing Hiroshima.

This thirteen-minute film-within-a-film may be thought of as documentary or a mockumentary, but either way it is formally almost indistinguishable from some of Resnais's earlier documentaries. Like *Night and Fog*, its temporal structure is fragmented through the juxtaposition of archival footage of past horrors and present-day footage of the sites of those horrors. Its point of view is fragmented through the juxtaposition of an image track that is relatively omniscient and a sound track that performs the clash between the outsider who (like Resnais and Duras) knows nothing of Hiroshima and the insider whose knowledge is incommunicable. And it is self-conscious in its formal rigor and its emphasis on the processes and problematics of historical representation.

Using a posttraumatic form of narration to deconstruct the opposition between documentary and fiction, *Hiroshima*'s prologue paves the way for a migration of posttraumatic cinema from one mode to the other. The remainder of the film explores the formal possibilities of a fictional posttraumatic cinema, which on the one hand undergoes an expansion by leaving behind the formal constraints of documentary footage, but on the other hand retains its indexical link to the reality of Hiroshima, through both the prior link to the prologue sequence and the continuing presence of the city as the shooting location for the fictional story. But even the fictional dimension itself does not preclude a kind of discursive or psychological documenting of the effects of historical trauma, largely through a revision of the flashback as a form for the representation of history and memory.[3]

The significance of the flashback in this regard was suggested in 1916 by the psychologist Hugo Münsterberg in his book *The Photoplay: A Psychological Study*: "[The photoplay] can act as our imagination acts. . . . In our mind past and future become intertwined with the present. The photoplay obeys the laws of the mind rather than those of the outer world."[4] While archival footage calls up the image of the past before the eyes of the spectator, and footage of historical sites and testimony can stimulate spectators to recall or construct an image of the past, the flashback can actually mimic those acts of recollection and imaging. As such, the flashback is the most common and most clearly marked cinematic analogue of historical consciousness in fiction films. As Maureen Turim suggests in her book *Flashbacks in Film*, the history of the flashback is at the same time a meta-history, charting the changing models of historical consciousness disseminated in films.[5] My question then becomes, in what ways has the flashback modeled a masterful, secondarized, or "narrative" (in Janet's sense) historical memory, and in what ways a posttraumatic one? How has the history of the flashback registered the traumatic histories of the Second World War and the Holocaust?

Walter Benjamin would have phrased the question differently. Does the history of the word *flashback* itself not suggest a series of links between the physical trauma of the industrial revolution, the psychological symptoms of trauma victims, and the fragmentation of temporality in cinema? The *Oxford English Dictionary* dates the word to 1903, when *Motoring Annual* used it to refer to an engine explosion that completely destroyed an automobile. *Flashback* next appeared as a cinematic term in the pages of *Variety* in 1916—interestingly enough, the same year Münsterberg's book appeared.[6] What the *OED* fails to point out is that the term began to migrate again during the 1960s, when it became a slang term for intrusive sensory memories of past drug-induced hallucinations. By 1969, it had been picked up by psychiatrists as the accepted term for these drug-induced memories.[7] By the 1970s, it was being used by Vietnam veterans to refer to their intrusive, hallucinatory memories of combat, and by 1980, this migration was reflected in the psychiatric literature.[8] Benjamin might have used this etymology to illustrate the way in which modernity and modern warfare exploded temporality, both psychologically and culturally.[9]

For the purposes of this argument, I will put aside the larger question of modernity, however, in order to focus on the flashback as the site of an analogy between posttraumatic psychology and posttraumatic cinema—or, between a disturbance in field of psychological imaging and a disturbance in the field of cultural imaging. I will begin by tracing the psychiatric history of the flashback, before turning to its emergence as a signifier of historical trauma in the cinema.

FLASHBACKS IN PSYCHIATRY

> [The positive effects of traumas] are attempts to bring the trauma into operation once again—that is, to remember the forgotten experience, or, better still, to make it real, to experience a repetition of it anew. . . . If this happens, it implies a domination by an internal psychical reality over the reality of the external world.
> —Sigmund Freud[10]

The discourse of the psychological flashback predates the rise of psychiatry during the nineteenth century.[11] Pierre Janet pointed out the similarity of what he called the "hysterical somnambulism" of his patients to Lady Macbeth's unconscious reenactment of the horrifying aftermath of a massacre. In Shakespeare's play, her behavior is eloquently described by two witnesses. "You see, her eyes are open," says the doctor. The gentlewoman replies, "Ay, but their sense is shut."[12]

This is how Janet described the hysterical somnambulist in 1907:

> We may see that he has not our dull memory of things, but that he sees the objects he speaks of, and really hears, feels, touches them exactly as if they were real. . . . The objects you thrust before their eyes do not in the least alter their dream, and do not in the least stop it. . . . To make yourself heard, you must dream with the patient and speak to him only words in accordance with his delirium.[13]

Another aspect of the posttraumatic flashback described by Janet is its tendency to be triggered by association. He described the case of his patient Irène, who was traumatized when she witnessed the death of her mother in bed. Subsequently, she became subject to episodes of unconsciously reenacting the death scene, which were triggered by her viewing a bed from a certain angle.[14]

The American psychiatrist Abram Kardiner was one of the first to describe in detail, in 1941, flashbacks engendered by the trauma of war, in this case the First World War:

> Some types of sensory disturbances are accurate hallucinatory reproductions of sensations originally experienced in the traumatic event. In this instance the symptom contains the idea, "I am still living in the traumatic situation." . . . The patients would live through their war scenes very vividly while in these trances. . . . The relationship with the external world was completely severed. Sensory stimuli on the skin and verbal suggestion had no effect. . . . In a few cases, some contact with the external

environment appeared to exist, except that the patients mistook situations and called individuals by wrong names.[15]

This latter type of disturbance, later called *pseudohallucination* by Mardi Horowitz, seems closer to Sol's flashbacks in *The Pawnbroker*.[16]

The soldiers that Kardiner treated had at least been prepared to fight for what was considered to be a patriotic cause. This was not the case for the Jews who survived the one-sided war of annihilation waged upon them by the Third Reich, though their flashbacks, as described here by the psychiatrists Henry Krystal and William Niederland in 1968, seem to resemble the combat flashbacks described by Kardiner.

> Almost ubiquitous were disturbances of memory. Many memories of persecution have become hypermnesic, at the same time occurring with such clarity and being so threatening that the patient cannot be sure that the old horrors have not, in fact, reappeared. . . . In the most intense panics, we observed episodes of confusion, disorientation, and also dreamlike states in which the patients believed themselves to be back in a concentration camp.[17]

After American psychiatry's encounter with traumatized Vietnam War veterans during the 1970s and 1980s, posttraumatic flashbacks finally began to be taken seriously enough to become the subject of numerous research studies. In 1985, Thomas Mellman and Glenn Davis interviewed twenty-one psychiatric inpatients diagnosed with PTSD—mostly Vietnam veterans—and found that nineteen reported having experienced flashbacks.

> Visual perceptions often consisted of faces associated with combat losses, the enemy, or jungle scenery. . . . Most hallucinations and illusions lasted seconds to minutes. Patients characterized the perceptual difficulty as "seeming real at the time," but reality testing was invariably intact within several minutes to an hour after the disappearance of the abnormal perception.[18]

As mentioned in Chapter 1, flashbacks have also been described recently by cognitive psychologists as a reversion from the most mature form of memory encoding, linguistic, to an earlier iconic form. These unassimilated iconic memories are less prone than linguistic memories to the processes of decay and mutation. They tend to remain fixed, rather, as literal recordings of past perceptions.

The same is true of posttraumatic dreams. The difference between the literal nature of posttraumatic dreams and the figurative or imaginary nature of normal dreams prompted Freud to exclaim, "This astonishes people far too little."[19] Cathy Caruth follows Freud in noting this difference between PTSD and other psychological disorders:

> It is indeed this truth of traumatic experience that forms the center of its pathology or symptoms; it is not a pathology, that is, of falsehood or displacement of meaning, but of history itself. If PTSD must be understood as a pathological symptom, then it is not so much a symptom of the unconscious, as it is a symptom of history. The traumatized, we might say, carry an impossible history within them, or they become themselves the symptom of a history that they cannot entirely possess.[20]

In what ways might the cinematic flashback be an analogue for the psychological flashback as a signifier of this impossible history? How might it be a cultural symptom of historical trauma? The cinematic flashback, for instance, would make it possible for the spectator not only to see Lady Macbeth's sensorimotor reenactments of the past from the point of view of the doctor and the gentlewoman, but also to see her revisualizations from her own point of view—to cross over the fictional threshold of subjectivity and, as Janet put it, to "dream with the patient." For if, as Freud suggested, the psychological flashback "implies a domination by an internal psychical reality over the reality of the external world," and if, as Münsterberg argued, "the photoplay obeys the laws of the mind rather than those of the outer world," then the cinematic flashback would in fact seem to be the perfect analogue for the posttraumatic symptom to which it lent its name.

FLASHBACKS IN FILM

When flashbacks began to appear in cinema after the turn of the century, they did not initially function as signifiers of trauma. They evolved between 1903 and the 1910s—not long after the emergence of the cinema itself—within an economic logic of the standardization and differentiation of films as products, a logic that left little room in this period for experimentation with posttraumatic forms of narration. Flashbacks allowed filmmakers to differentiate their products using a form of narration that was economical (much narrative information presented efficiently), pleasurable (moreso than the use of intertitles to present anterior plot information), and conducive to the development of more elaborate, novel-like stories.[21]

At the same time, standardization of films was deemed necessary in order to maximize efficiency. While providing needed differentiation, flashbacks were also perceived as threatening uncontrolled experimentation, audience confusion, and ultimately loss of profits.[22] Flashbacks themselves, then, had to be standardized. Their potential for disrupting the flow of the narrative had to be minimized. The resulting classical flashback form was, of course, anything but posttraumatic. A loss of mastery over time and point of view, and a shifting of attention from the story told to its telling, were not in order. On the contrary, any inherent disruptions of tense, mood, and voice caused by the flashback had to be smoothed over so that narrative mastery could be maintained.

What follows is a description of the stylistic features, and narrative and generic functions, of what I take to be the classical flashback, which was instituted during the 1910s, largely in Hollywood, and survived in Hollywood-influenced filmmaking throughout the world, with modifications, at least through the 1950s, if not to the present day.[23] In terms of narrative function, classical flashbacks convey information about the narrative past to the spectator, and often to characters as well. Flashbacks can be motivated by a remembering character, or presented directly, with no character focalization. In the case of focalized flashbacks, the memory may be sought or resisted by the rememberer. If the rememberer resists, often there is another character, an investigator-type, who seeks to have the rememberer remember.

A classical flashback did not simply occur at a given point in the story; its appearance was elaborately and redundantly prepared and announced by, first of all, certain basic elements of plot and dialogue. During a trial scene, for instance, a witness might be asked what she had seen. There would be a close-up of the witness talking, perhaps an intertitle in the case of a silent film, and then the flashback. These devices prepared the audience for a time jump, preventing reactions of confusion or disturbance.

The above is an example of a flashback motivated by a character's speech (even if, in silent film, that speech was not heard by the audience). In the case of a flashback motivated by an unspeaking character— what I would call an *interior flashback*, where the spectator is privileged over nonremembering characters in gaining access to the fictional space of the rememberer's visualization—the flashback might be announced by a close-up of the rememberer shifting her gaze and holding it on a blank spot or an object of memory.

Stylistically, the transitions into and out of classical flashbacks were clearly marked using optical effects, such as fades and dissolves. Musical cues, and sound effects such as echoing dialogue in talkies, were sometimes used as well.

Not only the onset of the classical flashback but also its content needed to be easily intelligible. The scene within the flashback either would be a return to an earlier scene, or would be made easily intelligible by dialogue, intertitles, or the context of the plot.

Finally, the narrative functions of classical flashbacks were generically coded. I would identify three broad, overlapping genres of classical flashback, which are loosely related to film genres in the usual sense. *Melodramatic flashbacks* contributed to the construction of a character, explaining the character's motivation within a present conflict and clarifying the action needed for narrative resolution. *Mystery flashbacks* revealed information previously withheld from the plot for purposes of suspense or comedy. And *biographical flashbacks* told life stories retrospectively, framing them in the present. As such, classical flashbacks played a key role in the teleological structure of narratives. The return of the past was motivated by the generically determined resolution of the plot.[24]

Through these narrative, stylistic, and generic boundaries, classical flashbacks prompted spectators to enjoy time shifts without losing a sense of mastery over time and point of view, or losing pleasure in the fiction by questioning the process of its narration.

An early example of a classical flashback occurs in *The Birth of a Nation*, when the Northerner Phil Stoneman is courting the Southerner Margaret Cameron. He looks at her, but she looks away, and then there is a flashback showing her brother, a Confederate soldier, dead on a battlefield. After the flashback, Margaret walks away from Phil, refusing him.

In several ways, this flashback is similar to Sol's flashback in *The Pawnbroker*. In both cases, the flashback is triggered by and interrupts the proposal of another character, from whom the rememberer looks away before flashing back. Neither memory is actively sought by the rememberer. Margaret's flashback, too, is interior, since she does not communicate her memory to Phil. And the content of Margaret's memory is potentially traumatic, in terms of both the personal loss of her brother and the collective experience of the Civil War.

Though the content of the flashback is potentially traumatic, however, at the formal level it is largely classical; it works to promote spectator mastery over the time shift. The flashback is announced in advance by an intertitle at the beginning of the scene: "Bitter memories will not allow the poor bruised heart of the South to forget." The transitions into and out of the flashback are marked by fade-outs. And the content of the flashback is easily intelligible, since it repeats an earlier scene.

In terms of genre, this is a melodramatic flashback functioning within a historical epic as a barrier to romance, which must be rectified by violence (the defeat of the "Negro militia" by the Klan) before narrative resolution can be achieved.[25]

After the First World War, a modernist reaction against classical cinema appeared in Europe; French, German, and Swedish films in particular began to feature nonclassical flashbacks.[26] An example of an early experiment with a modernist, posttraumatic form of flashback is *La Maternelle* (France, 1932). This is another focalized, interior flashback with traumatic content. Marie, a young girl abandoned by her mother, sees a couple kissing, and then flashes back to a scene of her mother kissing the man for whom she later abandoned the girl. This memory is signified by a shot lasting only half a second, and is immediately followed by five additional half-second flashbacks to other memories of abandonment.

Only two elements of this flashback sequence are even remotely classical. First, the spectator is given a modest preparation for the flashback by the appearance, just before it, of a memory image superimposed over the image of the kissing couple, accompanied by a dialogue flashback. Second, the contents of the six flashback shots are all repeated from earlier scenes.

Nonclassical elements are the absence of transitional markers and the use, instead, of simple cuts; the extreme brevity and discontinuity of the six shots, which severely limit their intelligibility; and the retraumatizing agency of the memories, which seem to return involuntarily and which cause the girl to attempt suicide at the conclusion of the flashback.

Generically, this is in many ways a typical melodramatic flashback. It leads directly to the resolution of the plot, in which Marie is rescued and happily reunited with her teacher who, it is implied, will adopt her. In other ways, however, the flashback works against melodramatic convention (or perhaps beyond it) to experiment with the construction of a subjectivity conventionally marginalized in film—that of a female child. This experiment consists in the fact that not only do the contents of the flashback allow the spectator to see what Marie remembers (and in each case from her visual point of view), but the form of the flashback also works to mimic the way Marie experiences her memories, and to reproduce that experience for the spectator.[27]

The flashback in *La Maternelle* exemplifies one of two strands in the history of the modernist flashback. While some films, especially German films like those discussed by Turim (*The Cabinet of Dr. Caligari*, *Variety*, and *Secrets of the Soul*) experimented primarily with the style of flashback content in their attempts to mimic the subjectivity of memory, *La Maternelle* experiments instead with the way its flashback is contextualized through editing and narrative construction. I will continue to stress this strand of the modernist flashback, since it is here that we find the flashbacks in *The Pawnbroker*.

A second wave of modernist cinema followed the Second World War. Indeed, the war—and especially the key traumas of the Holocaust and the bombing of Hiroshima—became the referent of some of these films' experiments in the representation of memory. Possibly the most influential modernist flashback in this period—and probably the most direct influence on the flashbacks in *The Pawnbroker*—was the first one in *Hiroshima, mon amour*. While the referent of the posttraumatic discourse in the film's prologue sequence is the bombing of Hiroshima, however, it is not surprising that the more subjectively and psychologically marked flashbacks that follow the prologue refer not to Hiroshima but to France, since the film's writer and director, and most of its producers, were French.

In the scene in question, the French woman stands smiling, looking at her Japanese lover, who is asleep on the bed of her hotel room in Hiroshima. The score is melodic, but a new, dissonant phrase arises and replaces the previous melody, with the old and new melodies briefly overlapping in a kind of musical dissolve. The shots continue as follows, all edited with simple cuts:

1. Reverse shot of the sleeping man, a medium shot in which we can see his hand upturned on the bed. His fingers twitch.

2. The woman. Her smile has faded, and she averts her gaze slightly away from the man.
3. Simple cut to a three-second flashback, showing a close-up of a man's twitching hand, then a fast pan to his bloody face, eyes open in death, kissed frantically by a woman.
4. Simple cut to the sleeping man, as before.
5. The woman, still remembering.
6. The man, waking.
7. The woman, still remembering. Then her facial expression changes again. She appears to come out of the memory, returns her gaze to him, and smiles again.

Only later does the spectator learn the meaning of the flashback—that during the Occupation the woman had a love affair with a German soldier who was shot dead by a sniper before her eyes.

This flashback is similar in some ways to the flashback in *The Birth of a Nation*. It is a focalized, interior flashback to the memory of a beloved soldier lying dead. And it is preceded by the rememberer averting her gaze from a romantic object and adopting a kind of remembering stare. But whereas the announcement of the flashback in *The Birth of a Nation* is made relatively obvious by the preceding intertitle about "bitter memories," the announcement in *Hiroshima* is relatively subtle. The only signal other than the change in the woman's gaze and facial expression is the preceding musical dissolve. As in *La Maternelle*, spectator preparation for the flashback is minimized.

This flashback is similar to the flashback in *La Maternelle* in two additional ways. First, it replaces the classical transition marks with simple cuts, the dissolve in this case having been displaced to the music track. Second, there is a suggestion that the woman's memory may not be fully voluntary. It seems to catch her unawares in a way that Margaret's memory in *The Birth of a Nation* does not, while it does not possess the retraumatizing agency of Marie's memories in *La Maternelle*.

To the flashback experiment in *La Maternelle*, *Hiroshima* adds two elements. First is a new way of making the flashback unintelligible. *La Maternelle* renders its flashback relatively unintelligible primarily through the extreme brevity and discontinuity of its six shots. The flashback shot in *Hiroshima* is slightly longer, but is still extremely short for its time, and its intelligibility is further diminished by the presence of a fast pan within the shot. But whereas the contents of the six flashback shots in *La Maternelle* are all repeats from earlier scenes, the content of the *Hiroshima* flashback is unfamiliar and uncontextualized by the plot, "left to dangle" unexplained, as Turim puts it, for another twenty minutes of screen time. Second, to the concept of the associative memory flashback employed in *La Maternelle* (a memory of the mother kissing triggered by the sight of a couple kissing) *Hiroshima* adds the device of the graphic match. A partial match between the present-time shot of the Japanese man's fingers twitching in sleep and the flashback shot of the German soldier's fingers twitching in death functions here as a cinematic analogy for associative memory.[28]

This flashback, too, is generically coded as melodrama, but in a weaker sense, lacking as it does the kind of framing by a narrative resolution that appears in *La Maternelle*. The woman's memory in *Hiroshima* constitutes not a problem to be solved, but an unresolvable existential condition. The flashback's status as an experiment in the mimicry and transmission of posttraumatic consciousness moves to the foreground as a primary motivation.[29]

The posttraumatic flashback, then, as elaborated in films like *La Maternelle* and *Hiroshima*, used a set of stylistic devices to transmit to the spectator a series of experiences that were, in turn, analogous to a series of characteristics of psychological trauma. First was the reduction of classical signals used to prepare the spectator for a time jump. This preparation of the spectator for the classical flashback may be thought of as analogous to the preparation for a blow that, according to Freud, engenders anxiety and prevents a reaction of "fright" and trauma. " 'Anxiety,' " Freud wrote, "describes a particular state of expecting the danger or preparing for it, even though it may be an unknown one. . . . I do not believe anxiety can produce a traumatic neurosis. There is something about anxiety that protects its subject against fright and so against fright-neuroses."[30] The posttraumatic flashback, on the other hand, worked to surprise the spectator with both the painful content of the flashback and, perhaps more important, the formal disturbance of the time jump.

Second was the use of the graphic match as an analogue of the associative triggering of psychological flashbacks.

Third was a cluster of devices that worked to provoke a cinematic analogy for the temporal disorientation of the trauma victim. The replacement of the classical transitional markers, like dissolves, by simple cuts; the extreme brevity of flashback shots; and the lack of redundancy and contextualization of the flashback content—these worked against the intelligibility of the classical flashback, and for the disorientation of the spectator.

The posttraumatic flashback employed a modernist fragmentation of tense, restriction of mood, and self-consciousness of voice. The classical sense of mastery over time was rejected, as cinematic temporality became subject to a profusion of relatively unpredictable and unintelligible time jumps. The classical omniscience and flexibility of point of view gave way as the spectator was repeatedly prompted to experience the temporal disorientation and emotional disturbance of the witness to traumatic events. And, as Turim suggests, repeated, formally disturbing time jumps denaturalized cinematic storytelling, and tended to promote spectator awareness of the process and means of narration.[31]

The posttraumatic flashback thus worked to create a disturbance not only at the level of content, by presenting a painful fictional memory, but also at the level of form. It registered the actual disturbances of traumatic experience, described earlier in this chapter, as a set of formal disturbances in the history of the flashback, as a rejection of the classical smoothing over of narrative time jumps, and as the provoking of an analogue posttraumatic consciousness in the spectator. As such, the posttraumatic flashback used a fictional form as a medium for the transmission of real traumatic experience.

Holocaust Flashbacks: *Sophie's Choice* and the Classical Flashback

The Holocaust does not impose inherent formal limits on flashbacks. Rather, the makers and viewers of films negotiate what Berel Lang has referred to as moral limits.[32] The Holocaust may have constituted a collective trauma, but it has remained available for representation through the discourse of narrative mastery, including the classical flashback. Surprisingly, the best example of a classical flashback with Holocaust content that I have found appeared not before the modernist experiments of *The Pawnbroker*, but seventeen years later. *Sophie's Choice* (United States, 1982) turns nostalgically back to a kind of "golden age" of the classical flashback as exemplified in a film like *Casablanca*, extending it from that earlier film's representation of the end of a love affair during the German Occupation of Paris—to Auschwitz.[33]

The protagonist of *Sophie's Choice* is Stingo, an aspiring writer in New York who falls in love with Sophie, a Polish Catholic survivor of Auschwitz. Stingo and the spectator discover the story of Sophie's past through a series of three flashbacks. In the scene before the second flashback, Stingo has discovered that Sophie has told him a lie about her past, claiming her father had been an anti-Nazi, when in fact he had been a pro-Nazi propagandist. He confronts her: "Sophie, I want to understand. I'd like to know the truth." There is a very slow camera move into a close-up of Sophie's face, as she says, "Oh the truth, I don't even know what is the truth after all these lies I have told." A lone recorder begins to play. Sophie's gaze begins to dart around the room, then comes to rest looking directly into the camera. "My father," she says, and there is a cut to a photograph of her father. "How can I explain how much I loved my father." There is a cut back to Sophie's face as she continues to speak, looking into the camera, and then a long flashback begins, presenting the story of her life before deportation, her arrest as a member of the resistance, and her deportation, with her two children, to Auschwitz.[34]

The spectator's preparation for the flashback in this scene is not just redundant; it is almost obsessive in its nostalgic return to the classical style. The time jump is announced by six separate devices: plot (Stingo confronts Sophie about her lie); dialogue ("I'd like to know the truth"); the camera move into Sophie's face; the onset of the recorder music; Sophie's changing gaze; and the appearance of the photograph as a memory object.

The content of the flashback is new, but it is far from disorienting. Not only is it fully contextualized by the plot, but it lasts half an hour, almost constituting a separate narrative-within-the-narrative, as in *Casablanca*, with occasional returns to Sophie's face or voice-over narration in the present. In this sense, it does not strive to mimic the subjectivity of memory itself, but is, rather, highly secondarized.

Indeed, while the content of the flashback belongs to Sophie, one could argue that its form belongs to Stingo. Unlike the other flashback scenes discussed here, this is not an interior flashback, but a flashback that illustrates the rememberer's verbal narration of her memory to an investigator character. The memory does not return involuntarily, but is instead deliberately excavated (again, as in *Casablanca*). There is no suggestion of excessive vividness or associative memory. All of this is consistent with the fact that the film's protagonist is not Sophie but Stingo. *Sophie's Choice* harkens back to the classical, literary coming-of-age story, or, more specifically, the story of the coming-of-age of the novelist, or *Kunstlerroman* (artist novel), which is highly teleological in the sense that the narrative is resolved when the protagonist becomes a novelist who can write his (classically male) own coming-of-age story. This coming-of-age consists in gaining knowledge of love and death, but Stingo's knowledge is doubled; not only does he fall in love with Sophie and then lose her to suicide, but through her, and through her memories, he gains a kind of vicarious knowledge of another order of death entirely, an order of death that belongs to the very continent that engendered the *Kunstlerroman* in the first place.[35] Sophie and her memories thus represent the mystery of the other, which the hero must investigate, solve, and transcend. Sophie's memory of Auschwitz may be "impossible" for *her*, as Caruth puts it (it finally kills her), but insofar as her memory is mediated by Stingo and his coming-of-age story, it actually makes *possible* the resolution of the narrative. Far from being presented formally as unassimilable, Holocaust memory in *Sophie's Choice* is assimilated generically to the hero's coming-of-age.[36]

HOLOCAUST FLASHBACKS: *THE PAWNBROKER*

> For me the dead were more real than the living.
> —Elie Wiesel[37]

The idea that the "impossible" form of Holocaust memory might be analogous to an entirely different form of cinema appears implicitly and explicitly in various writings on the Holocaust. It is implicit in Lawrence Langer's discussion of the fragmentation of temporality in oral histories of the Holocaust, the failure of survivors to be able to reconcile what Charlotte Delbo has called the "common memory" of normal life before and after the war with the "deep memory" of the Holocaust. Langer describes the temporality in one survivor's oral history as "a permanent duality, not exactly a split or a doubling but a parallel existence. He switches from one to the other without synchronization because he is reporting not a sequence but a simultaneity."[38] Langer might just as easily be describing the flashback scenes in *The Pawnbroker*, and the way they evoke less the sequential logic of the classical flashback than the simultaneous logic of crosscutting—the classical technique of cutting back and forth between scenes understood as occurring at the same time in two different locations.

The memory/cinema analogy is explicit in this passage from Susan Fromberg Schaeffer's *Anya* (1974), a first-person novel about a Holocaust survivor.

> My life was not continuous; it would never be continuous again. Something, the world, or history, had intervened like a terrible editor of a movie, snatching out handfuls of characters, changing the sets wildly, changing them back again. . . . And now my mind was doing it, too, cutting pieces of the film randomly with clumsy scissors, without anesthetic, and the victim never knowing anything had been taken. . . . The film which has recorded the story of my life was spliced one third through to an irrelevant reel by a maniac.[39]

One wonders whether Hugo Münsterberg could have predicted that his memory/cinema analogy would lead to this.

Wallant's 1961 novel, *The Pawnbroker*, also contains numerous references to cinema, as well as sometimes mimicking cinematic forms such as the flashback, crosscutting, the freeze frame, and the fade in its narrative style.[40] The following passage, describing the end of Sol's dream of an idyllic picnic with his family before their deportation, makes an explicit memory/cinema analogy.

> And then they stopped, every blade of grass froze, each of them was arrested in motion: David balanced impossibly on one short, sturdy leg, Ruth maintained her pose of reaching. All was silence; it was like a movie which had suddenly stopped while its projecting illumination continued. . . . And then it all began dimming; each face receded, the sunny afternoon turned to eternal twilight, dusk, evening, darkness.[41]

Wallant's description of a psychological flashback, however, makes no explicit cinematic analogy.

> Oh yes, yes, a nice, peaceful summer day; quiet, safe, full of people going about their business in the rich, promising heat. A dozing morning in a great city. He looked idly at the intricate landscape, his eyes lidded with boredom as he walked.
>
> Suddenly he had the sensation of being clubbed. An image was stamped *behind* his eyes like a bolt of pain. For an instant he moved blindly in the rosy morning, seeing a floodlit night filled with screaming. A groan escaped him, and he stretched his eyes wide. There was only the massed detail of a thousand buildings in quiet sunlight. In a minute he hardly

remembered the hellish vision and sighed at just the recollection of a brief ache, his glass-covered eyes as bland and aloof as before.[42]

While this passage makes no explicit cinematic analogy, it does emphasize the motif of eyes and vision, as does Wallant's single essay on writing, entitled "The Artist's Eyesight." As I will show, the filmmakers, in adapting the novel, exploited the connection between Wallant's eyesight motif and the formal dynamics of the cinematic gaze.

Here is how the film's editor, Ralph Rosenblum, describes the genesis of its flashback form.

> By 1962 people had put World War II and its atrocities behind them, and it was questionable whether audiences would be willing to reopen themselves to the stupendous evil that had squeezed the life out of its victims. What tricks of emotional penetration could Lumet perform that went beyond the well-known newsreel images of liberation bulldozers pushing piles of emaciated dead into mass graves? . . . The information is either too brutal to portray or else simply incapable of reaching us any more. The scriptwriters, Morton Fine and David Friedkin, must have known what they were up against, for in an unusual note to the director they asked that some more graphic way be found of representing memory. They feared the traditional flashback would not have the needed impact.
>
> The time was right for an overhaul of the flashback. In the thirties and forties flashbacks had been very popular and always happened in the same way. A sequence quieted down, Joan Crawford or Bette Davis said, "I remember . . ." or began reminiscing in a dreamy way about her first marriage, the camera moved in on her entranced face, an eerie "time" music saturated the sound track, a shimmering optical effect crept over the screen as if oil were dripping across it, and everyone in the audience knew, "Uh-oh, we're going into memory." What new film technique could be a more graphic way of representing memory than the traditional flashback? We knew from personal experience that memories, especially unpleasant ones, are not engaged in by a voluntary swan dive into the past. They intrude in flashes.[43]

If this passage is of limited value as a document of the complex real determinations of the flashbacks in *The Pawnbroker* (for one thing, it was presumably written years later), it is at least highly suggestive of the web of discourses in which those flashbacks have been embedded. First, the similarity to Resnais's retrospective comments on *Night and Fog* is striking.[44] Both texts argue that archival footage of the liberated camps had lost its effectiveness as a cinematic memory of the camps, and that, in order to be effective, new films required formal experimentation. This, of course, is a textbook modernist argument.

Second, Rosenblum's summary of the classical flashback functions · implicitly as a vivid critique of the formal conservatism of such flashbacks, and is a remarkably accurate description of the flashback in *Sophie's Choice*, which lacks only Rosenblum's dripping oil.

Third is Rosenblum's claim that the filmmakers "knew from personal experience" that some memories were not voluntary but rather "intrude in flashes," a claim that the film's director Sidney Lumet has also made.[45] This claim raises some questions. Had the filmmakers actually suffered from posttraumatic flashbacks? When Rosenblum says that unpleasant memories "intrude in flashes," does he mean that they flash up suddenly and involuntarily, or that they last only as long as a flash, or both? By rhetorically opposing memory flashes and voluntary memories, he gives a plausible motivation for the flashbacks' intrusiveness, but not for their split-second duration. In fact, I have seen no reference in the psychiatric literature to psychological flashbacks lasting less than several seconds, which, in cinematic terms, is significantly longer than a split second.

Finally, Rosenblum pushes the memory/cinema analogy a step further when he juxtaposes the word *flashback* as a cinematic term and the word *flashes* as a memory term. When his book on editing, containing the passage on *The Pawnbroker*, was published in 1979, it would still be several years before *flashback* would enter the psychiatric mainstream to refer to posttraumatic memories, and would become a clear marker of the memory/cinema analogy.

The psychiatrist Ernst Becker, however, anticipated this development in a 1969 article on *The Pawnbroker*. Becker wrote, "His mind is continually prey to obtrusive flashbacks, flashbacks to a world he has left, but which still claims him. Physically and externally he is here; inwardly and emotionally he is elsewhere." On the following page, Becker writes, "Nazerman's story is one that my generation has lived vicariously so many times, we had rather be spared the details. We almost are—the thing is handled with such perfect economy; we see only a few heart-rending and soul-rending flashbacks." Becker may have been the first to use the word *flashback* in both its psychological and cinematic senses, but failed to point out the significance of this semantic analogy.[46] Arguably, however, it was the film of *The Pawnbroker* itself that

first implicitly proposed—and demonstrated so vividly—the application of the word *flashback* to the psychological realm of posttraumatic
memory.

I will return now to the flashback sequence from *The Pawnbroker* described at the beginning of this chapter, in order to show how the film
both applied the posttraumatic flashback to the Holocaust and explored
its most extreme and systematic possibilities. First, there are virtually
no advance signals explicitly announcing the coming of the flashback,
nothing like the intertitle preceding the flashback in *The Birth of a Nation*, or the confrontation of the rememberer by an investigator character, as in *Sophie's Choice*. Neither is there an implicit musical signal,
as in *Hiroshima* and *Sophie's Choice*; the scene lacks music altogether. In
fact, there is only one classical signal, an implicit one: Sol's change of
expression, his adoption of a memory stare.

It must be said, however, that while the spectator's preparation for
the flashback is minimal within the scene itself, there is another form
of preparation at the level of the overall structure of the film. From the
film's very beginning, the spectator is rapidly tutored to understand the
flashes occurring at various points as interior flashbacks, to contextualize them as presenting Sol's memories of the Holocaust, and to expect
them from time to time. This tutored expectation certainly diminishes
the factor of surprise at the flashbacks' appearances, without, I would
argue, eliminating it altogether. Rather, an overall, vague sense of expecting flashbacks at an undetermined time may coexist with the shock
of each flashback's particular appearance.[47]

Second, *The Pawnbroker* takes the device of the graphic match as an
analogue for the associative triggering of posttraumatic memory a step
further than *Hiroshima*; here, the triggering of Sol's memory of his wife
by the sight of Mabel is presented by a precise graphic match of shots
of the two women, without an intervening shot of the rememberer as in
Hiroshima.

Third, *The Pawnbroker* arguably pushes spectator disorientation to its
limits. The content of the flashback is new; but while it is more contextualized by the overall narrative than the first flashback in *Hiroshima*, its
intelligibility is radically diminished by the extreme brevity of its first
appearance, and by the use of simple cuts. In fact, at a sixth of a second,
some of the flashes are too brief to be comprehended by the spectator.
It is only as they elongate in subsequent repetitions that they begin to

be intelligible. It is the brevity of these flashback shots that, more than any other stylistic device, I think, determined *The Pawnbroker*'s cultural effectiveness as a representation of the Holocaust and as a purveyor of posttraumatic cinema.[48]

Two possible influences on *The Pawnbroker*'s experiments with split-second flashbacks have already been cited: the filmmakers' personal experiences (which I tend to discount), and *Hiroshima, mon amour*. Rosenblum also cites the jump cuts in Godard's *Breathless* (1959), while a scene from Resnais's *Last Year at Marienbad* (1961) seems to have been the prototype for another of *The Pawnbroker*'s flashback sequences, though Lumet has denied the influence of European films altogether.[49] Lumet cites instead his own experience in live television, mentioning a sequence in one program that contained twenty-three cuts in one minute.[50]

In addition, having surveyed period reviews of *The Pawnbroker*, and found that the majority use the word *subliminal* to describe the split-second flashbacks, I would propose a fourth possible influence. Research on the use of subliminal stimuli in American advertising had been publicized in a 1957 book, *The Hidden Persuaders*, as a result of which the U.S. House of Representatives considered passing legislation banning subliminals. Apparently, the fact of subliminal film editing had entered the public imagination in this way, and influenced the reception of *The Pawnbroker*'s flashbacks, if not their production.[51]

These split-second flashbacks narrate Sol's point of view not only by showing the spectator what Sol visualizes, but also by prompting the spectator to experience that vision as Sol experiences it: as a disorienting, overwhelming intrusion. Since the film lacks an investigator character like Stingo to overcome the rememberer's resistance to memory, and to mediate it, it is the memories themselves that seem to overcome resistance, inflicting themselves directly on both Sol and the spectator. The spectator may even come to identify with Sol's resistance to the memories.

To make the lack of an investigator character even more poignant, there is a would-be investigator, the social worker Marilyn Birchfield, who tries to befriend Sol, and almost succeeds. Ultimately, however, none of the flashback memories is ever verbally narrated by Sol to another character. The other characters can be divided into the majority who never learn anything about Sol's memories, even as he experiences flashbacks in their presence, and a few—primarily Sol's sister and his lover, both Holocaust survivors themselves—who already know. On the one hand, there is the silence of the inability to speak, and on the other, the silence of already knowing. The spectator is put in the position of making an epistemological leap over a double barrier of external silence and internal resistance, to experience what the witness himself would prefer to forget.

Paradoxically, these split-second flashbacks tend both to increase spectator identification with the fictional protagonist, and to promote spectator awareness of the artificiality of the fiction. Flashes lasting only a sixth of a second threaten the spectator's ability to perceive the image, potentially prompting the question, "Why is the film showing me a flash so brief that I cannot comprehend it?" At this threshold of perception, the process of narration may be called into question, along with, perhaps, the visual basis of narrative cinema itself. As Cathy Caruth has argued with respect to *Hiroshima, mon amour*, the posttraumatic flashback's claim to representation is countered by what seems to be an even higher priority: the interruption of representation, the loss of visual mastery. Thus, an image—here, the image of the concentration camp—becomes an anti-image, blocking, or punching a hole in the chain of images. If narrative self-consciousness in *Night and Fog* is can be interpreted as a symbol of the body's reaction to shock, in *The Pawnbroker* it constitutes a quite literal link to the protagonist's condition—his blinding by vision.[52]

A corollary to the fragmentation of temporality through *The Pawnbroker*'s flashbacks is their articulation of trauma through the breakdown of the cinematic gaze. This breakdown, which is consistent with the eyesight motif in Wallant's novel, begins in the film's first scene, a dream sequence showing Sol's memory or fantasy of an idyllic, pre-Holocaust family picnic interrupted by the arrival of the Nazis. In this dream sequence, the members of Sol's family are bound together by their gazes at one another across the expanse of an open field. This binding includes the use of shot/reverse shot and eyeline matching to construct an exchange of gazes between Sol and his wife. At the end of the sequence, the family members' gazes are torn away from one another and directed toward the horrifying offscreen sight of the Nazis. In his dream, Sol thus represents his trauma as the breaking of the family gaze by the Nazis.

In the flashbacks that follow, Sol reenacts the breaking of this original gaze again and again. The present claims his gaze, but though he looks at Mabel, he sees only Ruth. Mabel says, "Look," but he hears "Willst du was sehen?" Shot/reverse shot and eyeline matching are brought to bear, but are undermined by temporal fragmentation. The shot of the gaze takes place in the physical reality of the present, but the reverse shot of the gaze's object takes place in the psychological imaginary of the past.

Not only do the flashbacks disable Sol's visual mastery over his surroundings, but, even within the Mabel/Ruth flashback, his victimization is presented as a loss of visual mastery. In the flashback, Sol is forced to look through broken glass at Ruth sitting naked in a cell, but she cannot see him, and his gaze is soon blocked by a soldier approaching her. Thus Sol's gaze, once a sign of mutual possession, has been broken and inverted into a sign of his loss of mutuality, his isolated possession by others—his trauma.[53]

As in *Hiroshima, mon amour*, the melodramatic coding of the flashbacks in *The Pawnbroker* is weakened by the discourses of both existentialism and trauma. Consistent with melodrama, *The Pawnbroker's* flashbacks reveal the origin of the protagonist's problem—here, especially, his refusal to teach the pawnbroking trade to his Puerto Rican assistant, Jesus, and his blindness to Jesus' resulting decision to join a plot to rob the pawnshop. Furthermore, the flashbacks clarify the action needed for narrative resolution: Sol's recognition of Jesus and of his responsibility to him, perhaps his acceptance of Jesus as a kind of substitute for the son he lost in the Holocaust.[54] Consistent with *Hiroshima's* existentialism, however, is both the weakening of the resolution of this melodramatic narrative—Sol's recognition of Jesus is too late to save him—and the failure of this weakened resolution to rectify Sol's memories. The film seems to recognize that nothing can rectify the content of Sol's memories. If anything can be rectified, it is the posttraumatic form of the memories, their tendency to blind Sol to the present. But it is ambiguous whether even this rectification can be inferred at the end of the film.[55]

In *Sophie's Choice*, the flashbacks' melodramatic coding is reinforced by their function in the solution of a mystery. The solution of the mystery of Sophie makes possible the resolution of Stingo's coming-of-age narrative. The posttraumatic time of Sophie's memories is accommodated to the "normal" (teleological) time of Stingo's present-day narrative. This binding of mystery to melodrama even operates to a limited extent in *Hiroshima, mon amour,* insofar as the Japanese man comes to play a mediating role in relation to the French woman's flashbacks similar to Stingo's role in relation to Sophie's. *The Pawnbroker,* on the other hand, does not construct Sol's past as a mystery; the flashbacks offer the spectator no pleasure in the solution of a mystery to offset their relaying of trauma. It is the spectator who is accommodated to the imperatives of memory, jerked back and forth across the gap separating the nonsynchronized and irreconcilable worlds of past and present, the gap separating the unreality of the living from the reality of the dead.

As generic function moves into the background as a motivation for the flashbacks, one of the things that moves into the foreground is the film's experimentation with the cinematic mimicking of psychological flashbacks. In fact, *The Pawnbroker* goes further than *La Maternelle, Hiroshima,* and any other film of which I am aware in its systematic efforts to mimic psychological flashbacks precisely, and to link these efforts to a systematic representation of PTSD at the level of content.[56] The film presents Sol as a kind of PTSD case study, complete with symptoms of emotional deadening, avoidance of trauma-associated stimuli, difficulty with anniversaries of traumatic events, and feelings of helplessness and shame. Rod Steiger is particularly effective in his use of facial expressions to convey the intrusive, hypervivid, and retraumatizing nature of Sol's flashbacks. *Hiroshima,* on the other hand, made a significant contribution to posttraumatic cinema at the level of form without linking this contribution to the presentation of characters suffering from PTSD at the level of content.[57]

The contribution to posttraumatic cinema of *The Pawnbroker's* flashbacks is clearly not due to their content, to their representation of the Holocaust per se.[58] But even their formal mimicking of psychological flashbacks is less significant, I would argue, than their status as a disruption of the classical flashback, and of the audience's expectations of flashbacks in mass-distributed films of the mid-1960s. The trauma of the Holocaust registered in *The Pawnbroker* less as an image of the camps, less even as the psychological accuracy with which that image intrudes on the present as an analogue of the psychological flashback, than as a visceral experience of shock. Formal disruption in *The Pawnbroker* is no mere aesthetic experiment; it is the cinematic symptom of a disruption in history.

Crucial to *The Pawnbroker*'s effectiveness as a posttraumatic film was its position within the history and economics of the American film industry. The 1960s were a time of relative instability in the industry, when a handful of vertically integrated studios no longer controlled the market, demand and profits were down, and independent productions made up an increasing proportion of mass-distributed films. The time was ripe for mass-distributed films to experiment with new forms, such as those coming out of the French New Wave, live television, and advertising (subliminals). As a New York-based, independently produced, mass-distributed American film, *The Pawnbroker* was well positioned to take advantage of this opportunity. Posttraumatic flashbacks would have had less of an effect in a full-fledged experimental film, where extreme formal experimentation would have been expected. In a more mainstream studio film, on the other hand, posttraumatic flashbacks would have been viewed as too risky. Situated in the avant-garde of mainstream American film, however, *The Pawnbroker* was able to borrow the posttraumatic flashback from *Hiroshima, mon amour* and import it into American film culture in such a way as to deliver a formal shock to a mass audience.[59]

Within a few years—and probably due largely to the influence of *The Pawnbroker*—the posttraumatic flashback had entered the narrative repertoire of mainstream film, at least as a recognizable alternative to the classical flashback.[60] As this cinematic analogue for psychological and historical experience became a fixture in the Western cultural landscape, its shock value decreased. The avant-garde of posttraumatic cinema migrated to new locations.

5   István Szabó
and Posttraumatic Autobiography

IN THE previous chapter, I argued that a film need not be a documentary in order to document historical trauma. *Hiroshima, mon amour* and *The Pawnbroker* experimented with the use of posttraumatic narration to register historical trauma in fiction, expanding the techniques of posttraumatic narration through the semiotic flexibility of the fiction film. István Szabó, Hungary's most successful filmmaker of the past four decades, subsequently extended the possibilities for registering historical trauma in the fiction film through the genre of autobiographical fiction. In an informal trilogy composed of his second, third, and fourth features, Szabó built on Resnais's experiments in posttraumatic narration to recall and record his own witnessing of historical trauma—both his personal losses as a Hungarian Jew growing up under Nazism and then communism, and the collective losses of his city, his country, his generation, and his fellow Jews.

Father, Love Film, and *25 Fireman Street* combine the figurative power of the posttraumatic fictional narration that Resnais initiated—the image of the present as a signifier of the past, the flashback, the film-within-the-film—with a testimonial power related, after a fashion, to that of the Wiener film: the urge to reproduce and disseminate an image of historical reality. Documentary footage like the Wiener film mechanically records and reproduces real images of historical events, but is severely limited by the historical possibilities of filming under extreme conditions. The autobiographical fiction film renders both less and more than documentary footage. Its recording and reproduction of the historical image is mediated by memory, fictionalization, and reenactment; but, at the same time, the autobiographical fiction film transcends the limitations of documentary filming, penetrating a broader range of historical realities—from the public realm of the crowd, to the intimate realm of the family, to the imaginary realm of memories, fantasies, and dreams.

111

I want to make a distinction, however, between, on the one hand, films written and directed by witnesses, and on the other hand, films based on written accounts—diaries, memoirs, or autobiographical novels—that are adapted to film by nonwitnesses. Adaptations are more common, partly because their division of labor is better suited to the structure of mainstream film industries. There are a limited number of Holocaust survivors who are in a position to write and direct mainstream films, and who are willing to make autobiographical ones and able to get them financed and distributed. Some examples of successful adaptations of autobiographical Holocaust works by nonsurvivor filmmakers are *The Diary of Anne Frank* (United States, 1959), *The Garden of the Finzi-Continis* (Italy, 1971), and *Europa, Europa* (Germany/France, 1991).[1]

In the subgenre to which Szabó's trilogy belongs, however, the memories of witnesses are articulated not only by the content of the films narrowly defined but also by their style and their form of narration. This subgenre therefore raises a question of historical representation not raised by adaptations. How can the mental language of traumatic historical memory be translated into the concrete, audiovisual language of cinema? How can witnessing become film? This is not to say that nonwitnesses may not grapple with similar questions of film language in representing traumatic historical memory, as did Alain Resnais and the makers of *The Pawnbroker*. In the case of the autobiographical film, however, the question of translation assumes a particular form, insofar as it focuses on an individual person: the witness/filmmaker. Indeed, Szabó's trilogy is significant not only because of its particular translation of one witness's experience of recent Hungarian history into a fascinating form of cinema, but also because of its demonstration of autobiography—and the figure of the autobiographer—as a highly productive site for the examination of a set of questions of historical representation. Looking at the trilogy simply as a text, we might say that it could have been produced by any author, individual or collective. But looking at it as a symbolic act grounded in cultural history, we cannot escape the fact that it was produced by a particular Hungarian Jew.

The subgenre of autobiographical Holocaust films and videos began to congeal in the early 1980s, through a small group of mostly low-budget European, American, and Israeli fictional works, as well as documentaries.[2] These works receive little attention in the two existing books on international Holocaust films, which emphasize more main-stream films; they have received no critical attention as a genre. One earlier autobiographical Holocaust film, however, is discussed extensively in both books: *The Last Stage* (Poland, 1948), a fiction feature written and directed by Wanda Jakubowska, a Jewish survivor of Auschwitz.[3] I contend, however, that the formal and discursive paradigms of the autobiographical Holocaust film were established not by Jakubowska alone, but by three major Eastern European filmmakers—Jakubowksa, Roman Polanski, and István Szabó. The realism of *The Last Stage* may have made it more recognizable as an autobiographical Holocaust film, but to miss the autobiographical discourse on the Holocaust in Szabó's more modernist trilogy is to miss what may be the most productive body of work in the genre.

JAKUBOWSKA'S REALIST PARADIGM, AND POLANSKI'S ALLEGORICAL ALTERNATIVE

The Last Stage / Ostatni Etap is based on the true story of a Jewish prisoner in Auschwitz—known as "Mala"—who was executed for her role in the resistance.[4] While it does not tell Jakubowska's own story, the critical discourse on the film asserts that its realism stems from Jakubowska's personal memories of Auschwitz. The challenge Jakubowska faced in translating this material into cinema is suggested in a quote from the filmmaker: "People who had not been in the concentration camp did not understand. And no wonder. What had happened there far surpassed the capacity of normal, human understanding. But it had to be understood, and well understood, so that it might never happen again."[5]

If, in her reference to Auschwitz surpassing normal understanding, Jakubowska implicitly or symptomatically invokes the discourse of trauma, how, then, does *The Last Stage* respond to the problem of representing the trauma of Auschwitz? It falls back on the narrative conventions of the realist historical film, albeit the socialist variant. The film's strictly linear temporal structure undergirds a teleological narrative of fascist domination overcome by socialist resistance. The onset of fascist domination is established within the first shot. In a normal, happy street scene, we see a loving father and daughter. Within seconds, the Nazis have swept through the scene, rounded up as many people as possible, and put them in trucks, bound, presumably, for Auschwitz, which is revealed in the next shot, and which constitutes the setting for the rest of the film. The film goes on to tell the story of Polish-Jewish deportee Marta Weiss (a fictionalized version of Mala)—her selection by the Nazis as a Polish/German interpreter, her introduction to the women's camp, her recruitment into the women's socialist resistance, her escape from the camp, and her eventual arrest. The film concludes with the scene of her public execution and martyrdom, interrupted at the last minute by a formation of fighter planes flying over the camp, heralding the coming liberation. Just as the first scene represents fascism as an interruption of capitalism, so the final scene poses the next stage—the "last stage"—of the dialectic of history as the interruption of fascism by socialism.

Point of view in *The Last Stage* is highly flexible and omniscient. Classical editing establishes the space of Auschwitz with a high-angle shot, proceeding to break the camp down into the private spaces where the guards strategize the prisoners' subjugation and the prisoners conspire to resist, and the public space of the camp's main square (*Appellplatz*), where these two classes starkly conflict. Frequent crane shots showing masses of prisoners in formation circled by their captors do double duty for the film's realism. They both highlight the narrative omniscience of the film, and emphasize the physical realism of its mise-en-scène; the shots were filmed on location at Auschwitz, reportedly using 3,500 Auschwitz survivors as extras.[6]

With this unself-conscious linear temporality and omniscient point of view, *The Last Stage* works to overcome the trauma of that which "far surpassed the capacity of normal, human understanding," marshaling the discourse of socialist realism to master the memory of Auschwitz, to make it "understood, and well understood."[7]

Remembering his life after his liberation from Auschwitz and Buchenwald, Elie Wiesel articulated a different approach to the problem of translating memory into narrative.

> I knew that the role of the survivor was to testify. Only I did not know how. I lacked experience, I lacked a framework. I mistrusted the tools, the procedures. Should one say it all or hold it all back? Should one shout or whisper? . . . How does one describe the indescribable? . . . And then, how can one be sure that the words, once uttered, will not betray, distort the message they bear? So heavy was my anguish that I made a vow: not to speak, not to touch upon the essential for at least ten years.[8]

Roman Polanski outdid Wiesel, however. He did not "speak" about it—that is, make a film about it—for fifty-six years. As a Jewish child, Polanski escaped the liquidation of the Krakow ghetto, survived the remainder of the war passing as a member of a Catholic family, and lost his mother to Auschwitz. He did not explicitly refer to this subject matter in his films, however, until late in his career—in *The Pianist* (2001), which, however, is based not on his own autobiography but that of the pianist, Wladyslaw Szpilman, who escaped from the Warsaw (not the Krakow) ghetto. On the other hand, it is not difficult to argue, contrary to Polanski's own statements, that practically his entire oeuvre constitutes the allegorical projection of the Krakow ghetto onto a series of other settings: a boat (*Knife in the Water*), an apartment (*Repulsion*) or apartment building (*Rosemary's Baby*, *The Tenant*), a castle (*The Fearless Vampire Killers*), a peninsula (*Death and the Maiden*), even another ghetto (*Chinatown*).[9]

The point of view of the helpless victim trapped in a claustrophobic space and threatened by a steadily increasing menace, horrifying and surreal, is encapsulated in the opening scene of Polanski's *Cul-de-Sac* (1966). The setting is Lindisfarne, an island off the coast of England that becomes a peninsula at low tide. During one such low tide, two men are driving on the road out to the end of the peninsula. One has been shot in the leg. The car dies, and the uninjured man goes on foot for help, leaving the injured man alone in the car. The tide begins to rise, a layer of water gradually covering the entire landscape as the injured man calls for help. The road is finally submerged, and the car begins to float away.

Compare this scene to the following childhood memory from Polanski's autobiography.

> [My sister] took me to the window [of our apartment] and pointed. Some men were at work on something right across the street. It looked like a barricade. "What are they doing," I asked. "They're building a wall." Suddenly it dawned on me: they were walling us in. . . . What was once a pleasant outlook—a quiet street leading into an open square with trees—had now become a cul-de-sac.[10]

Lacking explicit autobiographical references, however, Polanski's allegorical films are of limited use as a form of Holocaust autobiography.

SZABÓ

Between the transparency of Jakubowska and the opacity of Polanski lies the translucent modernism of Szabó. Born in 1938, Szabó was a Jewish child living in Budapest between 1941 and 1945, during which time about 100,000 Budapest Jews were massacred by Hungarian Nazis, and about 435,000 Hungarian Jews outside Budapest were deported to Auschwitz, where 90 percent were immediately gassed to death. Szabó was among the many Budapest Jews who were hidden by Christians during the worst period, the winter of 1944–45. Both his parents survived the massacres, but his father, a doctor, died of a heart attack at the time the city was liberated.[11]

Szabó became the most successful Hungarian filmmaker from the late 1960s to the present. During the late 1950s, Hungarian cinema had begun to emerge from a period of strict Stalinist control. Miklós Jancsó, with his experimental, epic approach to Marxist historiography, emerged as the first internationally recognized representative of a new Hungarian cinema. Szabó, with a more psychological approach to history, was the second.

Szabó, who both writes and directs his films, has, like Polanski, repeatedly downplayed the autobiographical elements of his films in his statements about them, emphasizing instead their representation of various collective subjectivities: Hungarian, Central European, or at times universal.[12] Since he has said little publicly about his personal history, it is difficult to establish exactly how autobiographical his films are. However, while he may never have made a strictly or transparently autobiographical film, it is clear, based on the few public statements he has made about his personal history, as well as on my interview with his colleague, Gyula Gazdag, that elements of Szabó's own and his family's history appear persistently in his first four features, and occasionally thereafter.[13]

All of Szabó's first four films feature the actor András Bálint, who seems to have functioned loosely as a fictional substitute for the filmmaker himself. In *The Age of Daydreaming* (1964), Bálint stars as a young radio engineer, a job Szabó once held.[14] The fact that the protagonist's father is dead is an incidental detail in this first feature, but is elevated to the central problem of Szabó's second feature, *Father* (1966), in which Bálint plays a character known only as Takó, which resembles Szabó's own name. Szabó used his own former residence for the exterior shots of the apartment building in which Takó lives.[15]

In *Love Film* (1970), the protagonist played by Bálint is once again fatherless, and remembers having been hidden during the war. *25 Fireman Street* (1973) seems to be based largely on the historical experiences of Szabó's and his wife's parents.[16] In one plot strand, a Dr. Baló and his wife and son are forced into separate hiding places during the war. Mrs. Baló and the boy survive, but Dr. Baló dies of a heart attack during the liberation. Of course, the name Baló once again has a familiar ring; Szabó's former residence reappears as well.

After *25 Fireman Street*, Szabó turned away from autobiography to a large extent. His international reputation was cemented by *Mephisto* (1981), which won the Academy Award for Best Foreign Language Film. *Mephisto* was the first film in another informal trilogy by Szabó— followed by *Colonel Redl* (1985) and *Hanussen* (1988)—that is indicative of his shift away from autobiography. As opposed to the earlier trilogy of semiautobiographical Hungarian productions, in Hungarian, written by Szabó essentially alone, and featuring the Hungarian actor András Bálint, the films in this second trilogy are based on the life stories of other individuals, are international co-productions, in German, only co-written by Szabó, and starring the Austrian actor Klaus Maria Brandauer. Aspects of autobiography do return in Szabó's later work, notably in *Meeting Venus* (1991), which is based on Szabó's experiences as an opera director, and, less directly, in *Confidence* (1979), about a Socialist hiding in Budapest in 1944–45.[17]

The embrace of autobiography as a form of revolt against repressive cinematic conventions links Szabó to a range of other postwar filmmakers and film movements, especially the French New Wave and François Truffaut's *The 400 Blows*, whose influence Szabó cited by including a poster for it in *The Age of Daydreaming*. The role of autobiography in Szabó's films becomes most problematic where it overlaps with the representation of Jewish identity and the Holocaust, for reasons I will suggest below. These subjects tended to be repressed, displaced, and disguised in his films until *Sunshine* (2000), which is his first film to explicitly represent Hungarian Jews and their fate during the war, but which is neither autobiographical nor, I would argue, posttraumatic in its form of narration.[18] Paradoxically, Szabó first entered the canon of Holocaust cinema not for his earlier, autobiographical films but for his later, less personal film, *Mephisto*, which represents the experience not of a victim but of a collaborator, and which occupies a prominent place in Annette Insdorf's book on Holocaust films, *Indelible Shadows*.[19] Holocaust memory actually structures Szabó's earlier trilogy, however, at the level of subtext. The significance of the trilogy as a form of Holocaust autobiography and posttraumatic cinema has been eclipsed by the canonization of *Mephisto* on the one hand and of *The Last Stage* on the other.

Szabó has been known as a Hungarian filmmaker, and a European filmmaker, but only recently a Jewish one. It should not come as a complete surprise that the leading Hungarian filmmaker is a Jew (although it may be considered lucky that he survived the war). Even after the genocide, Jews continued to play an important role in Hungarian cultural life. Memories of Nazism and fears of continuing anti-Judaism make one hesitate to speak of the importance of Jews among the European intelligentsia. An effect of this chapter, then, is to declare that Jews survived in Europe, that they exist, that they are making films. István Szabó speaks for the surviving Jews of Hungary in a way that no one else does, through the power of mass-distributed images and sounds. His films make a crucial contribution to both Hungarian and Jewish history; indeed, they show that the two histories are inextricably intertwined.

The Holocaust in Hungary

In order to see through the surface of Szabó's trilogy to the subtext, and to understand the trauma that governs the relations between the two levels, one must know some details of the trauma itself, of the process by which Jews were excluded from the Hungarian nation socially, culturally, and physically.

During the mid-nineteenth century, the Hungarian aristocracy used Jews to address national problems of economic backwardness and ethnic conflict. Jews were granted civil rights in exchange for their contributions to the development of the country's economic and social life. The price required was their thorough assimilation into Hungarian culture. Thereafter, Jews had to reject "Jewish values" and embrace "patriotic" ones in order to be accepted into mainstream society. Many simply converted to Catholicism. Under these conditions, Jews did enter the mainstream, and made major contributions to Hungarian society and culture.[20]

Conditions changed, however, after the short-lived 1918 communist takeover, at which time Jews constituted about 6 percent of the national population. The right-wing, anti-Jewish dictator Miklós Horthy ousted the Communists in a 1919 counter-revolution that involved the massacre of thousands of Jews and leftists.[21] Many Jews emigrated at that time; those who stayed became even more patriotic and assimilated.

During the interwar period, from 1919 to 1941, a series of laws enacted by the Horthy regime removed the Jews' civil rights.[22] Fascist ideology began to enter the mainstream of national literary life, and what had been a strong but encouraging force for assimilation became a violent stream of condemnation.[23]

Hungary's 1941 alliance with Nazi Germany inaugurated a period of bloodletting for the whole nation, and a period of genocide for the Jews. Hungarian participation on the eastern front was a disaster. As Germany began to lose the war, Hungary became increasingly wary of the alliance, and secretly approached the Allies to sue for peace. In 1944, Germany occupied Hungary and set up a sympathetic government of Hungarian Nazis. However much the Occupation might have been viewed as a national tragedy, there was little active resistance. The deportation of the approximately 435,000 provincial Jews to Auschwitz in trains of cattle cars took only four months. It was a sudden and massive extermination, even by Nazi standards. The deportation from Hungary had been conceived by the German occupiers; its planning was primarily, and its execution exclusively, carried out by Hungarian authorities.[24]

Plans to complete "the Final Solution" in Hungary by deporting the approximately 230,000 Jews in Budapest to Auschwitz were interrupted by the progress of the war. Allied bombing of the city began in April 1944, and the entire population spent much of the next ten months of siege warfare in cellars, starving and freezing. In June, most of the Jews were concentrated into "yellow star houses" throughout the city.[25]

In October, Hungarian Nazis (who called themselves the Arrow Cross) initiated a reign of terror against Budapest's Jews and other perceived enemies. Jews were shot throughout the city; many were taken to the banks of the Danube and shot into the river.[26] In December, the Soviet army encircled the city, and bombardments and house-to-house fighting ensued. The Arrow Cross continued its reign of terror until the city was completely liberated in February 1945.

After the liberation, about 144,000 Jews remained in Budapest, the largest Jewish community left in former Nazi-occupied Europe. Liberation did not mean the end of anti-Judaism in Hungary, however. Anti-Jewish pogroms in 1946 and the repression of the Jewish community by the socialist state after 1948 resulted in a renewal of Jewish assimilation, with many Jews denying their Jewish origins, and raising their children largely in ignorance of the Holocaust and of what had happened to their families during the war. As in all the nations of the Soviet bloc, the official Hungarian narrative of the war stressed the crimes against the nation committed by Germany and a few Hungarian collaborators, repressing the memory of crimes against the Jews, and the more widespread Hungarian complicity in those crimes. This narrative held a virtual monopoly on the public discourse of the war from the immediate postwar period until the early 1990s, after the fall of the socialist state, when it had to compete with the discourses of Jews, neo-Nazis, and others.[27]

The Holocaust was referred to in only a very small number of Hungarian films before Szabó began to elaborate some kind of cinematic discourse of Jewish memory in 1966. The few films that did refer to the Holocaust did so within strict ideological limits, articulating not the point of view of the victims, but rather the myth of a heroic Hungary that protected its Jews, who were stereotyped as children, women, or weak men wearing glasses (as in *Somewhere in Europe*, 1947; *Keep Your Chin Up*, 1954; *Budapest Spring*, 1955; *Two Half-Times in Hell*, 1962; and *Darkness in Daytime*, 1963). The first inkling of the victim's point of view appears at the beginning of *Dialogue* (1963), directed by János Herskó, a Jew who survived slave labor during the war.[28] The protagonist is introduced at the beginning of the film as she is peering out through the barbed wire of a concentration camp, before being assimilated into a set of postwar political and romantic conflicts. The assistant director was István Szabó.

FATHER

Father/Apa begins with documentary footage of war-torn Budapest: a series of shots of the Chain Bridge—the first bridge built over the Danube to join Buda and Pest during the 1840s, forming the capital city—broken, bombed by the Germans in their flight from the city in

1944–45, in order to stop the advancing Soviet army. This documentary sequence transitions seamlessly into fictional footage of the funeral of Takó's father. The dialectic of this opening sequence—the real and the fictional, the public and the private, the collective losses of the war and the personal loss of the father—initiates and binds the set of discourses that structure the narrative that follows.

At its most explicit level, *Father* is Takó's coming-of-age story, narrated by the adult Takó. The first half of the film concerns his childhood neurosis in response to his father's death: his obsession with his lost father, his fantasy that his father had been a communist partisan hero, his lies, his misbehavior. The second half of the film cuts to Takó's young adulthood as a college student, and alternates between scenes of Takó continuing to act out this childhood neurosis, and scenes in which he works through the neurosis, accepts the reality of his father's life and death, and comes of age. This plot resolves quite neatly with a scene of Takó standing at peace over his father's grave.

At this explicit level, Takó is marked as different from other boys. At the implicit level, however, he is marked as the same. The personal problem of Takó's lost father is symbolic of a national problem of Takó's/Szabó's generation: the problem of the postwar generation individuating from the oppressive legacy of the previous generation and assuming its place as the next link in the chain of history. The previous generation is symbolized by a pair of father figures: on the one hand, the murderous Hitler, and on the other hand, the hypocritical Stalin (or his representative in Hungary, Rákosi), who defeats Hitler and sets himself up as a false "good" father. Takó's coming-of-age is a metaphor for the coming-of-age of his generation: the shedding of the need for the oppressive father figures of the past, and the acceptance of the reality of one's own adulthood.

Father, as I have characterized it thus far, does not appear to be a posttraumatic film. The double teleology of the explicit personal and implicit generational coming-of-age narratives seems to leave no room for an unresolved narrative of Holocaust trauma. And yet I would argue that there are three sets of symptoms indicating the existence of an unresolved trauma lingering beneath the surface of the film.

First are some bits of dialogue occurring in two different scenes that create apparently unresolvable inconsistencies in the narrative. The first bit of symptomatic dialogue occurs in the first half of the film, in a scene in which Takó's mother takes him to the movies. The feature (significantly, Chaplin's *The Great Dictator*) is preceded by a newsreel showing the execution of Arrow Cross men after the liberation. Seeing a shot of a noose being fitted around a condemned man's neck, Takó asks his mother, "Why were they hanged?" She answers, "They killed a lot of people. They wanted to kill us too. They condemned your father, but he managed to escape." The camera then tracks in to Takó as he turns to stare at his mother, apparently deeply affected by this statement. What follows is Takó's first fantasy of his father as a partisan, heroically escaping. With the resolution of the narrative, however, the question remains: why did Takó's mother say the Arrow Cross wanted to kill Takó's father, not to mention Takó and his mother as well? (In fact, the mother's statement, "They wanted to kill us too," suggests that they are Jewish, since the only entire families the Arrow Cross "wanted to kill" were Jews.)[29]

The second bit of symptomatic dialogue occurs in the latter part of the film, when the adult Takó is investigating the truth of his father's past. Visiting the town where his family had lived during the war, he explores a cellar, saying, "That's where father hid. No, I only made up that story. Or is it true?" These words not only perpetuate the enigma, but also recognize it as an enigma, as well as hinting at the possibility that Takó's father may have hidden for some reason other than his having been a partisan.

I propose that these apparent inconsistencies in *Father* are the cinematic equivalent of Freudian slips, behaviors that appear to be accidental, but that are revealed by analysis to be signifiers of repressed thoughts. If the film functions in a way that is analogous to the functioning of the Freudian subject, then I would argue that these inconsistencies point to Szabó's repressed autobiography of the Holocaust. And at the core of this repressed narrative is the fact that the protagonist's father was victimized because he was a Jew.[30] If, in the explicit personal narrative, the protagonist's neurosis marks him as different from other Hungarian boys, and in the implicit generational narrative he is the same, then here, in the repressed narrative of the Holocaust, the protagonist's difference returns, but in another form. It returns not as a personal neurosis following the loss of the father, but as a collective trauma: the trauma of the Hungarian Jews, symbolized not by the physical loss of the father, but by his preceding loss of Hungarian citizenship as a Jew, his having been marked for exclusion and extermination by his fellow Hungarians, his having been, as Gusztáv Kosztolányi put it, "cast out of the body of the nation."[31]

The second major symptom of a repressed Holocaust autobiography in *Father* is the film's iconography of castration, an iconography that cannot be fully explained by the film's narrative of personal neurosis, I argue, but that requires an additional explanation rooted in historical trauma.[32] This iconography begins in the very first images of the film: the documentary footage of the broken Chain Bridge. Of course, the image of the bridge is not inherently a phallic symbol. This iconography emerges only with the film's subsequent addition of images and motifs that form a pattern, and after this pattern is then put into the context of the film as a whole and its historical significance.

The pattern continues in the second scene, in which Takó's father's black coffin and the hole that awaits it transfer the symbolism of castration to the father himself. One of Takó's defenses against his resulting neurosis is visualized in a flashback scene in which he remembers his father in a state of phallic plenitude: in vigorous motion, lifting Takó into the air, and accessorized with objects that the boy later fetishizes: a leather jacket, a briefcase, glasses, a cigarette. At the end of the film, Takó dreams that he is searching for his father. He is told his father is in one room after another, but each room is empty. The hole that signifies the father's physical and symbolic/phallic destruction in the funeral scene reappears here to signify the return of Takó's phallic crisis. But the dream has a happy ending: Anni tells him she is pregnant. Takó has asserted his own phallic identity.

The film's concluding shot of Takó standing at peace over his father's grave resolves the phallic crisis articulated in the funeral scene. The hole has been filled and covered over by the body of the son.

Of course, at one level, *Father*'s iconography of castration can be explained with reference to Takó's personal narrative, revolving around the crisis brought on by the death of his father, or even with reference to the implicit national narrative, revolving around the phallic crisis of a generation. It is the initial image and continuing motif of the bridge, however, that carries the film's iconography of castration to a third level: Budapest's collective trauma of the winter of 1944–45. The initial image of the broken bridge refers to Nazi violence explicitly and indexically; it is a literal record of that violence. As such, it places the entire narrative under the sign of historical reality, so that while the bridge may be recruited as a symbol for Takó's personal phallic crisis, that crisis always implicitly refers back to a collective historical trauma.

The bridge, however, signifies not one historical disaster but two, linked but discreet. One is the disaster of the city and the nation as a whole: their victimization by the Germans, especially the Germans' severing of the link that constitutes the capital. And insofar as the integrity of the city and nation is understood symbolically as a phallic integrity, the broken bridge that signifies their victimization becomes an icon of castration.

The scene that links the bridge to a second disaster occurs in a sequence in the latter part of the film that refers explicitly to the Holocaust. This sequence, which constitutes the third major symptom of Szabó's repressed Holocaust autobiography in *Father*, contains three scenes, the first of which has Takó playing an extra in a Holocaust film. He and several of his friends have six-pointed stars sewn onto their lapels, and then join a column of "Jews" being herded across the rebuilt Chain Bridge by "Arrow Cross" extras. But the director keeps yelling "cut," shrieking from the top of his crane that the extras are not getting it right, that they are treating a tragic scene as if it were a comedy.

The second scene in this sequence shows Takó and his friends sitting pensively at a café on Margaret Island, after the film shoot, with the Danube in the background. One of Takó's friends talks about the strangeness of his relationship to the war in which his father fought. "I hardly remember the war," he says, "except for a few faint memories: dead horses, bombings."

In the third scene of the sequence, Takó and his girlfriend, Anni, another "Jewish" extra, walk along the bank of the Danube while she monologues about her ambivalence toward her actual Jewish identity. "For years I denied that my father died in a Nazi camp. I'd make up a story rather than admit I was Jewish. I finally realized the futility of it, and I faced reality. . . . Sometimes I still feel ashamed and pretend not to be Jewish. I am Hungarian, am I not?" The monologue takes up two minutes of screen time.

It is in this one sequence, when the Holocaust surfaces to the level of explicit, if marginalized, narrative, that *Father* adopts aspects of the posttraumatic cinema originated by Resnais. The Danube flows through the entire sequence, functioning as a present-tense signifier of past trauma similarly to the way Auschwitz functions in *Night and Fog*. Its presence implicitly calls up memories of the war associated with those initial shots in which the river flows past the bombed bridge. When Anni and Takó walk along the riverbank, they pass near the spot where Jews were shot into the Danube. The film makes no explicit or implicit reference to this fact; the river flowing behind Anni only symptomatically links her words to that trauma. At the same time, the continuous, eye-level movement of the camera as it follows Anni recalls the formal evocation of the witness's point of view in both *Night and Fog* and *Chronicle of a Summer*.

Also similar to Resnais is the contrast drawn in this sequence between the eloquence of the Danube as a mute signifier of historical trauma and the failure of conventional realist film techniques that attempt to represent traumatic events directly. The comic film-within-the-film scene recalls both *Night and Fog*'s assertions of representational failure and *Hiroshima*'s film-within-the-film scenes—the Japanese film clips that try so hard to dramatize the bombing realistically that they end up seeming oddly unrealistic, and the actress's peace film, the obviousness of which seems inadequate to the vicissitudes of a postatomic reality. Szabó's film-within-the-film scene seems to cover over the past rather than evoke it, just as the repaired Chain Bridge on which the scene takes place seems to cover over the earlier image of the bridge destroyed.

By explicitly linking the Chain Bridge to the Holocaust, this sequence suggests that the iconography of castration that originated in the opening shots of the bridge extends to the Holocaust as well. But in what sense might the father's victimization *as a Jew* be understood, in this repressed narrative, as a symbolic castration? I would suggest that this understanding is symptomatic of a core Hungarian Jewish (and perhaps more generally Ashkenazik) belief: that when Jews were granted full rights as Hungarian citizens, Jewish men were given the keys to a specifically phallic national identity. And when Jews were rejected as Hungarian citizens during the war, that phallic identity was lost. The Holocaust as Jewish male loss of citizenship constitutes both a trauma and a symbolic castration insofar as it is an assault that violates and irreversibly alters the integrity of the self.[33]

In the latent text of *Father*, then, the three meanings of the father coexist. He is simultaneously an individual father whose death precipitates a personal crisis for the protagonist, the symbol of a history whose overbearing weight causes a generational crisis, and an emblem

Illustration 5.1. *Father*: the destroyed Chain Bridge as an icon of the trauma of Budapest.

of Hungarian Jewish trauma. But Hungarian Jewish trauma carries its own form of censorship. While Hungarian Jews who settled outside Hungary after the war had some opportunities to represent their trauma openly, those who stayed in Hungary did not. In order to pass as true Hungarians, they had to sacrifice their Jewish identity, and first and foremost their memories of the Holocaust. In the French production, *Shoah*, the problem of the erasure of memory could be worked on freely by the text. *Father*, however, was produced in the context of a society in which the very anti-Judaism that produced the trauma in the first place remained undisturbed, having been papered over, so to speak, by the antifascist rhetoric of socialism. The only cultural space available for the representation of the Hungarian Holocaust was reserved for socialist platitudes; there was no space for a reckoning with trauma. Therefore, in the manifest text of *Father*, Holocaust trauma is repressed, but returns indirectly in the form of Freudian slips in the dialogue and an iconography of castration, and returns directly in a series of explicit representations that are confined to a single posttraumatic sequence, and displaced from the protagonist's narrative to that of his marginal-

Illustration 5.2. *Father*: the rebuilt Chain Bridge becomes an icon of Jewish trauma.

ized girlfriend. Holocaust trauma returns in these symptomatic forms to challenge the film's claims of personal and generational resolution, and to suggest that Szabó's/Takó's generation cannot come of age until it confronts the memory of the Holocaust.

One of the most remarkable things about *Father*, however, is the way it not only represses Szabó's autobiography of the Holocaust, but also simultaneously and insistently subverts that repression by calling the spectator's attention to it, and to the repressed material. Of course, according to Freud, all psychological symptoms do this to an extent. I would argue, however, that *Father* not only contains symptoms of its repressed material, but also self-consciously points them out. This is clearly demonstrated in the film's most self-conscious sequence, the film-within-the-film sequence described above. Anni not only embodies Takó's repressed and displaced Jewish identity, but explicitly identifies the problem of its repression, telling him, "I'd make up a story rather than admit I was Jewish."

A less clearly marked but perhaps even more telling moment occurs at the beginning of the sequence, when the "Jewish" extras are standing

Illustration 5.3. *Father*: Anni embodies the difficulty of Jewish memory in Hungary. In the background is the Danube, site of Jewish massacres in 1944–45.

in a column on the street, waiting for the filming to begin. Takó sees a bus passing by, full of passengers, and then folds his arms, covering up the six-pointed star on his lapel.[34]

LOVE FILM

Love Film / Szerelmesfilm, like *Father*, is a narrative of memory containing within it a subnarrative of Holocaust memory. But whereas, in *Father*, traumatic memory appears indirectly as symptoms, in *Love Film* it appears directly. As in *The Pawnbroker*, its engine is the modernist flashback developed by Resnais in *Hiroshima, mon amour*. *Love Film* is not a thoroughly posttraumatic film the way *The Pawnbroker* is, in which all the flashbacks are focalized by a character suffering from PTSD. It is, rather, a Proustian meditation on memory. Given Szabó's and Hungary's history, however, it is not surprising that memories of the Holocaust appear in the film, and assume a posttraumatic form.

In the present, a young man, Jáncsi, played by Bálint, is traveling by train from Budapest to France to visit his childhood sweetheart,

Illustration 5.4. *Father*: Tako, playing a Jewish extra in a Holocaust film, covers his yellow star.

Kata. The narrative is dominated by a complex flashback structure— Jáncsi's memories of his and Kata's lives, triggered by the journey, and encompassing the same period of Hungarian history encompassed by *Father*, from the Second World War through the 1956 uprising against the Soviet Union. Some of the flashbacks present peaceful memories of Jáncsi's and Kata's childhoods. Some take place during the German Occupation of Budapest, when Jáncsi is sent into hiding and his father dies. Other flashbacks present his young adult romance with Kata before, during, and after the '56 uprising, and her subsequent escape to France.

Again, two discourses emerge in addition to that with which I am chiefly concerned. First is a romantic coming-of-age story focusing on the development of a relationship from childhood to young adulthood, a crisis in that relationship, and the challenge of reconciling youthful romance with the realities of adulthood.

Second is a meditation on the collective problem of emigration in Hungarian society. This problem intersects with the romantic problem insofar as it precipitates the crisis in Jáncsi and Kata's relationship, but it also stands for the rupturing of Hungarian society by emigration generally.

The third discourse is the Proustian one, dealing with the phenomenon of memory, and the way both pleasant and unpleasant memories are triggered and layered in the present. One extended flashback sequence in the film consists of ten segments:

1. In the present, Jáncsi is traveling by train to France.
2. Flashback A: Jáncsi remembers a time that Kata took him to a Budapest train station to meet some friends before the '56 uprising.
3. Flashback A continued: During the '56 uprising, Jáncsi and Kata are accidentally caught in an exchange of gunfire between Hungarian rebels and Soviet troops on a Budapest street. They are separated, hiding on opposite sides of the street. A close-up of Jáncsi peering across the street, trying to spot Kata.
4. Shot of a photograph of Bözsi, a young woman who was Jáncsi and Kata's childhood swimming teacher.
5. Flashback B: 1944–45. In this brief flashback, German soldiers come into Bözsi's apartment and take her husband. He is wearing a Hungarian army uniform, which suggests that he is being rounded up as a deserter, a common occurrence at the time.[35] Bözsi resists and is taken also. Sounds of gunfire in the background. As she is taken away, there is a close-up of her feet being dragged over the pavement. She is wearing sneakers and white socks.
6. Flashback C: Sometime after the war, Mr. Hackl, an old man who knew Bözsi, addresses the camera: "I remember she wore sneakers and white socks. Her husband shouted, 'Don't talk German!' For poor Bözsi abused them in German."
7. Flashback B continued: Bözsi and her husband are shot in a firing squad. The segment consists of a single shot lasting about two seconds.
8. Two photos of Bözsi.
9. Flashback A continued: the '56 uprising. The gunfire ceases, and Jáncsi finds Kata. Each discovers that the other was thinking of Bözsi while they were separated.
10. The present: Jáncsi is on the train.

The representation of associative memory evident in this sequence is common to both Proustian and posttraumatic discourse. The train in the present triggers the memory of the train station before '56. Gunfire and the momentary separation of Jáncsi and Kata in '56 trigger the memory of Bözsi's execution for refusing to be separated from her husband. For Szabó, as for Resnais, history exists not in the past but in the present, in memories waiting to be triggered by association.

Also common to Proustian and posttraumatic discourse is the distinction between voluntary and involuntary memory. Flashback A is voluntary, triggered by Jáncsi's pleasurable confinement on the train, which affords him the luxury of memory. Flashback B is involuntary, triggered by crisis. In Proust, both the remembering and what is remembered take place under conditions of peaceful, bourgeois existence. In the first flashback of *Hiroshima*, the conditions of remembering are peaceful, but the content of the memory is violent. In *Love Film*, what triggers the memory of one historical disaster is another historical disaster, with the remembering taking place literally in the middle of a battle. For Szabó, recent Hungarian history is experienced as a series of disasters layered on top of one another, where each new layer triggers memories of the older ones. Perhaps the clearest indication of this layering of traumatic memory is the fact that, in the brief flashback shots of 1944–45 described above, it is impossible to determine whether the gunfire, which is the only sound heard, is taking place within the flashback or in the framing scene of 1956. The sounds of the two periods become confused for the spectator just as the feelings associated with those periods become confused for the characters.

A third inheritance from Proust is the transformation of memory from a bracketed plot device into the basic mode of narration. Whereas the explicit discourse of *Father* is dominated by the generic coming-of-age story, in *Love Film* that generic story moves into the background, and memory itself comes into the foreground as the main subject of the film.

What Szabó adds to the discourse of memory that originated in Proust is the notion of what the French sociologist Maurice Halbwachs called "the social frameworks of collective memory."[36] In Proust, as in Bergson, memory is determined by the individual, in whose mind it lies intact and dormant, waiting to be triggered. *Hiroshima* concerns two opposed realms of memory: the individual memory of the French woman, as in Proust, and the collective memory of Hiroshima, which the Japanese man never narrates as a personal story, but which appears in the form of visual documents. In *Hiroshima*, the realms of individual and collective memory approach one another, but their meeting is perpetually deferred.

In *Love Film*, Szabó confronts the Proustian notion of individual memory with Halbwachs's notion of its social frameworks, and places them both under the sign of historical trauma. First, Jáncsi's memory of Bözsi is mediated by photographs, which literally intervene between the shots of remembering and the shots of what is remembered. Second, Jáncsi and Kata's simultaneous remembering of Bözsi suggests Halbwachs's theory that the individual maintenance of memories depends on their reinforcement by other rememberers. Third, the shot of Mr. Hackl's testimony suggests that the image of Bözsi's execution is not a representation of something Jáncsi witnessed himself, but rather something he imagined later, based on what Mr. Hackl told him. In fact, the correspondence between what Jáncsi visualizes and what Mr. Hackl describes is imperfect; she wears sneakers and white socks just as Mr. Hackl describes, but does not abuse the men in German. Furthermore, the image of Bözsi's death is repeated two other times in the film, each time staged slightly differently. Thus, the only direct image of violence associated with 1944–45 that appears in the film is not presented as an "authentic" representation, but rather as a complex memory construction, mediated by other representations. In *Father*, social frameworks of memory appear only symptomatically, as a pressure applied by national memory on Jewish memory, displacing it to the level of symptomatic discourse. *Love Film* thematizes those frameworks.

While posttraumatic memory is presented more directly in *Love Film* than in *Father*, its autobiographical Jewish content is once again displaced. One repeated flashback presents Jáncsi's memories of being separated from his parents during the German Occupation, and taking refuge in a hospital, and later with Kata's family, all of which could have happened to Szabó as a Jew hiding from the Arrow Cross. But the explanation for Jáncsi's hiding offered by the film is that his father is a deserter. Deserters were in fact targeted by the Arrow Cross, in much smaller numbers than were Jews, but their families were not targeted or forced into hiding.

As in *Father*, however, Szabó leaves a clue to the displaced narrative of Jewish trauma. One of the main influences on *Love Film* is the autobiographical novella *Under Gemini*, by the Hungarian poet Miklós Radnóti. *Under Gemini* describes Radnóti's prewar train journey from France to

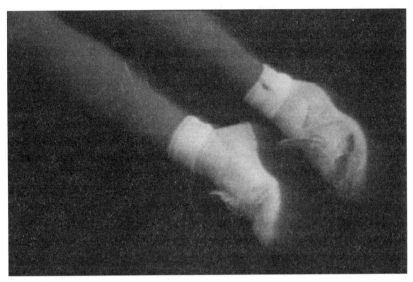

Illustration 5.5. *Love Film*: Jáncsi's memory of Bözsy's execution is mediated by Mr. Hackl's testimony: "I remember she wore sneakers and white socks."

Hungary as a catalyst of memories, one of which concerns his childhood witnessing of the public execution by firing squad of a First World War deserter. Szabó signals this influence by showing a copy of the book, which Jáncsi gives to Kata as a gift.[37]

But Szabó's reference to *Under Gemini* signifies much more than just a plot influence. Radnóti was a Jew who converted to Catholicism but was nevertheless subject to anti-Jewish legislation in Hungary. As a Jewish slave laborer in 1944, he wrote a series of short, devastating poems on scraps of paper, testifying to the atrocities he witnessed and suffered, before being shot into a mass grave by a Hungarian guard. When his body was dug up, the poems were found and published. Radnóti became famous as a national poet/martyr, but the Jewish identity of his life and death was repressed.

The presence of *Under Gemini* in *Love Film* signifies Radnóti's status as a model for Szabó—a model of the Hungarian Jewish autobiographer who is offered success as a national artist at the expense of his Jewish identity. Radnóti accepted the offer. The Holocaust spelled the end of his life anyway, but for Szabó it spelled, in a sense, the beginning. Radnóti thus stands for the condition of Szabó's artistic birth: the simultaneous necessity and impossibility of repressing one's Jewish autobiography.[38]

As the explicit representation of the Hungarian Jewish Holocaust is displaced onto Anni in *Father*, so in *Love Film* it is displaced onto another marginal female character. Kata has asked Jáncsi to bring a photograph of Bözsi with him to France, since Kata knows a Hungarian woman there who may have seen Bözsi after her arrest. Kata and Jáncsi show her the photograph. "No, that's not the one," the woman says.

> The girl I remember was my age and had fair hair. She was next but one to me when we were shot at. She didn't know why she and her husband had been taken from the Gestapo to the Arrow Cross. It's terrible how clearly I remember that day. We were marched to the Danube. There were people in the street. A woman turned away. A man stopped and kept looking at us. He wore a Hussar-style coat.[39] Two women laughed. One of them wore a beret. They lined us up on the embankment after having taken away our shoes, coats, and sweaters. We stood with our backs to the Danube on the pink stone of the bank, and in front there was the railing of the promenade. In the fog, that railing stood out so clearly that I'll never forget it. That was the last thing I saw of Budapest. Then I think I saw that, one after the other, they were falling into the Danube, and that very quickly the whole thing was coming toward me. I felt a violent urge to go to the toilet. I couldn't hold it back. And it was really the iron railing I saw last. Instinctively I fell backwards into the water before having been hit. Someone fell on me, but I knew I was alive and that I had to swim under water, as far as possible. I heard the shots but luckily the fog was dense. When I lifted up my head, I couldn't see anything. I swam on and on past the last bridge of Budapest. Then, in a peasant house I told them that my fiancee had died on the front and that I had wanted to kill myself. I asked for warm clothing. I had a ring on my hand; I gave it to them for the clothes and some money. Then I set out on foot toward Yugoslavia. It's like a story, isn't it? "Once upon a time."

The word *Jew* is never spoken, but the Jewish identity of the woman is implicit, since only Jews were shot en masse into the Danube.

The posttraumatic deformation of time in *Love Film* takes the form of a pressure on the editing, specifically on shot length. The two most violent events narrated in the film are Bözsi's execution and this woman's near execution. The former is represented by a shot lasting two seconds, and is consistent with the flashbacks in *Hiroshima* and *The Pawnbroker*. The latter is represented by a shot lasting almost five minutes, and is consistent with the testimonial long takes of *Chronicle of a Summer*, *Father* (Anni's monologue), and *Shoah*. It is as if traumatic events were incapable of being represented in a normal-length shot, their return being dominated, once again, by the dialectic of not enough/too much. Surely it is not accidental, however, that, of the two representations of execution in *Love Film*, only the one marked as non-Jewish, Bözsi's, is narrated directly through images and sounds, whereas the one marked as Jewish is narrated indirectly through verbal description, as if unable to break through to the status of the directly representable.

25 *FIREMAN STREET*

Whereas, in *Love Film*, historical memory is represented by flashbacks, in *25 Fireman Street/Tüzoltó utca 25* it is represented by dreams. The film takes place during the course of a long, hot night in Budapest, during which the residents of a single apartment building are plagued by dream-memories of pain and loss spanning thirty years. This is Szabó's first feature film without a protagonist played by András Bálint. The story presents, rather, a fabric of memories dreamed by various residents of the building, in and around which most of the film takes place. Two middle-aged female characters are featured: Mária and Irma. Mária is based on Szabó's mother; her son, a relatively minor character, is played by Bálint.

A long, middle portion of the film represents 1944–45 as the core of Mária's and Irma's memories. Mária's family displays a range of reactions to their persecution (for reasons unspecified): petitioning the authorities for exceptions based on patriotic service, hiding jewels, giving away clothes and furniture to neighbors for safe keeping, panic, suicide. Finally, they are evicted by members of the Arrow Cross, including their neighbor Vilma. Their remaining possessions are seized, and they are ghettoized and strip-searched. The men are sent away for slave labor.

Irma hides three fugitives in the attic. She fears betrayal from neighbors, turns additional fugitives away, and endures more than one raid by a looting Arrow Cross gang searching for "deserters, escapees, dubious persons." The bombing of the city begins. "No one will ever believe it happened," Irma says to herself. "It will pass. We won't even dream about it." She wakes from her dream, crying, "I want peace, only

Illustration 5.6. *Love Film*: a Jewish woman remembers being shot into the Danube.

peace. Give me a simple day, a day without headaches, a night without dreams."

The liberation of Budapest: Mária is surrounded by death. Lacking medicine, her husband dies of a heart attack. After the liberation, Vilma asks Irma to sign an affidavit in her defense, stating Vilma knew Irma had hidden fugitives but did not report it. Irma signs the affidavit. So many people have died, or emigrated like this woman: "Dear Mária. São Paulo, June 17. It's no use. It doesn't matter where you go. I'm 4,000 meters above sea level, at half an hour's ride from a village, in a lovely place and in relative peace, and even so I cannot sleep."

This last film contains the most explicit and centralized representation of the Hungarian Jewish Holocaust in Szabó's trilogy. References to the persecution of Mária's family, to petitioning the authorities for exceptions based on patriotic service, to the hiding and giving away of possessions, to suicide, eviction, ghettoization, and slave labor can only be explained by the Jewish identity of Mária's family. Explicit indicators, such as the word *Jew* and six-pointed stars, however, are left out, so that spectators are free to associate Mária's experience with the Hungarian

Jewish experience, or to dissociate the two. (Of course, the name *Mária* is associated with Catholicism.)

Paradoxically, at the same time that the Holocaust rises to the fore in *25 Fireman Street*, the autobiographical impulse gives way further to the representation of collective memory. In *Father*, memory is a dialogue between three discourses, subsumed under the point of view of a single character. In *Love Film*, the memory of the autobiographical protagonist begins to enter into dialogue with the memories of other characters, like Kata and Mr. Hackl. In *25 Fireman Street*, the transformation is complete. The role of the remembering protagonist is replaced by the role of the building itself, which functions as a witness to the collective memory of its inhabitants. The social frameworks of collective memory, which appear as symptoms in *Father*, and as the context of the protagonist's point of view in *Love Film*, here become the very structure that binds the narrative. The Hungarian Jewish Holocaust at last assumes its place as a memory that is distinct yet inextricably bound up with the collective memory of the nation's suffering. The memories of individual residents may differ, but they are woven together as if into a single posttraumatic dream.

Conclusion

Autobiography is not a simple vehicle of posttraumatic memory and history. The arguments presented above do not rely upon the romantic notion of the author as the sovereign creator of a unified and organic work, a notion that seems inconsistent with the fractured and involuntary aspects of posttraumatic consciousness. However, neither do these arguments embrace a structuralist or poststructuralist focus on discourse that is completely divorced from the realm of individual creativity. Rather, I have sought the complex relations between the autobiographer on the one hand and the realms of collective and discursive memory on the other. One way of looking at the model of authorship implied here is as a field of productive paradoxes centering on an individual artist.

One of these paradoxes involves the relationship between fact and fiction. On the one hand, Szabó's trilogy repeatedly references certain immutable facts of traumatic personal and collective memory: the death of the father, the massacre of the Jews, and so on. On the other hand, the trilogy not only mediates these facts through a series of fictionalizing techniques (e.g., condensation, repression, displacement), but also thematizes this mediation of memory through the representation of symptomatic behavior, photographs, dreams, social frameworks, and films-within-films. For example, Szabó, like Resnais, frequently includes documentary footage in his fiction films, but in addition *Father*, like *Hiroshima, mon amour*, juxtaposes documentary not only to the fiction of the film itself but also to the "fiction" of the film-within-the-film, thus thematizing the relationship between the two. This paradoxical relationship even appears in the dialogue when Anni says, "I'd make up a story rather than admit I was Jewish," and when the woman at the party in *Love Film* says, "It's like a story, isn't it? 'Once upon a time.'" Szabó acknowledges the contradictory aspects of traumatic memory— its truthfulness and its distortion.[40]

It is Szabó's modernism that allows him both to thematize the paradoxes inherent in the trilogy and to engage in such delicate negotiations between discourses of memory that sometimes come into conflict. Through the narrative techniques discussed above, he manages to slip through the ban on Jewish memory in the Hungarian mainstream in order to represent a variety of Holocaust experiences. One of the prices of this accomplishment is the narrative splitting off of these various experiences from one another. Throughout the trilogy, references to ghettoization, to hiding, to forced labor, to massacres on the streets and along the riverbank, and finally to Auschwitz—as a symbol of the fate of the Hungarian Jews outside Budapest, as well as of the Jews in general—are presented in disconnected fragments, thus obscuring the fact that all were aspects of the broader phenomenon of the Jewish genocide.

This historical dissociation certainly had an ideological cause: the unofficial ban on Jewish memory in the Hungarian mainstream. There may have been an additional cause of the particular split between references to events in Budapest and references to events outside Budapest. The Jewish experience of 1944–45 in Budapest is the trauma that forms the core of Szabó's trilogy, and that the trilogy works the hardest to admit. It may be that knowledge of the totality of the Holocaust—of "Auschwitz"—was largely excluded from the historical consciousness of the trilogy both because of the *possibility* of its exclusion (Szabó's knowledge of it would have been indirect) and because of the *necessity* of its exclusion (to admit this inconceivably massive trauma on top of the local trauma of Budapest may have felt like emotional suicide).

If Szabó's trilogy fails to make this link within Jewish memory, it succeeds in making the link between personal memory, national memory, and Jewish memory, and does so against great odds. For while the personal trauma of Szabó's autobiography is bound to both national and Jewish collective traumas, the dominant ideology dictated that in order to narrate the national, one had to repress the Jewish. It is to Szabó's credit that he would not obliterate the aspect of his autobiography that made him different—his victimization not only by the Germans but also by his fellow Hungarians. Rather, he insisted on testifying as both a Hungarian and a Jew; he insisted on both commonality and difference; he insisted that a traumatized nation admit the trauma of its own victims; indeed, he created a new, specifically cinematic link between these two inextricably bound histories of trauma.

6   Postmodernism, the Second Generation, and Cross-Cultural Posttraumatic Cinema

SHOAH WAS arguably the culmination of the modernist, post-traumatic cinema on which the book has focused thus far. It may have felt like the end of the line for Holocaust cinema, but of course it wasn't. The phenomenal success of Steven Spielberg's *Schindler's List* (1993) launched the dissemination of an unprecedented quantity of films, television programs, and other media about the Holocaust, including the massive database of survivor oral histories collected by Spielberg's Shoah Foundation, and three Academy Award winners for Best Documentary: *The Long Way Home* (1997), *The Last Days* (1998), and *Into the Arms of Strangers: Stories of the Kindertransport* (2000).

What has become of posttraumatic cinema under these conditions, particularly since the cultural modernism that supplied posttraumatic cinema with so much of its form between 1955 and 1985 has become increasingly displaced or absorbed by postmodern culture, of which the profusion of Holocaust images since *Schindler's List* may itself be a symptom? If postmodern films present the Holocaust less as a reality (like realist films) or a memory (like posttraumatic films) than as a collection of recycled images, where does this leave the project of posttraumatic cinema? As the reality of images increasingly dominates all other forms of reality, can images still be said to repeat a trauma that originated in historical reality?

This chapter will examine two relatively recent works representing historical trauma in a postmodern vein: *Schindler's List* and *History and Memory: For Akiko and Takashige.* This pairing crosses a series of boundaries, however (in good postmodern fashion), that require preliminary discussion. First is the boundary between documentary and fiction film, mapped in this book as the boundary between the first four chapters, which deal primarily with documentary, and the fifth and sixth, dealing with fiction. Just as this boundary in the book is marked by a discus-

140

sion of *Hiroshima, mon amour*, which contains and interrogates the distinction between the two forms, so this final chapter on postmodernism will renew the documentary/fiction question, in a way that is consistent with postmodernism's further weakening of the distinction between them. Not only is *Schindler's List* essentially a fiction film and *History and Memory* essentially nonfiction, but each work, like *Hiroshima, mon amour*, contains contradictory elements. *Schindler's List* is a fiction based on fact, but concludes with a nonfiction segment showing *Schindlerjuden* (Jews saved by Schindler) placing stones on Schindler's grave in Israel, accompanied by the actors who played them in the film. *History and Memory*, on the other hand, is a nonfiction work that contains some fictionalized and reenacted segments.

Second is the distinction between what Hal Foster has called *reactionary* and *resistant* postmodernisms. Foster argues that reactionary postmodern works repudiate the critical energies of modernism and celebrate the status quo; I will argue that *Schindler's List* belongs in this category. *History and Memory*, on the other hand, I identify as a resistant postmodern work that does not depart from modernism so much as it extends the movement's critical energies in an altered form, while repudiating certain of its elitist postwar developments.[1]

A third distinction can be mapped onto this second: the distinction between film and videotape. Film has often been identified as a key medium of reactionary postmodernism, most notably by Fredric Jameson.[2] Certainly the relatively high expense of film—*Schindler's List* reportedly cost $23 million (not high in Hollywood terms, but astronomical in relation to *History and Memory*)—tends to make it more useful for those with an economic stake in the status quo.[3] Moreover, the technology of film projection may have a tendency to draw spectators toward fantasy and away from critique. Videotapes like *History and Memory*, on the other hand, can be produced much more cheaply; tape thus tends to be the medium of choice for marginalized groups. Tape—with its "coldness," omnipresence, and ease of quotation through dubbing—may be an even more inherently postmodern medium than film. It is fitting, then, that we turn to videotape for the first time here in this final chapter.

The fourth boundary crossed in this chapter may be the most difficult for some historians of the Holocaust to accept: *History and Memory* is not about the Holocaust, but rather the internment of Japanese Americans in the United States during the Second World War. Some may view my inclusion of the tape in this book as implying a universalization of the Holocaust, equating it to all other instances of historical oppression. I am aware that the Nazi camps and the U.S. camps were profoundly different—to begin with, for the basic reason that there was no mass murder of Japanese Americans. I include *History and Memory* for two reasons, however.

The first reason has to do with my interest in what I will call *second-generation trauma*—vicarious trauma experienced by the children of trauma survivors, known as the second generation. I argue that second-generation cinema can demonstrate the continued relevance of post-traumatic cinema beyond the decline of modernism and into the rise of postmodern culture. This second-generation cinema can function not only as a representation of the specific experiences of children of survivors, but also as an especially intense manifestation of the broader phenomenon that Ellen S. Fine has termed *absent memory*, whereby an entire generation (postwar French Jews in Fine's article) suffers from the memory of an event it did not experience.[4] I have seen glimpses of a postmodern, second-generation discourse in a few films and videos about the Holocaust. And yet, as the child of a Holocaust survivor who has made a video about my own experience of second-generation memory, what I have been surprised to discover is that *History and Memory*, while not about the Holocaust, actually represents the phenomenon of second-generation Holocaust memory—both in itself and in its intersection with postmodernism—more powerfully, for me, than any work about the Holocaust that I have seen. I have therefore decided to, in effect, trust the work, follow its lead, and analyze the consequences.

At the same time, this decision dovetails with my belief, mentioned in the Preface, in the necessity of avoiding both the anti-Jewish trap of denying the specificity of the Holocaust and the opposite trap of allowing the memory of the Holocaust to isolate Jews from non-Jews and their own traumatic histories. It is possible, without equating distinct historical traumas, to appreciate the fact that filmmakers like Tajiri may have partly learned how to represent their own histories from posttraumatic Holocaust films, just as Jewish filmmakers like Claude Lanzmann partly learned how to represent Jewish trauma from non-Jewish filmmakers like Alain Resnais. This can be viewed negatively as an appropriation or transgression; I choose to view it positively as a natural historical process of cross-cultural influence.

SCHINDLER'S LIST AND REACTIONARY POSTMODERNISM

Let me begin with a slightly more thorough definition of postmodernism. Following Jameson, I would begin with the notion of postmodernity as a late capitalist phase in which the production of images and their attendant apparatus increasingly supplants the production of hard goods. With the dissemination of television and then computers, these images have come to stand less and less for some other reality, and have become more and more their own reality—simulacra: signifiers without referents. Postmodernism is the cultural mode specific to this historical period, although it coexists with preexisting modes, and also blends with them, rendering a realist postmodernism and a modernist postmodernism.[5] According to Jameson, a primary feature of postmodern culture is pastiche: the nostalgic and ahistorical quotation of dead styles, devoid of the critical energies of parody and satire.[6] This postmodern culture supports capitalism by creating more demand for its products and discouraging social critique.

Whereas Jameson stops there, Foster opposes to this reactionary postmodernism a resistant postmodernism that uses quotation not for an ahistorical nostalgia but to deconstruct and revolutionize the simulacra of postmodern capitalism.

Schindler's List (1993) was not the first postmodern film to represent the Holocaust. Probably the most significant earlier example, as mentioned in Chapter 1, was Syberberg's *Hitler: A Film from Germany* (1977), discussed as a postmodern work by Eric Santner and other critics. I have chosen not to discuss this important work, however, because it is not consistent with my focus on the trauma of Holocaust victims. *Hitler* focuses, rather, on the melancholic loss of national identity in defeated Germany. The Holocaust itself is dealt with somewhat marginally, and not at all from the victims' point of view. Perhaps it is no accident that it was in Germany, where the desire to avoid remembering the Holocaust was most deeply ingrained at a national level, that postmodernism was adopted relatively early as a major, self-conscious form for representing the Second World War era. Syberberg's *Hitler*, Fassbinder's *Lili Marleen* (1981), and Reitz's *Heimat* (1984) demonstrate an affinity between the postmodern fascination with the simulacrum and the desire to avoid certain painful historical realities. The significance of *Schindler's List*, on the other hand, is that it was the first major work to adopt a postmodern form to represent the trauma of Holocaust victims—and, moreover, to emanate from a filmmaker who identified himself as a Jew.[7]

Discussing the postmodernism of *Schindler's List* is complicated, however, by the film's aura of realism, both formally and in terms of the public discourse surrounding the film. We are not dealing here with the kind of self-conscious postmodern pastiche that will draw any spectator's attention, present even in a few recent Hollywood productions like *Natural Born Killers* (1994) and *Moulin Rouge* (2001). The blatant postmodernism of these films that take place in an ahistorical world of simulacra may make them fascinating symptoms of contemporary society. *Schindler's List*, which takes place in a compellingly realistic historical world, is more than a symptom, however; it has changed the way one of the most significant events in modern history is remembered. Its postmodernism may be less blatant, but it is arguably more influential.[8]

Pastiche in *Schindler's List* consists, first of all, of the quotation of other films, the two most significant of which are *Night and Fog* and *Shoah*, since they are probably the two most respected prior Holocaust films (tellingly displaced, now, by *Schindler's List* itself). Like *Night and Fog*, *Schindler's List* represents the past by framing black-and-white footage between color segments, with a graphic match linking the initial cut from monochrome to color. (In *Night and Fog*, the graphic match cuts from the fence at Auschwitz to a line of German soldiers; in *Schindler's List*, it cuts from candle smoke to train smoke.) It also contains a scene in which the camera lingers on huge piles of Jews' stolen suitcases, eyeglasses, shoes, and the like, an image first made famous in *Night and Fog*.[9] *Schindler's List* borrows directly from *Shoah* the image of a Polish bystander using a throat-cutting gesture to inform a trainload of Jews of their fate in the death camp. A scene showing Jews trying to escape from the Krakow ghetto via the sewers seems indebted, in both its mise-en-scène and its chiaroscuro lighting, to two previous Polish films dealing with the German Occupation: *Border Street* (1948) and *Kanal* (1956), the latter directed by Andrzej Wajda, whom Spielberg consulted.[10]

The most significant non-Holocaust-related film quotation in *Schindler's List* is *Citizen Kane*. Spielberg has acknowledged that his conceptualization of the Schindler character was influenced in a general way by the character of Charles Foster Kane; both are larger than life figures who become rich, who contain both good and evil, and whose motivation is ambiguous. Both also specialize in the production of simulacra—Kane in fake headlines, Schindler in what he calls "the presentation," by which he means his ability to create a successful business by first creating the image of one. (*Citizen Kane*, it seems, may have had postmodern tendencies *avant la lettre*.) The thematic influence of *Kane* also carries over into a stylistic influence. The beginnings of both films establish their protagonists' ambiguity or mystery by showing only parts of their bodies, delaying the showing of their faces for some time. And a scene of Schindler and Stern unpacking in Schindler's new factory office seems to be modeled after scenes of Kane and Bernstein (as well as Leland) in Kane's newsroom; both use deep space, low angles revealing the ceiling, and side lighting to show the Christian protagonist in his office with his Jewish assistant.[11]

In fact, critics of *Schindler's List* (including myself) almost seem to be competing in a game of spot-the-quotation, spurred on by the pastiche style of Spielberg and of the culture at large. Bryan Cheyette may be the winner, citing *Strike* (1924), *Targets* (1968), *The Godfather* (1972), *Apocalypse Now* (1979), and Wajda's *Korczak* (1990), in addition to some of those already mentioned.[12]

Pastiche in *Schindler's List* extends beyond individual film quotes to whole styles, genres, and modes of film. Rather than taking sides in the old debate about realism versus expressionism as the appropriate form for Holocaust representation, Spielberg juggles both forms.[13] Numerous crowd scenes adopt the rough, handheld documentary style that originated in cinéma vérité and direct cinema and has become ubiquitous as a signpost of "realism" in contemporary television dramas. On the other hand, several scenes adopt the expressionistic chiaroscuro lighting of film noir. This style is used most impressively in the scene in which a trainload of female *Schindlerjuden*, inexplicably diverted to Auschwitz, arrives at the Birkenau ramp at night, and their faces are bathed in train smoke and lit by laser beam-like rays of light shooting through the boxcar slats. As Michael Rothberg has observed, the two scenes most focused on the genocidal aspects of the Holocaust that the main thrust of the narrative avoids (by focusing on an exceptional case of rescue)—the Krakow ghetto liquidation and the Auschwitz arrival—split the difference between realism and expressionism.[14]

The dominant genres at work are the historical epic and docudrama. The epic genre becomes especially pronounced in scenes showing a lone Schindler poised like Moses above large crowds of Jews.[15] Schindler's final scene, on the other hand, is an obvious attempt at the catharsis of melodrama, complete with emotional breakdown and string orchestra accompaniment.[16] Finally, the color scenes framing the story at the beginning and end of the film depart from dramatic narration altogether for what may be considered less a documentary than a ritual mode of cinema.

Aside from pastiche, other postmodern elements in the film include the nostalgic use of black and white;[17] the use of digital effects, for example, to erase modern structures from the Krakow skyline;[18] the mixing of high art (European art cinema) and low art (Hollywood genre cinema);[19] and the thematization of representation generally ("the List") and, more specifically, the role of representation in capitalism ("the presentation").[20]

In the discourse surrounding the film, too, there is a tendency to weaken the distinction between levels of reality. Spielberg's colleague Jeffrey Katzenberg seems to have merged Spielberg with Schindler when he said of the film that "enough of the right people will see it that it will actually set the course of world affairs. Steven is a national treasure. I'm breakin' my neck lookin' up at this guy."[21] And Spielberg himself disturbingly reduced "the Final Solution" and the Nielsen ratings to one level when he dedicated his Best Director Oscar "to the six million who can't be watching this among the two billion that are watching this telecast tonight."[22]

The question is, how does postmodern pastiche in *Schindler's List* function in relation to the question of trauma? The film certainly shows plenty of potentially traumatizing images, particularly images of Jews being summarily shot to death, often at point blank range in the head. As Alain Resnais has suggested, however, after a certain point, images of atrocity don't have "a very striking effect on people,"[23] and this may be particularly true for a generation of viewers who have been inundated with an unprecedented volume of extreme images in the media—who have, perhaps, "seen it all." The question, therefore, becomes: what kind of experience of these images does the film promote in its audience through the narrative form it gives them?

One hint that Spielberg has repudiated the posttraumatic form that began with *Night and Fog* and culminated in *Shoah* lies in the way the quotes from the two films are incorporated into *Schindler's List*. Switches from black and white to color in *Night and Fog*, first of all, were historically motivated, since the vast majority of the available archival footage was in fact monochrome, whereas color film was more widely available in 1955. The color switches functioned as a historically logical stylistic extension of the overall posttraumatic temporal structure of the film, in which temporal movement was repeatedly interrupted, the spectator was jerked from present to past and back again, and the epistemological certainty of both strands was problematized. The color switches in *Schindler's List*, on the other hand, have no corresponding historical motivation. Black and white is dehistoricized as pure style. Rather than interrupting the narrative, it flows along a chronological continuum with a high degree of epistemological certainty, framed by the ritualized use of color only at the beginning and end of the film.

Images of piles of Jews' belongings in *Night and Fog* also served the posttraumatic discourse of the film, since they demonstrated the magnitude of a past loss that could not be represented directly, but only indirectly through its traces in the present. In *Schindler's List*, on the other hand, these images take place in the past, and function not in place of an absent image of the unrepresentable, but in addition to the presence of numerous images of what is, for Spielberg, perfectly representable. A similar point can be made about the throat-cutting gesture, which Lanzmann used to represent not only the moral ambiguity of bystanders in the past, but also its unconscious return in present memory. Spielberg, on the other hand, incorporates it as a historically authentic yet narratively compelling detail.

Schindler's List quotes these moments of modernist-posttraumatic cinema the better to co-opt their aura as icons of the Holocaust, while repudiating and reversing their discursive function. The new discourse into which they are inserted combines the historical mastery (and trauma avoidance) of classical realism with postmodern pastiche. As has been pointed out by several scholars, quotation in *Schindler's List* does not interrupt the flow of the narrative with a modernist self-consciousness, but rather blends seamlessly into that narrative with the unself-consciousness of realism. It functions both to reinforce the authenticity of the film (on the postmodern assumption that the past is more real if it looks like past films) and to set the film up as the ultimate and authoritative Holocaust film that absorbs and replaces all previous Holocaust films.[24]

Just as *Schindler's List* repudiates the self-conscious voice of the modernist-posttraumatic films it quotes, so too does it repudiate those films' posttraumatic fragmentation of time and restricted point of view. The linear temporality of the film encourages spectator mastery over time, and leads to a classical telos: the redemption of the Christian male hero and the capitalist ethos he represents.[25] Even the two brief color segments fit into this chronology and telos, rather than interrupting them. The first represents prewar Jewish society; the second, the saved remnant paying tribute to the hero who saved them.

Schindler's List does not position the spectator within the restricted point of view of the victims, but rather switches among points of view: that of the victimized Jews, that of the Nazi victimizer Goeth, and, above all (literally), that of Schindler, whose point of view is almost omniscient. In some respects, point of view is structured vertically. We may be with Schindler the rescuer on a hilltop looking down at the ghetto being liquidated; we may be with Goeth the victimizer on his hilltop balcony, looking down at the camp through a rifle scope; or we may be down below with the Jews, often in handheld style.

In other respects, point of view is structured according to an inside/outside logic, with the Jews trapped inside the ghetto or camp, and Germans like Schindler or Goeth positioned outside, or free to come and go. The discourses of realism and omniscience should, in theory, enable the audience to accompany the Jews into the darkest and most hermetically sealed spaces of their victimization, as when a (typically Spielbergian) little boy jumps into a camp latrine to hide from a selection. These discourses reach a crisis point, however, when the Schindler women are sent into the Auschwitz gas chamber. As a handheld camera follows the naked women in their forced walk toward the open doors of the chamber, some spectators may be wondering whether Spielberg's realism is so self-confident that he would dare to show *this*, or whether he will finally succumb to the modernist position of *Night and Fog* and *Shoah*—that no matter how close one tries to get to the victims' point of view, there is a limit of what can be directly represented. Spielberg proceeds to play a kind of aesthetic game with this question. At first, the film seems to continue along realist lines, as we watch the women walk through the doors and into the chamber. But then this realism is called into question, as there is a cut, and we are back on the other side of the anteroom, looking at the doors. Perhaps, we think, the film will succumb to the modernist position after all, and the fate of the women will not be directly shown. As the doors are shut, however, the camera proceeds to track forward to the peephole in the door, and the shot ends by looking through the hole at the women visible inside. This suggests the shocking possibility that the dilemma will be resolved neither with the point of view of the victims nor with the blockage of any view, but rather with the point of view of the victimizers. When we then cut back into the chamber with the victims, it is almost a relief that we will not be positioned as SS murderers. A series of shots shows the panicked women waiting for gas, and then water spraying from showerheads. Finally we cut to the women, now dressed, leaving the building and staring over their shoulders at a column of Jews in the background who are filing into the gas chamber building. This time the camera does not follow them inside, but tilts up to show the chimney spewing smoke. The sequence thus concludes with a nod to the modernists, showing only the entrance and exit of the "true" gas chamber, but not the inside. This, then, is another of the film's postmodern strategies: it resolves the dilemma of a point of view inside the gas chamber not by committing itself to a realist "yes" or a modernist "no," but by playing a yes/no game—by quoting both strategies.[26]

While *Schindler's List* does contain certain discreet stylistic features of posttraumatic cinema—images of piles of Jews' belongings and of an Auschwitz chimney as indirect signifiers of genocide, a color scene showing present-day signifiers of the past—these features do not contribute to a posttraumatic discourse in the film. Rather, they constitute postmodern quotations of posttraumatic cinema within the framework of a classical realist narrative structure, in which linear chronology, omniscient point of view, and unself-conscious quotation promote the sense that an authentic history has been experienced, mastered, and memorialized.

Second-Generation Trauma, Resistant Postmodernism, and *History and Memory*

Schindler's List was made by filmmakers with no direct relationship to the Holocaust in order to make an audience also lacking any such direct relationship feel as if they had witnessed the real thing. *History and Memory* (1991), on the other hand, makes no attempt to provide a sense of witnessing the past as real, but articulates the personal experience of the videomaker, Rea Tajiri, whose mother and other family members were interned in the Japanese American camps before she was born. In what way might the children of the survivors of historical trauma—and their cultural productions—become witnesses to that trauma?

> The amputated are left only with phantom pains, but who can say that the pain felt in a hand that one no longer has is not pain. These latter-day Jews are like people who have had a hand amputated that they never had.

These words—written by the French psychiatrist Nadine Fresco in her 1984 article "Remembering the Unknown," one of the best pieces of writing on the second generation—suggest that second-generation memory can be thought of as a postmodern phenomenon because it functions as a kind of simulacrum, the memory of an event that was never witnessed.[27] And it is a very powerful kind of simulacrum because, unlike the collective memory of past events in general, second-generation memory is more than something one is simply aware of or is affected by; it actually organizes major aspects of one's identity.

Mental health professionals continue to debate the question of whether and how trauma affects the second generation. The notion of "intergenerational trauma" was initially viewed as "preposterous." During the 1960s, however, case studies began to be published arguing that individual children of survivors were vicariously traumatized by the Holocaust.[28] As empirical studies were conducted in subsequent decades, some researchers rejected the theory that children of survivors were traumatized "directly" by the Holocaust, suggesting instead that any effects upon the children were "indirect"—caused only by the compromised parenting styles of traumatized survivors—and therefore no different from the effects of parenting compromised by other causes. Nanette C. Auerhahn and Dori Laub, on the other hand, accept the existence of these "indirect" effects, but maintain the existence of some "direct" effects as well. "Children both pick up on the defensive structures of traumatized parents and intuit the repressed, dissociated, and warded off trauma that lurks behind the aggressive and traumatic overtones that are found in adults' parenting styles."[29] In other words, children are affected not only by the compromised parenting they receive, but also by the specific content of the memories—explicitly or implicitly transmitted—that caused the compromised parenting. "We maintain," they write, "that children of survivors are witnesses to the Holocaust."[30]

Neither the Tajiri tape nor the Fresco article to which it is uncannily similar, however, makes the case that the second-generation memory phenomena they describe conform to a clinical definition of PTSD. Rather, they point to a nexus of experiences, some of which can be identified as symptoms—at times, perhaps, muted—of PTSD.

One of the characteristics of the phenomenon described by Fresco that is relevant to *History and Memory* is the parents' verbal silence about past events whose overwhelming nature is communicated to the children nonverbally. One of Fresco's subjects related:

> Until I was about 10, I didn't know that my mother was Jewish. Her whole family had been exterminated, all of them had disappeared, almost without a trace. Since she had never told me, and since no one had ever spoken to me as a Jewess, it was something I lived through in silence. When I was 10, I put all my clues together. I had found a box of photographs of my mother's family at the back of a wardrobe behind three suitcases. And I realized she had a brother who looked very much like me. Then I went and told her that I knew she was Jewish, and that set off one of those terrible attacks she had all the time. My father said to me: "If you realized she was Jewish, you only had to come and tell me, you didn't have to go and upset her." I didn't do it again. I had done it to put a name on what had been happening every day for years without my understanding it.[31]

One of the child's responses to the paradoxical coexistence of omnipresent memory and parental silence is the phenomenon of untraceable memory. Again, one of Fresco's subjects: "There are things that I have always believed and thought on that subject, but I don't know when I picked them up. I must have learnt somewhere what happened to [my aunt] after Drancy [a French concentration camp], but I don't know how, or when, or from whom. I must have found out about it, then forgotten. I buried it, I don't know where."[32]

Another response to silence is a second-generation obsession with the past, described by Fresco as "the fascination exerted on them by the mystery in which they played no part. The blindspot of some primal scene, the place of concentration where death took place is also, for them, the only way out in which they can find an access to the life that existed before their birth."[33] Works like *History and Memory* may be thought of as attempts on the part of the author to work through this obsession, as well as to work through the sense of having been "exiled from identity"[34] or "deported from meaning."[35]

Several films articulating (in very different ways) the kind of second-generation Holocaust trauma described by Fresco have been made by the Belgian filmmaker Chantal Akerman and the American filmmaker Abraham Ravett. Pier Marton's video *Say I'm a Jew* (1984) and my own *Second Generation Video* (1995) are also relevant, as is, in a different but related format, Art Spiegelman's comic book *Maus* (1980–91).[36] All of these works contain features of modernist-posttraumatic cinema, and certainly warrant further study as such. Moreover, all but the Akerman films were produced in the United States. This indicates a shift from the first decades after the war, when U.S. filmmakers shied away from the Holocaust and it was primarily in Europe that both realist and post-traumatic cinemas of the Holocaust emerged. *Schindler's List* marked (though it did not single-handedly cause) the penetration of Holocaust memory further than ever before into the U.S. public sphere, and a grad-ual shift in the balance of Holocaust representation away from Europe and toward the United States. As a part of this process, the posttrau-matic cinema of the Holocaust has become increasingly displaced by the realist, monumentalist discourse of films like *Schindler's List* and the veritable tidal wave of Holocaust and Second World War memorial cin-ema it inspired, much of it produced by Spielberg himself.[37]

Posttraumatic cinema has not disappeared, however. It has largely migrated from the realm of the European art film, in which it origi-nated, to the realms of experimental film and video—much of it based in the United States—and of what Laura U. Marks has called *intercul-tural cinema*, accompanied by a broadening of subject matter to include the collective and second-generation memories of racial, colonial, and sexual trauma that have largely preoccupied the films and videos of these genres.[38] This migration has been paralleled by a broadening of research on intergenerational trauma, which initially focused on chil-dren of Holocaust survivors, and has now spread to the following range of traumas among the many discussed in the *International Handbook of Multigenerational Legacies of Trauma* (1998), edited by Yael Danieli, an expert in Holocaust trauma: the Armenian genocide, Japanese Amer-ican internees, atomic bomb survivors, combat veterans, Stalinism, the Cambodian genocide, Native Americans, the descendants of American slavery, Third World repressive regimes, domestic violence, and AIDS.[39]

Strategies of autobiography and resistant postmodernism have played a prominent role in the new experimental works dealing with the memories of these traumas. *History and Memory* demonstrates one way in which posttraumatic cinema has been sustained and transformed in the process.

Tajiri's experimental, documentary, autobiographical discourse of historical trauma has a variety of predecessors. First is the basic formal impulse of avant-garde or experimental film throughout its history: the rejection of the coherent diegesis of mainstream cinema, and the desire to subvert that form and/or to create a completely different audiovisual form. Second is the autobiographical tendency within that movement that arose in the work of some post–World War II United States filmmakers, such as Jonas and Adolfas Mekas, Stan Brakhage, James Broughton, Hollis Frampton, Robert Frank, and Jerome Hill. Perhaps most relevant to *History and Memory* is Jonas Mekas's *Reminiscences of a Journey to Lithuania* (1971), a diary film in which Mekas records a trip to his country of origin and remembers, among other things, his deportation to a Nazi concentration camp for his support of the resistance. Third is the rise of women's experimental cinema during the 1970s, like films by Amalie Rothschild, Ilene Segalove, and Su Friedrich, in which autobiography, and especially the investigation of the filmmaker's relationship with her mother, played a prominent role. A work that stands out is Friedrich's *The Ties That Bind* (1975), part of which deals with her mother's memory of growing up in Nazi Germany.[40] This aspect of *History and Memory* is especially significant given the fact that all the posttraumatic Holocaust films discussed in the book thus far were written and directed by men, and focus on male protagonists and documentary subjects.

Last is an increased attention to history through its fragmented images, which arose in the 1980s in some experimental works by James Benning, Alexander Kluge, Godard and Miéville, Marc Karlin, Woody Vasulka, and Lynn Hershman Leeson.[41] Perhaps most relevant within this development is Black British film and theory of the late 1980s, especially the films *Territories* (1985), *The Passion of Remembrance* (1986), and *Handsworth Songs* (1987), and the writings of Kobena Mercer and other theorists. Mercer has extended Foster's notion of resistant postmodernism to define an experimental cinema that uses quotation not as an affirmative, nostalgic, authenticating, or authoritative pastiche, but as a self-conscious and critical form of historiography. Mercer draws on the writings of Mikhail Bakhtin, Homi Bhabha, Dick Hebdige, and Paul Gilroy to explain the recycling and mixing of images, styles, and modes of discourse in these films. He argues that this strategy has multiple functions: it acknowledges the importance of media representations in history; it critiques the misrepresentation of oppressed groups in mainstream media; it critiques "corrective" realism as an oppositional cinematic strategy; and it acknowledges the group's position outside and between the dominant economies of representation. These films reproduce false media images of the group's history; juxtapose and frame those images so as to make their falsehood "speak"; and use these strategies of juxtaposition and framing to acknowledge (indeed, to celebrate) the films' own status not as ahistorical simulacra, but as resistant discourses emerging between the cracks of hegemonic discourses.[42] This strikes me as a good description of the resistant postmodernism of *History and Memory*.

History and Memory: For Akiko and Takashige is an approximately thirty-minute experimental tape about Tajiri's family's memories and her own second-generation memory of the Japanese American internment.[43] In the weeks after the Japanese attack on Pearl Harbor, the U.S. War Relocation Authority interned over 110,000 people of Japanese ancestry, two-thirds of whom were U.S. citizens, constituting more than 90 percent of the Japanese American population. Allowed to bring only what they could carry, whole families were sent first to temporary camps, like the Salinas Rodeo Grounds where Tajiri's mother was sent, and then to one of ten permanent camps, primitive and desolate, where they remained for up to four years. Tajiri's mother ended up in the camp at Poston, Arizona.

I would describe the form of *History and Memory* as a collage made up of the following kinds of material: documentary footage shot by Tajiri; clips from propaganda films, feature films, and illegal footage of the camp at Topaz, Utah, shot by the internee David Tatsuno; photographs; drawings; documents; text printed on the screen; and fictionalized and reenacted segments—all edited together into a complex and often multilayered structure threaded with Tajiri's own voice-over. The major themes are Tajiri's desire for knowledge about her mother's internment; her mother's silence or difficulty in speaking about it; her fascination with the only memory fragment of the internment that she heard her mother speak of as a child; her journey to Poston; and the role of film in representing or misrepresenting the internment.

There are things which have happened in the world while there were cameras watching, things we have images for. There are other things which have happened while there were no cameras watching which we restage in front of cameras to have images of. There are things which have happened for which the only images that exist are in the minds of the observers present at the time. While there are things which have happened for which there have been no observers, except for the spirits of the dead.

History and Memory engages all the forms of memory described by Tajiri in the above voice-over from the tape. It reproduces documentary images of the events; it reproduces restagings of the events; it presents original restagings; it uses audiotaped testimony to describe events lacking an image; it uses crawling text to narrate events that might have been witnessed only by the spirit of Tajiri's grandfather; and it uses Tajiri's voice-over to articulate her own memories and thoughts.

Perhaps the reason so many different forms of memory must be brought together to produce the tape is because of the lack of any single memory source that gives access to an adequate truth of what happened. Indeed, it is this very failure of memory that makes it necessary for a work to be produced that can search among and between inadequate sources in order to address an elusive but painful history. The most immediate failure of memory that seems to have necessitated the tape is Tajiri's mother's silence, which blocks Tajiri's access to "the images that exist only in the minds of the observers present at the time." In an audiotaped interview, Tajiri's mother claims that the reason she has forgotten almost everything about her internment is simply that it happened so long ago, but then goes on to suggest a more plausible reason by telling the story of a woman whose memories of internment caused her to "lose her mind." The following text crawls over this interview: "She tells the story of / what she does not remember / But remembers one thing: / Why she forgot to remember." This recalls a line in the Fresco article, "One remembers only that one remembers nothing."[44] Trauma thus appears, in the story of the woman who "lost her mind," as an origin of Tajiri's search for knowledge, and of her production of the tape.

Lacking an adequate parental image of the internment, Tajiri structures her search for memory around an untraceable image.

I don't know where this came from, but I just have this fragment, this picture that's always been in my mind. My mother, she's standing at a faucet, and it's really hot outside, and she's filling this canteen, and the water's really cold, and it feels really good, and outside the sun is just so hot, it's just beating down, and there's this dust that gets in everywhere, and they're always sweeping the floors.

These words are accompanied by a slow-motion dramatization of the image described, with Tajiri playing the role of her mother. Fragments of this dramatization recur throughout the tape.

The second-generation obsession with the past is articulated in this voice-over from the middle of the tape:

> I began searching for a history, my own history, because I had known all along that the stories I had heard were not true, and parts had been left out. I remember having this feeling growing up that I was haunted by something, that I was living within a family full of ghosts. There was this place that they knew about. I had never been there, yet I had a memory for it. I could remember a time of great sadness before I was born. We had been moved, uprooted. We had lived with a lot of pain. I had no idea where these memories came from, yet I knew the place.

While the verbal language of voice-overs, audiotaped interviews, and crawling texts struggles with the dilemma of an imageless second-generation memory, a variety of existing film images representing the

Illustration 6.1. *History and Memory*: untraceable memory.

past appear in the tape within a discursive framework that comments on their historical meaning. There is documentary footage of the Pearl Harbor attack from both U.S. and Japanese sources, the Tatsuno film of the Topaz camp, and out-takes from U.S. Signal Corps footage of the internment. It's not clear, though, to what degree the Signal Corps footage is staged propaganda, like the more obviously propagandistic clips from *Japanese Relocation* (1942, Department of War Information) and *The Way Ahead* (War Relocation Authority). Clips from the following fiction films appear: *From Here to Eternity* (1953), *December 7th* (1943), *Yankee Doodle Dandy* (1942), *Bad Day at Black Rock* (1954), *The Teahouse of the August Moon* (1956), *Come See the Paradise* (1990), and the Japanese film *Hawai Mare Okino Senjo Eigwa* (1942). Other references to Hollywood are a discussion of *Mississippi Burning* (1988), and images of movie stills included in a segment about Tajiri's sister. While most of the clips are commented upon by the tape only implicitly, two are commented upon explicitly. Signal Corps footage of a canteen at the Salinas Assembly Center is accompanied by an audiotape of Tajiri's mother watching the footage and replying that there was no canteen at Salinas. And clips from *Come See the Paradise*, a Hollywood movie about the internment, are accompanied by a voice-over of Tajiri's nephew reading his review criticizing the film as paternalistic.

Whereas *Schindler's List* inserts quotes from modernist films into a realist narrative for an unself-conscious pastiche effect, *History and Memory* inserts quotes from realist films into a modernist narrative as a self-conscious form of critique. These quotes are not used to make the work seem more authentic, as in *Schindler's List*, but rather to thematize the problematic nature of "authentic" memory both for second-generation individuals who grew up with the sense of personally remembering things that happened before we were born, and for those whose knowledge of the events stems only from media representations. Postmodern collage actually becomes a "realistic" form for representing historical consciousness in an age in which that consciousness is increasingly dominated by the media.

History and Memory adopts certain techniques of posttraumatic temporality from *Night and Fog* and *Shoah*. As in *Night and Fog*, there are segments containing images of the past as well as segments in which the camera investigates or wanders through the present-day sites of past events (the Salinas Rodeo Grounds and Poston), searching for traces or acknowledging the loss of traces. As in *Shoah*, there is witness testimony, some of it symptomatic of the original trauma, as when Tajiri's mother speaks of the woman who "lost her mind." Tajiri's camera, like Lanzmann's, reenacts past events as well, though for a somewhat different purpose. When Lanzmann's camera reenacts the victims' trip from the Chelmno church in the gas vans, it is to act out a posttraumatic identification with death. When Tajiri's camera reenacts her mother's journey to Poston, there is a greater element of working through trauma, since Tajiri explicitly films it as a gift for her mother, who was prevented from seeing the view on the original journey. The reenactment is intended to assist the survivor in healing.

Both Lanzmann and Tajiri also use reenactments by people, but, again, differently. Lanzmann adopts a fictional mise-en-scène (the barbershop) in order to transform a witness's testimony into an unconscious reenactment. He thereby attempts to preserve the pure documentary appearance of his film, especially insofar as he does not inform the audience of the fictional nature of the mise-en-scène. Reenactment in *History and Memory*, on the other hand, as exemplified in the scene of the mother at the faucet, explicitly rejects the documentary form in favor

Illustration 6.2. *History and Memory:* untraceable memory.

of fictional dramatization. With the explicit mixing of documentary and fictional forms, reenactment in *History and Memory* thus assumes a more postmodern character.

Whereas tense in *Night and Fog* and *Shoah* has a strict quality—strict alternation in the former, strict present tense in the latter—*History and Memory*, again in a more postmodern vein, mixes multiple present and past tense registers, cutting rapidly from one to the other. Images of the past are neither concentrated into extended blocks that interrupt the image of the present, as in *Night and Fog*, nor banished from the present to return as an invisible haunting, as in *Shoah*. Rather, they are admitted as fragments into a new kind of cinematic tense, where the present exists as a framework within which these fragmented representations of the past circulate, collide, and dialogue. This is the resistant postmodern historiography of a new genre.

Point of view in *History and Memory* is clearly structured around the author's autobiographical position, a position that is defined by the obsessive search for memory. This is most obvious in segments using first-person pronouns and the names of family members to bind words and images to the autobiographical subject. However, even when "impersonal" artifacts are presented, the autobiographical link remains insofar as the artifacts can be understood as evidence uncovered by the author in her search for memory. The collapsing of the impersonal into the personal is most explicit in the scene in which Tajiri narrates her discovery of the origin of her mother's mysterious bird carving. Searching through photographs at the National Archives, she found a photo of a Poston bird carving class in which the tiny image of her grandmother's face appears in the crowd.

Spatially, point of view is organized around the journey to Poston, the geographical center of the trauma. There is, of course, no documentary image of Tajiri's mother's original journey to Poston. There are hardly any documentary images of her family's internment at all; the only such images that appear in the tape are an illegal photograph of her mother at Poston, and one of her grandmother, in addition to the bird carving photo. Indeed, the missing image of the internment—symbolized in the tape by the mother's description of the drawn blinds in the deportation train that prevented her from seeing out—seems to have motivated the entire profusion of substitute images that constitutes the tape. Substituting for the real image of the original journey are the opening title sequence of *Bad Day at Black Rock*, which shows Spencer Tracy's train

Illustration 6.3. *History and Memory*: an image from *Bad Day at Black Rock* substitutes for the missing image of the mother's deportation train.

journey across the desert to investigate the fate of a missing Japanese American internee (the sequence is shown repeatedly in *History and Memory*, in a way that reminds me of the repeated train shots in *Shoah*); a scene from *Come See the Paradise* in which a woman on a deportation train asks "why are the blinds down?"; and Tajiri's footage of her car trip to Poston. The tape ends with the camera panning the barren desert landscape of Poston, which may symbolize not only the devastation of the Japanese American community but also, paradoxically, the fertile ground of second-generation memory. Indeed, *History and Memory* is but one of many texts in which the children of survivors of historical trauma feel they must journey back to encounter the original scene of devastation in order to move forward with their lives.

Temporally, point of view is organized around the faucet memory—which is to say, Tajiri's memory of her mother's memory. The tape's penultimate sequence, before the final panning over the Poston desert, is its first iteration of the entire faucet scene, which has previously been shown only in fragments. It is accompanied by Tajiri's voice-over:

My sister would say how funny it was. When someone tells you a story, you create a picture of it in your mind. Sometimes the picture will return without the story. I've been carrying around this picture with me for years. It's the one memory I have of my mother speaking of camp while we grew up. I overhear her describing to my sister this simple action, her hands filling a canteen out in the middle of the desert. For years I've been living with this picture, without the story, feeling a lot of pain, not knowing how they fit together. But now I found I could connect the picture to the story, I could forgive my mother her loss of memory, and could make this image for her.

This is one of the most profound cinematic expressions of the healing of not only second-generation trauma but all trauma. Here the tape works to heal the traumatic split between iconic and linguistic memory that van der Kolk and van der Hart describe; it stitches together the fragmented images characteristic of posttraumatic memory; and it bridges the intergenerational gap of silence through a creative act; all with a self-consciousness of the work's own role as not just a representation but, as in *Shoah*, an intervention in the desperate struggle for memory.[45]

Modernist cinema represented the image as a problematic substitute for reality, and eventually gave rise to a postwar cinema that grappled with the difficulty of representing historical trauma. *History and Memory* demonstrates a resistant postmodern cinema that acknowledges the extent to which reality is increasingly composed of images, and that grapples with the difficulty of representing second-generation trauma—a trauma that, although it is experienced as an image, nevertheless continues to hurt.

History and Memory does not function, however, like a postmodern version of *Night and Fog*, as a relatively singular starting point for a new cinematic discourse. One of the factors that made *Night and Fog*, and much of the modernist, posttraumatic cinema that followed it, so effective was its straddling of the boundary between avant-garde and mainstream cinema. The avant-garde energy of the discourse gave it the ability to excavate repressed memories and originate new, posttraumatic formal strategies; its engagement with mainstream cinematic forms and distribution channels allowed it to reach a relatively large audience and to have a significant effect on collective memory. Partly as a result of this cinema, posttraumatic historical consciousness has found a place in the public sphere. *History and Memory*, on the other hand, is a relatively marginal work, screened primarily in college classrooms, though not as frequently as *Night and Fog* was in its day.

What, then, is the role of cinema now in relation to the public discourse of historical trauma? Perhaps it is to guard against the omnivorous tendency of mainstream culture to co-opt and neutralize discourses that would challenge the status quo, that would confront the public with unpleasant realities that are not amenable to quick, easy, or commodifiable solutions. To a great extent, this co-optation has already taken place with respect to the discourse of the Holocaust, as evidenced by films like *Schindler's List* and *Life Is Beautiful* (1998). *History and Memory* serves as a reminder, emanating from the margins of film culture, of the persistence of historical trauma in our lives, and of the ability of the cinema to represent, and perhaps even to help heal, that trauma. Moreover, it serves as a reminder to those who live with the memory of the Holocaust of our link to other groups, living with other traumatic memories. The reciprocal relationship between *History and Memory* and the posttraumatic cinema of the Holocaust—what Tajiri's tape has inherited from those Holocaust films, and what it has given in return—demonstrates something that Cathy Caruth proposes in her book, *Unclaimed Experience*: "the way in which one's own trauma is tied up with the trauma of another, the way in which trauma may lead, therefore, to the encounter with another, through the very possibility and surprise of listening to another's wound."[46]

Notes

Preface

1. François Truffaut, "Rencontre avec Alain Resnais," *Arts et Spectacles* 22 February, 1956, 5. Reprinted in Richard Raskin, ed., *Nuit et Brouillard by Alain Resnais* (Aarhus, Denmark: Aarhus University Press, 1987), 139.

2. The figures of Marceline, Sol, and Anni are what Jean Cayrol called "lazareans." For Cayrol—poet, novelist, concentration camp survivor, and author of the commentary in *Night and Fog*—lazareans were those who, after Lazarus, had figuratively returned from death to wander, remember, and monologue in seemingly endless and alienated circles. Other film characters with lazarean qualities are Herman Broder in *Enemies, A Love Story* (1989), adapted from Isaac Bashevis Singer's novel, the family portrayed in *Brussels-Transit* (Belgium, 1980), and, perhaps after a fashion, many of Chantal Akerman's protagonists.

3. I follow Lawrence Langer in my use of the word *admitting*. See his *Admitting the Holocaust: Collected Essays* (New York: Oxford University Press, 1995).

I repeatedly use the term *Western* to limit the scope of cultural effects discussed here, not in order to exclude non-Western societies, but in order to distance my argument from claims of the universal significance of the Holocaust. I find such claims to be ahistorical, and to repress the differences between Western and non-Western societies. This is not to say that the Holocaust has not had an effect on non-Western societies, but simply to acknowledge that that effect has been significantly different in terms of depth, breadth, and substance. This difference is illustrated in a scene from *Chronicle of a Summer*, touched on in Chapter 3, in which two Africans living in France have no idea why Marceline, a French Jewish deportee, has numbers tattooed on her forearm. Some viewers might conclude that the Africans' knowledge of history is faulty; one might, however, conclude that their historical knowledge is understandably shaped by a different history.

4. Hayden White, *The Content of the Form: Narrative Discourse and Historical Representation* (Baltimore: John Hopkins University Press, 1987).

5. I prefer the term *anti-Jewish* to the term *anti-Semitic*. For me, the advantage of the latter term's familiarity is outweighed by the disadvantage of its conflation of racism against Jews and Arabs.

CHAPTER 1. INTRODUCTION TO FILM, TRAUMA,
AND THE HOLOCAUST

1. It will never be known how many were killed; the 10 million figure is
nothing but a tragic approximation. It derives from the following figures and
sources: 3.5 million Jews killed in extermination camps, mostly by gas, from
Israel Gutman, ed., *Encyclopedia of the Holocaust* (New York: Macmillan, 1990),
463; 1.25 million Jews killed by *Einsatzgruppen*, from Gutman, *Encyclopedia of the
Holocaust*, 438; 600,000 Jews killed in ghettos, from Raul Hilberg, *The Destruction of the European Jews* (New York: Holmes & Meier, 1985), 1219; 3.3 million
Soviet POWs killed, from Gutman, *Encyclopedia of the Holocaust*, 1192; 750,000
miscellaneous victims of the concentration camps, from Gutman, *Encyclopedia
of the Holocaust*, 313; 500,000 Soviets killed by *Einsatzgruppen*, from Abraham
J. Edelheit and Hershel Edelheit, eds., *History of the Holocaust: A Handbook and
Dictionary* (Boulder: Westview, 1994), 224; 200,000 Gypsies killed, from Guenter
Lewy, *The Nazi Persecution of the Gypsies* (New York: Oxford University Press,
2000), 222; 100,000 deemed physically or mentally disabled killed in euthanasia
centers, from Edelheit and Edelheit, *History*, 229. Most of these figures have been
contested; at times, much higher figures have been given.

It was Zoe Burman, formerly of the film department of the U.S. Holocaust
Memorial Museum, who told me that the Wiener film is unique.

2. The transcript of the Wiener interview, which was conducted by Ester Ha-
gar, is entitled "Mr. Wiener Interview Re. Libau." A copy is held by the film
department of the U.S. Holocaust Memorial Museum in Washington, D.C., as is
a copy of the film itself. The following citations refer to the interview transcript.
"Well, they're killing Jews there": 7. "It was about this time that Himmler outlawed the filming of any activities related to the extermination of Jews": 4. "They
were depressed . . .": 17.

The June 1941 start date of *Einsatzgruppe* exterminations comes from Gutman, *Encyclopedia of the Holocaust*, 438. The December 1941 start date of gassing
comes from ibid., 462.

3. An acknowledged shortcoming of this book is the lack of discussion of
any Israeli films. While I do not believe Israeli films have played a prominent
role in posttraumatic cinema globally, I have not seen enough of them to determine the extent to which they may have been influenced by posttraumatic
cinema elsewhere, or found their own way of responding to the trauma of the
Holocaust. The Holocaust has not been a major focus of Israeli cinema, although
in recent years there have been a number of films about the second generation,
a subject covered in Chapter 6. See Ilan Avisar, "Personal Fears and National
Nightmares: The Holocaust Complex in Israeli Cinema," in *Breaking Crystal:
Writing and Memory After Auschwitz*, ed. Efraim Sicher (Urbana: University of
Illinois Press, 1998), 137–59.

4. Theodor Adorno, "Cultural Criticism and Society," in *Prisms*, trans.
Samuel and Shierry Weber (London: Neville Spearman, 1967), 34.

5. I do not mean to imply that cinema and television are interchangeable. While a television program such as *Holocaust* and a film such as *Schindler's List* are comparable to an extent in terms of classical realist narration, as I will suggest, my subsuming of the television program under the rubric of cinema implies a repression of the specificity of television and its relation to trauma that will not be redressed in these pages.

6. For one introduction to the concept of the classical realist film, see Robert Stam, Robert Burgoyne, and Sandy Flitterman-Lewis, eds., *New Vocabularies in Film Semiotics* (New York: Routledge, 1992), 184–89. This can be a useful approach to certain kinds of mainstream productions, especially historical productions such as *Holocaust*. On the other hand, its effectiveness is limited in terms of both breadth and depth. It applies to genres such as historical films better than to genres such as musicals or horror films. And within the genres to which it does apply, it is so general as to repress significant aspects of films and differences between them. This older concept of classical realism has begun to be supplanted by more nuanced scholarship, such as Julia Hallam and Margaret Marshment's *Realism and Popular Cinema* (Manchester: Manchester University Press, 2000).

7. Elie Wiesel, "Trivializing the Holocaust: Semi-Fact and Semi-Fiction," *New York Times*, 16 April 1978, sec. 2: 29. The reference to the series' "cheapness" is on p. 1.

8. Berel Lang, "The Representation of Limits," in *Probing the Limits of Representation: Nazism and the "Final Solution,"* ed. Saul Friedlander (Cambridge, Mass.: Harvard University Press, 1992), 305.

9. Wiesel's approach to the question of film and the Holocaust is echoed, in many ways, in both existing books on international Holocaust films: Annette Insdorf, *Indelible Shadows: Film and the Holocaust* (New York: Cambridge University Press, 1989), and Ilan Avisar, *Screening the Holocaust: Cinema's Images of the Unimaginable* (Bloomington: University of Indiana Press, 1988).

10. Andreas Huyssen, "The Politics of Identification: *Holocaust* and West Germany," *New German Critique* 19 (1980): 117–36.

11. A similar approach appears in numerous works by Thomas Elsaesser, including his "Subject Positions, Speaking Positions," in *The Persistence of History*, ed. Vivian Sobchack (New York: Routledge, 1996), 145–83; and in Miriam Bratu Hansen, "*Schindler's List* is not *Shoah*: Second Commandment, Popular Modernism, and Public Memory," *Critical Inquiry* 22, no. 2 (1996): 292–312; reprinted in *Spielberg's Holocaust: Critical Perspectives on Schindler's List*, ed. Yosefa Loshitzky (Bloomington: Indiana University Press, 1996), 77–103.

12. Wiesel "Trivializing," 29.

13. This is not to say that knowledge or suspicion of mass murder was limited to direct witnesses, nor that Hitler had not hinted at such drastic measures for years, nor that supporters of Hitler, Nazism, or the Third Reich bore no responsibility for the crimes. On the secrecy of the death camps, see Hilberg *Destruction*, 962–67.

14. On Charles Sanders Peirce's notion of the indexical sign, see Peter Wollen, *Signs and Meaning in the Cinema*, 3d ed. (Bloomington: Indiana University Press, 1972), 122–23.

15. Christian Metz, *The Imaginary Signifier*, trans. Celia Britton, Annwyl Williams, Ben Brewster, and Alfred Guzzetti (Bloomington: Indiana University Press, 1975–82), 45.

16. Of course, the rise of electronic and digital media has somewhat displaced film's significance as an analogue of perception and fantasy.

That for me the cinema witnesses the physical reality of the Holocaust first, and the mental reality as a subsequent effect, results from the fact that I speak from the victim's position. In some German discourse on the Third Reich, on the other hand—for instance, in Syberberg's film *Hitler: A Film From Germany*—one finds the reverse. For Syberberg, the cinema begins by witnessing Nazism as a fantasy; the physical reality of the Holocaust comes later, if at all. This demonstrates the importance of not confusing the two discourses by putting them both under the single rubric of a discourse of the Holocaust.

17. For a useful, article-length introduction to the history of trauma research, see Bessel van der Kolk and Onno van der Hart, "The Intrusive Past: The Flexibility of Memory and the Engraving of Trauma," in *Trauma: Explorations in Memory*, ed. Cathy Caruth (Baltimore: Johns Hopkins University Press, 1995), 158–82.

18. The explicit/implicit/symptomatic framework comes from David Bordwell, *Making Meaning: Inference and Rhetoric in the Interpretation of Cinema* (Cambridge, Mass.: Harvard University Press, 1989), 8–9.

19. Susannah Radstone, ed., "Trauma and Screen Studies," *Screen* 42, no. 2 (2001): 188–216, with articles by Radstone, Thomas Elsaesser, E. Ann Kaplan, Maureen Turim, and Janet Walker. Elsaesser, Kaplan, Walker, and Anton Kaes have forthcoming books on the topic, and Kaplan and Ban Wang also have a forthcoming anthology.

20. For overviews of trauma studies, see James Berger, "Trauma and Literary Theory," *Contemporary Literature* 38, no. 3 (1997): 569–82; and Geoffrey Hartman, "On Traumatic Knowledge and Literary Studies," *New Literary History* 26, no. 3 (1995): 537–63.

21. See Michael Rothberg's discussion of Lacan's theory of trauma and the real, and Hal Foster's use of that theory, in his book *Traumatic Realism: The Demands of Holocaust Representation* (Minneapolis: University of Minnesota Press, 2000), 137–38.

22. Cathy Caruth, *Unclaimed Experience: Trauma, Narrative, and History* (Baltimore: Johns Hopkins University Press, 1996), 114–15.

23. Santner, "History Beyond the Pleasure Principle: Some Thoughts on the Representation of Trauma," in *Probing the Limits of Representation*, ed. Saul Friedlander, 143–54.

24. Angelika Rauch, "Post-Traumatic Hermeneutics: Melancholia in the Wake of Trauma," *Diacritics* 28, no. 4 (1998): 111–14.

25. Julia Kristeva, "The Pain of Sorrow in the Modern World: The Works of

Marguerite Duras," *PMLA* 102, no. 2 (1987): 138–52; Elaine Scarry, *The Body in Pain: The Making and Unmaking of the World* (New York: Oxford University Press, 1985).

26. Maurice Blanchot, "N'oubliez pas!" *La Quinzaine litteraire* 459 (1986): 12.

27. The often-cited Himmler quote can be found in Saul Friedlander, *Memory, History, and the Extermination of the Jews of Europe* (Bloomington: Indiana University Press, 1993), 105, where it is discussed at length.

28. Erik Barnouw, *Documentary: A History of the Non-fiction Film*, 2d rev. ed. (New York: Oxford University Press, 1993), 102–3.

29. The Camouflage Squad is described by former Treblinka guard Franz Suchomel in *Shoah*, transcribed in Claude Lanzmann, *Shoah: The Complete Text of the Acclaimed Holocaust Film* (New York: Da Capo, 1995), 99–100.

30. Elie Wiesel, *Night*, trans. Stella Rodway (New York: Bantam, 1986), 30.

31. Sigmund Freud, *Beyond the Pleasure Principle*, trans. and ed. James Strachey (London: Hogarth, 1955), 12–13, vol. XVIII of *The Standard Edition of the Complete Psychological Works of Sigmund Freud*.

32. American Psychiatric Association, *Diagnostic and Statistical Manual of Mental Disorders*, 4th ed. (Washington, D.C.: American Psychiatric Association, 1994), 424–29.

33. Lisa MacCann and Laurie Anne Pearlman, "Vicarious Traumatization: A Framework for Understanding the Psychological Effects of Working with Victims," *Journal of Traumatic Stress* 3, no. 1 (1990): 131–49.

34. Walter Benjamin, "The Work of Art in the Age of Mechanical Reproduction," *Illuminations* 219–54. Benjamin, A German Jew, was twice detained in internment camps in Occupied France, fled to Spain in 1940, was arrested by Spanish authorities, and died—either by suicide or of natural causes—before he could be sent back to France.

35. On the reaction to the liberation of the camps among liberators and the public in the United States, see Robert H. Abzug, *Inside the Vicious Heart: Americans and the Liberation of the Nazi Concentration Camps* (New York: Oxford University Press, 1985). For one argument on the significance of the films of the liberated camps, see Nicolas Losson, "Notes on the Images of the Camps," trans. Annette Michelson, *October* 90 (1999): 25–35.

36. K.R.M. Short and Stephan Dolezel, *Hitler's Fall: The Newsreel Witness* (New York: Croon Helm, 1988), 43–44.

37. Susan Sontag, *On Photography* (New York: Anchor, 1990), 20. I have run across a number of descriptions of reactions to the concentration camp films, but none as striking as this. While of course the differences between film and photography are important, I do not believe they specifically problematize the use of the Sontag quote as a substitute for the reaction to films.

38. By stressing the role of representation in trauma, I do not mean to embrace an exogenous, universal, or poststructuralist definition of it. My definition is still consistent with empirical research insofar as this crisis is only caused by extreme events, at least in people who are not already mentally ill.

39. Shoshana Felman and Dori Laub, M.D., *Testimony: Crises of Witnessing in Literature, Psychoanalysis, and History* (New York: Routledge, 1992). For one critique of Felman and Laub, see Dominick LaCapra, "Lanzmann's *Shoah*: 'Here There Is No Why,' " *Critical Inquiry* 23, no. 2 (1997): 245–48.

40. On PTSD in Holocaust survivors, see Henry Krystal, ed., *Massive Psychic Trauma* (New York: International Universities Press, 1968).

41. The earliest study of film-induced stress of which I am aware is R. S. Lazarus et al., "A Laboratory Study of Psychological Stress Produced by a Motion Picture Film," *Psychological Monographs* 76 (1962). Following several studies by Lazarus and colleagues, Mardi Jon Horowitz continued this strand of research. See his articles "Psychic Trauma: Return of Images After a Stress Film," *Archives of General Psychiatry* 20 (1969): 552–59; and "Stress Films, Emotion, and Cognitive Response," *Archives of General Psychiatry* 30 (1976): 1339–44, co-written with Nancy Wilner. The quote describing *Subincision* comes from page 554 of the earlier Horowitz article. The term *analogue trauma* comes from Mark I. Davies and David M. Clark, "Predictors of Analogue Post-Traumatic Intrusive Cognitions," *Behavioral and Cognitive Psychology* 26 (1998): 303–14. Research on film-induced stress until 1979 is summarized in J. Patrick Gannon, "The Traumatic Commercial Film Experience: An Extension of Laboratory Findings on Stress in a Naturalistic Setting" (Ph.D. diss., California School of Professional Psychology, 1979), 8–14.

42. A more psychoanalytically oriented approach to the question of the effects of treating Holocaust survivors can be found in Yael Danieli, "Therapists' Difficulties in Treating Survivors of the Nazi Holocaust and Their Children" (Ph.D. diss., New York University, 1981). Danieli proposes the existence of a form of countertransference not to the patient but to the Holocaust itself. See p. 129.

43. MacCann and Pearlman, "Vicarious Traumatization," 142.

44. Much of my anecdotal evidence for vicarious trauma induced by viewing atrocity films relates to *Night and Fog*. It includes my own childhood memory of seeing the film at my synagogue; numerous similar stories told to me by acquaintances; numerous brief references in a variety of published sources; and even a representation in another film: Margarethe von Trotta's *Marianne and Juliane* (1981). In the 1999 film *8mm*, the protagonist could be interpreted as suffering from vicarious trauma induced by the viewing of a snuff film.

45. This is not to reduce different experiences of trauma to one level, as Felman and Laub do, but rather to acknowledge that they do share common features in discourse.

46. LaCapra, *Representing*, 173–74.

47. LaCapra, "Lanzmann's *Shoah*," 267.

48. For a discussion of the classical realist historical film, see Keith Tribe, "History and the Production of Memories," *Screen* 18, no. 4 (1977–78): 9–22.

49. Gerard Genette, *Narrative Discourse: An Essay in Method*, trans. Jane E. Lewin (Ithaca: Cornell University Press, 1980), 26–32.

50. I am adapting the term *secondarized* loosely from Freud's concept of "secondary revision," defined by Laplanche and Pontalis as the "rearrangement of a dream so as to present it in the form of a relatively consistent and comprehensible scenario." In *Totem and Taboo*, Freud himself compares secondary revision to other kinds of processes: "There is an intellectual function in us which demands unity, connection and intelligibility from any material, whether of perception or thought, that comes within its grasp." The point, however, is that trauma defies this function. See Sigmund Freud, *Totem and Taboo*, trans. and ed. James Strachey (London: Hogarth, 1950), 95, vol. XIII of *The Standard Edition of the Complete Psychological Works of Sigmund Freud*; quoted in Jean Laplanche and J. B. Pontalis, *The Language of Psycho-analysis*, trans. Donald Nicholson-Smith (New York: W. W. Norton, 1973), 412.

51. On Janet's theory of narrative memory, see van der Kolk and van der Hart, "Intrusive Past," 159–64.

52. Hypermnesia: "unusually exact or vivid memory." William Morris, ed., *The American Heritage Dictionary of the English Language* (Boston: Houghton Mifflin, 1969), 647.

53. Krystal, *Massive Psychic Trauma*, 30–31. One of the things that makes films like *Shoah*, *The Pawnbroker*, *Love Film*, and *25 Fireman Street* posttraumatic is that "the reconstruction of the persecution period" in them is precisely "a slow, laborious, and painful procedure."

54. Van der Kolk and van der Hart, "Intrusive Past," 163–64, 172–75.

55. Ibid., 172.

56. Robert Gronner, in "Discussion: Similarities and Differences Between Survivors of the Hiroshima Disaster and Nazi Persecution," in Krystal, *Massive Psychic Trauma*, 197.

57. William G. Niederland, "An Interpretation of the Psychological Stresses and Defenses in Concentration Camp Life and the Late Aftereffects," in Krystal, *Massive Psychic Trauma*, 62.

58. My model of posttraumatic tense, mood, and voice is similar to Laurence J. Kirmayer's model of dissociation as a rupture in narrative coherence, voice, and time. See his article "Landscapes of Memory: Trauma, Narrative, and Dissociation," in *Tense Past: Cultural Essays in Trauma and Memory*, ed. Paul Antze and Michael Lambek (New York: Routledge, 1996), 181.

59. Walter Benjamin, "On Some Motifs in Baudelaire," in *Illuminations*, by Benjamin, trans. Harry Zohn (New York: Harcourt, Brace, & World, 1968), 157–202. Freud's theory of trauma is discussed on 162–64.

60. See Richard Prouty's Benjaminian discussion of trauma in *Menilmontant*, in "The Well-Furnished Interior of the Masses: Kirsanoff's *Menilmontant* and the Streets of Paris," *Cinema Journal* 36, no. 1 (1996): 3–17.

61. A fascinating earlier film that experimented with a variety of forms for articulating a posttraumatic memory of the Holocaust is *Unzere Kinder/Our Children* (Poland, 1948). This film deserves further discussion, but I am not including that discussion here because, as a Yiddish film, its posttraumatic

experimentation occurred, both economically and formally, outside the main-stream European and U.S. realist and modernist cinemas on which the book focuses. See Ira Konigsberg, "*Our Children* and the Limits of Cinema: Early Jew-ish Responses to the Holocaust," *Film Quarterly* 52, no. 1 (1998): 11–18.

62. Paul Virilio would argue that these traumas were not in fact discrete his-torical events, but, rather, aspects of one event: the ongoing development of "total war," or, as Omer Bartov calls it in a less radical argument, "industrial killing." See Paul Virilio, *War and Cinema*, trans. Patrick Camiller (New York: Verso, 1989); and Omer Bartov, *Murder in Our Midst: The Holocaust, Industrial Killing, and Representation* (New York: Oxford University Press, 1996).

63. It is certainly possible that other cinematic discourses of trauma have arisen in response to other historical events. Anton Kaes, for example, is writing a book on Weimar cinema and First World War trauma.

A few disclaimers are called for in my use of the word *discourse*, however. First, I am using the term in the relatively broad sense defined above, rather than in the specifically Foucauldian sense. Second, while the phenomenon in question was more focused than a broadly defined response, it did not possess the coherence of a movement or the longevity of a genre. Third, I have found no evidence that this discourse was consciously, intentionally, or explicitly linked to the psychiatric discourse of trauma at the point of production or, in most cases, at the point of reception; I assume that it was usually produced in an intuitive or unconscious manner.

Of course, this kind of argument can easily become circular. Is there really a discourse of trauma in these films, or do I see in them only what I presuppose to be there? Let me address this question with a fourth disclaimer. I do not in-tend for my argument to depend on a naive positivist faith in the psychiatric discourse of trauma as a true description of reality, even if that discourse itself does at times adopt an attitude of scientific certainty. I do hope to demonstrate in the following chapters that the films in question were in part responding to a common phenomenon associated with the memory of the Holocaust, a phe-nomenon that the psychiatric discourse of trauma has described at least in a more empirical and systematic fashion than can be found anywhere else.

64. Santner, "History," 144.

65. Personal correspondence from Henry Krystal, 1 June 2000.

66. Friedrich Nietzsche, *On the Genealogy of Morals*, trans. Walter Kaufmann and R. J. Hollingdale (New York: Vintage, 1989), 61.

67. Geoffrey H. Hartman, "Holocaust Testimony, Art, and Trauma," in *The Longest Shadow: In the Aftermath of the Holocaust* (Bloomington: Indiana Univer-sity Press, 1996), 151–72.

68. Saul Friedlander, "Trauma and Transference," in *Memory, History, and the Extermination of the Jews of Europe* (Bloomington: Indiana University Press, 1993), 117–38. LaCapra also articulates this view, without, however, fully endorsing it: "[One] may insist that any attentive secondary witness to, or acceptable ac-count of, traumatic experiences must in some significant way be marked by

trauma or allow trauma to register in its own procedures." LaCapra, "Lanzmann's *Shoah*," 244.

69. Caruth, *Unclaimed*, 2. A question that this book does not address is what
role trauma may have played in earlier paradigm shifts in film form. Griffith
certainly represented traumatic events in many of his films—both the public
trauma of the Civil War and the "private" traumas of abused women. Did the
representation of these traumas play a significant role in the transition from
early cinematic forms to the classical feature film? An article that suggests a relationship between the development of Griffith's style and the representation of
trauma is Russell L. Merritt, "Mr. Griffith, *The Painted Lady*, and the Distractive
Frame," *Image* [Rochester] 19, no. 4 (1976): 26–30.

CHAPTER 2. *NIGHT AND FOG* AND THE ORIGINS OF POSTTRAUMATIC CINEMA

1. Charles K. Krantz, "Alain Resnais' *Nuit et Brouillard*: A Historical and Cultural Analysis," *Holocaust Studies Annual* 3 (1985): 109.

2. David Weinberg, "France," in *The World Reacts to the Holocaust*, ed. David S.
Wyman (Baltimore: Johns Hopkins University Press, 1996), 15.

3. Henry Rousso, *The Vichy Syndrome: History and Memory in France since 1944*
(Cambridge, Mass.: Harvard University Press, 1991), 25.

4. Anne Wieviorka, "On Testimony," in *Holocaust Remembrance: The Shapes of
Memory*, ed. Geoffrey H. Hartman (Cambridge, Mass.: Blackwell, 1994), 26–27.

5. Rousso, *Vichy Syndrome*, 26.

6. Pierre Francés-Rousseau, *Intact aux yeux du monde* (Paris: Hachette, 1987),
53; quoted in Wieviorka "On Testimony," 27–28.

7. Weinberg, "France," 20.

8. Ibid., 21.

9. Colombat, *The Holocaust in French Film* (Metuchen, N.J.: Scarecrow, 1993),
13–14.

10. Rousso, *Vichy Syndrome*, 228–29.

11. Details on the production of the film come from Richard Raskin, *Nuit
et Brouillard by Alain Resnais: On the Making, Reception, and Functions of a Major
Documentary Film* (Aarhus, Denmark: Aarhus University Press, 1987), 25–30.

12. Krantz, "Renais' *Nuit*," 116–17. Also repressed in the film is the history
of French collaboration in the deportations. The film includes a photograph of
the French concentration camp Pithiviers, where foreign-born Jews were held
by French authorities for deportation. In the original photograph, used in the
version of the film sent to the French board of censors for approval, a guard
visible in the foreground is clearly identifiable by his cap as a French officer.
The censors requested the removal of the photo. In a compromise, the image of
a wooden beam was superimposed over the cap. See Raskin, *Nuit*, 30.

13. Raskin, *Nuit*, 52. My translation.

14. Bill Nichols, *Representing Reality: Issues and Concepts in Documentary* (Bloomington: Indiana University Press, 1991), 34–35.

15. A 16mm print of an English language version of *The Death Camps* is held by the National Center for Jewish Film at Brandeis University.

16. For a historical survey of the compilation film, see Jay Leyda, *Films Beget Films* (New York: Hill and Wang, 1964). For a more theoretically informed case study, see Carl R. Plantinga, *Rhetoric and Representation in Nonfiction Film* (New York: Cambridge University Press, 1997), 200–213.

17. It is misleading to place the Jews last since, in terms of liquidation specifically, they were the primary target. This was a common problem in Holocaust discourse before the 1970s in Western Europe, and the 1990s in Eastern Europe. The fact that the filmmaker was himself a Jew makes the problem a bit more disturbing.

18. The photo is reproduced in Yitzhak Arad, ed., *The Pictorial History of the Holocaust* (New York: Macmillan, 1990), 194–95. The date is given in Edelheit and Edelheit, *History,* 173.

19. On the representation of Jews as uncivilized in the Warsaw ghetto footage, see Lucy S. Dawidowicz, "Visualizing the Warsaw Ghetto," *Shoah: A Review of Holocaust Studies and Commemorations* 1, no. 1 (1978): 5+.

20. The question of the moral implications of the documentary gaze in different contexts is discussed in Vivian Sobchack, "Inscribing Ethical Space: Ten Propositions on Death, Representation, and Documentary," *Quarterly Review of Film Studies* 9, no. 4 (1984): 283–300. The averted gaze of the passing Jews in the Warsaw ghetto footage suggest a horrific variation on the themes of the crowd, the gaze, modernity, cinema, and fascism in Benjamin's writing.

21. Nichols, *Representing Reality,* 56–68.

22. At times I refer to Resnais as the author of *Night and Fog* and other films he directed. This is common in writing on Resnais because, although he did not write his own screenplays, he did choose his screenwriters carefully, work closely with them, and retain a great deal of artistic control over the films he directed.

23. There is a difference between my argument, here, about the *evidentiary* primacy of the image in realist historical documentary and my earlier argument about the *explanatory* primacy of the commentary.

24. Resnais's encounter with Brecht's theories is noted in John Francis Kreidl, *Alain Resnais* (Boston: Twayne, 1977), 34.

25. For Resnais, as for other modernists, the interest in opera as a synergistic collaboration of theater and music indicated a desire to bring a variety of media into the cinema as independent contributors that would be combined but not submitted to a predetermined hierarchy.

26. Marc Bloch, *The Historians' Craft,* trans. Peter Putnam (New York: Vintage, 1953), 46; quoted in Lynn A. Higgins, *New Novel, New Wave, New Politics: Fiction and the Representation of History in Postwar France* (Lincoln: University of

Nebraska Press, 1996), 28. Bloch, a Jew and co-founder of the Annales School of history, was a Resistance leader and was executed by the Gestapo in 1944.

27. Bettina Knapp, *French Novelists Speak Out* (Troy, N.Y.: Whitson, 1976), 25.

28. Jean Cayrol, *Miroir de la rédemption* (Neuchâtel: Editions de la Baconnière, 1944); quoted in Knapp, *French Novelists*, 22.

29. Elie Wiesel, *A Jew Today*, trans. Marion Wiesel (New York: Random House, 1978), 15–16.

30. Jean Cayrol, *Foreign Bodies*, trans. Richard Howard (New York: G. P. Putnam's Sons, 1960), 76.

31. Herman Rapaport, "Duras' Aurelia Steiner, or Beyond Essence," in *Auschwitz and After: Race, Culture, and "the Jewish Question" in France*, ed. Lawrence D. Kritzman (New York: Routledge, 1995), 313–31.

32. Maureen Turim, *Flashbacks in Film: History and Memory* (New York: Routledge, 1989), 214.

33. Rene Predal, *Alain Resnais* (Paris: Minard, 1968); cited in Naomi Greene, *Landscapes of Loss: The National Past in Postwar French Cinema* (Princeton: Princeton University Press, 1999), 31.

34. Turim, *Flashbacks*, 79–84.

35. Leo Bersani and Ulysse Dutoit note that the sound tracks of a number of Resnais's films begin with this kind of solo, hollow drumbeat, and trace this practice to French theatrical history. This, then, would be another example of Resnais's synergistic formal practice, and, insofar as it connotes a certain artificiality relative to classical cinema, his films' self-consciousness. See Leo Bersani and Ulysse Dutoit, *Arts of Impoverishment: Beckett, Rothko, Resnais* (Cambridge, Mass.: Harvard University Press, 1993), 167.

36. The French text of the commentary can be found in Raskin, *Nuit*, 72–130. When the English translation in the film's subtitles seems adequate, I have used it. When not, I have done my own translation.

37. Knapp, *French Novelists*, 25.

38. Cathy Caruth, "Trauma and Experience: Introduction," in Caruth, *Trauma*, 7–8.

39. Erich Auerbach, *Mimesis: The Representation of Reality in Western Literature* (Princeton: Princeton University Press, 1953), 534–35.

40. Hayden White, "Historical Emplotment and the Problem of Truth," in *Probing the Limits of Representation*, ed. Saul Friedlander, 50–52.

41. Without the opportunity to shoot his own footage and thus expand his formal vocabulary, Resnais would probably never have agreed to make the film.

42. Resnais's debt to Sartre is evidenced by the fact that two of his later films quote the existentialist: *La Guerre est finie* and *Stavisky . . .* See James Monaco, *Alain Resnais* (New York: Oxford University Press, 1979), 112–13, 175.

43. Alain Robbe-Grillet, "Alain Robbe-Grillet," in *Three Decades of the French New Novel*, ed. Lois Oppenheim (Urbana: University of Illinois Press, 1986), 23–24.

44. Some observations about this passage. First, the subtitle deemphasizes this implication of the spectator by translating "il y a nous" (there are those of us) to simply "there are those." Second, the passage implicitly refers to the Algerian War of Liberation. Third, the phrase, "those of us who pretend to believe this only happened at a certain time and in a certain place," risks crossing the line separating a progressive attitude toward colonialism from an overgeneralization of the Holocaust.

45. Roland Barthes, *Writing Degree Zero*, trans. Annette Lavers and Colin Smith (New York: Hill and Wang, 1968), 5–6.

46. On Blanchot's anti-Judaism between 1936 and 1938, see Jeffrey Mehlman, *Legacies of Anti-Semitism in France* (Minneapolis: University of Minnesota Press, 1983), 6–22.

47. *On vous parle* (1947) is the first novel in Cayrol's trilogy, *Je vivrai l'amour des autres.*

Chapter 3. *Shoah* and the Posttraumatic Documentary after Cinéma Vérité

1. Linda Williams defines the postmodern historical documentary in "Mirrors Without Memories: Truth, History, and the New Documentary," *Film Quarterly* 46, no. 3 (1993): 9–21. Bill Nichols gives his definition of the new historical documentary in *Blurred Boundaries: Questions of Meaning in Contemporary Culture* (Bloomington: Indiana University Press, 1994), 92–106. There, and in his *Representing Reality*, he seems to regard *Shoah* less as an example of the new form than as a precursor, although I would make the case for its being more than that. Paula Rabinowitz defines the reflexive historical documentary in *They Must Be Represented: The Politics of Documentary* (New York: Verso, 1994), 16–32. Janet Walker defines the posttraumatic documentary in "The Traumatic Paradox: Documentary Films, Historical Fictions and Cataclysmic Past Events," *Signs* 22, no. 4 (1997): 803–25.

2. For a critical discussion of the early history of cinéma vérité and its technological determinants, see Nichols, *Representing*, 271–72, note 7.

3. Barnouw, *Documentary*, 253–54.

4. The necktie microphone and tape recorder are mentioned in Ellen Freyer, "Chronicle of a Summer—Ten Years After," in *The Documentary Tradition: From Nanook to Woodstock*, ed. Lewis Jacobs (New York: Hopkinson and Blake, 1971), 441.

5. For a discussion of documentary interview forms, see Nichols, *Representing*, 50–53.

6. Ibid., 44; emphasis in the original.

7. Weinberg, "France," 21.

8. Ibid., 22.

9. Ibid., 22, 30.

10. Ibid., 22.

11. Ibid., 28.

12. Ibid., 27.

13. An additional documentary, Straub and Huillet's *Fortini-Cani* (1976), seems to have explored some of the same terrain as *Night and Fog, The Sorrow and the Pity,* and *Shoah.* I have not had an opportunity to see the film, which presents footage of the present-day site on which a group of Italian partisans were massacred by the Nazis. J. Hoberman compares it to *Shoah* in his " 'Shoah': Witness to Annihilation," *Village Voice,* 29 October, 1985, 46. Some other relevant historical documentaries from this period—which represent other historical events, however—are *In the Year of the Pig* (United States, 1969, see Nichols, *Representing,* 48); and, from Cuba, *Hombres de Mal Tiempo* (1968, see Julianne Burton, "Democratizing Documentary," *The Social Documentary in Latin America,* ed. Julianne Burton [Pittsburgh: University of Pittsburgh Press, 1990], 68–69) and *Muerte y vida en El Morillo* (1971, see ibid., 73–74).

14. Koch, "The Angel of Forgetfulness and the Black Box of Facticity: Trauma and Memory in Claude Lanzmann's Film *Shoah,*" trans. Ora Wiskind, *History and Memory* 3, no. 1 (1991): 119–32; LaCapra, "Lanzmann's *Shoah.*"

15. For a definition of acting out, see Laplanche and Pontalis, *Language of Psycho-analysis,* 4.

16. This point is made by Thomas Elsaesser in his article "Subject Positions," 178. Fackenheim is quoted in Claude Lanzmann, "From the Holocaust to the Holocaust," *Telos* 42 (1979–80): 141.

17. James Young, *Writing and Rewriting the Holocaust: Narrative and the Consequences of Interpretation* (Bloomington: Indiana University Press, 1988), 163.

18. See Hansen, "*Schindler's List.*"

19. Koch, "Angel of Forgetfulness," 130.

20. Lanzmann, *Shoah,* 161.

21. My argument here is indebted to a similar argument made by Shoshana Felman in her article "The Return of the Voice," 205.

22. Freyer, "Chronicle," 441.

23. Lanzmann, *Shoah,* 107–8.

24. Koch, "The Aesthetic Transformation of the Image of the Unimaginable," *October* 48 (1989): 20–21.

25. I would segment *Shoah*'s denoted subject matter as follows: (1) destruction of traces; (2) deportation; (3) arrival at extermination camps; (4) early phase of extermination; (5) later phase of extermination; (6) failure of resistance to stop extermination; (7) failure of testimony to stop extermination; (8) failure of Warsaw ghetto uprising to stop extermination.

26. Lanzmann gives the figure of 400,000; *Shoah,* 1. Edelheit and Edelheit estimate the number at 152,000 to 310,000; *History,* 294.

27. Lanzmann, *Shoah,* 3.

28. On the elimination of bones at Chelmno, see Srebnik's testimony in Lanzmann, *Shoah,* 10–11.

29. Of course, *unerase* is not a word. And yet it seems to me that the unerasure of memory is precisely the main goal of *Shoah*. The word *retrieval* comes close to what I mean by *unerasure*, but it is both too general and too conclusive. (*Undelete* comes close, too, but is too conclusive and too specific to computers.) I see unerasure as a highly specific form of activity that logically precedes retrieval. And while erasure is by definition a complete removal that leaves no traces and thus cannot be undone, I would argue that no real erasure is completely successful. There are always traces, either of what was erased, or of the erasure itself.

30. Lanzmann, *Shoah*, 86–88.

31. Quoted in LaCapra, "Lanzmann's *Shoah*," 264. Lanzmann's term "non-places of memory" ("*non-lieux de la memoire*") is a play on the term "places of memory" ("*lieux de memoire*"), discussed by French historian Pierre Nora in his influential introduction to his anthology, *Realms of Memory: Rethinking the French Past*, English edition edited and with a foreword by Lawrence D. Kritzman, trans. Arthur Goldhammer (New York: Columbia University Press, 1996).

32. Ora Avni, "Narrative Subject, Historic Subject: *Shoah* and *La Place de l'Etoile*," *Poetics Today* 12, no. 3 (1991): 513.

33. Lanzmann, *Shoah*, 2.

34. Ibid., 88–89.

35. My discussion of the church scene is partly indebted to Felman, "Return of the Voice," 258–68.

36. Claude Lanzmann, "Les Non-lieux de la mémoire," in *Au sujet de "Shoah": Le Film de Claude Lanzmann*, ed. Michel Deguy (Paris, 1990), 291; quoted in LaCapra, "Lanzmann's *Shoah*," 264–65.

37. Lanzmann, "Les Non-lieux de la mémoire," 290–91; quoted in LaCapra, "Lanzmann's *Shoah*," 255.

38. Simon Louvish mentioned this image in his review of *Schindler's List*. "I shall remember Spielberg's film as a superbly crafted work by an intelligent professional director. But I shall recall much more powerfully Jan Karski, *Shoah*'s Polish courier, refusing to remember and walking out of the frame, leaving me to contemplate what horrors endure in a man's mind so fresh for over 30 years. It is that empty chair, not Spielberg's sound and fury, which raises the hair on the back of my neck." "Spielberg's Apocalypse," *Sight & Sound* 4, no. 3 (1994): 15.

39. The self-consciousness of testimony in *Shoah* is discussed in Young, *Writing*, 161–62.

40. Some other striking examples of self-consciousness in the film are the scene of Lanzmann's hidden camera interview of former Treblinka guard Franz Suchomel, with its exceedingly distorted interview footage, and its shots of Lanzmann's surveillance van and the unstable image on the hidden camera monitor; and Auschwitz survivor Armando Aaron's amazing comment when asked by Lanzmann why so many Christians gathered in the street to see the deportation of the Jews of Corfu: "Pour voir le cinéma" (to see the show).

41. The Lanzmann statement is in his article "Why Spielberg Has Distorted the Truth," *Guardian Weekly*, 3 April 1994, 14.

42. LaCapra, *Representing*, 205.
43. Van der Kolk and van der Hart, "Intrusive Past," 163.

CHAPTER 4. *THE PAWNBROKER*
AND THE POSTTRAUMATIC FLASHBACK

1. Edward Lewis Wallant, *The Pawnbroker* (New York: Harcourt Brace Jovanovich, 1961). According to film editor Ralph Rosenblum, the three-year distribution delay possibly resulted from a lack of distributor interest, and certainly from censorship problems associated with the nudity in the flashback scene described below. See Ralph Rosenblum and Robert Karen, *When the Shooting Stops . . . The Cutting Begins* (New York: Viking, 1979), 164.
No stills from *The Pawnbroker* or *Schindler's List* are included in this book because the copyright owners, Universal and Paramount respectively, charge steep commerical licensing fees even for nonprofit academic publications such as this one.
2. Robert Hughes, "*Hiroshima, mon amour*: A Composite Interview with Alain Resnais," *Film: Book 2; Films of War and Peace* (New York: Grove, 1962), 50.
3. One could pursue an alternate path in searching for ways in which fiction films departed from realism in order to attempt to respond to the trauma of the Holocaust. Instead of focusing on the temporal strategies of films like *Night and Fog, Hiroshima, mon amour, The Pawnbroker*, and, later, Szabó's *Love Film* and *25 Fireman Street*, one could focus on the use of expressionistic mise-en-scène in the Czech films *Distant Journey* (1949), *Transport from Paradise* (1962), and *The Fifth Horseman Is Fear* (1965). Of course, this would require a different way of theorizing posttraumatic cinema. On these Czech films, see Ilan Avisar's chapter, "Stylistic Approaches to the Representation of the Holocaust on the Screen: the Czech Cinema," in *Screening the Holocaust*, 52–89.
4. Hugo Münsterberg, *The Film: A Psychological Study* (New York: Dover, 1970 [1916]), 41.
5. Turim, *Flashbacks*, 17–18. Turim discusses *The Pawnbroker* briefly in her book, and at somewhat greater length in her article "The Trauma of History: Flashbacks Upon Flashbacks," *Screen* 42, no. 2 (2001): 205–10. Our approaches are distinct but complementary, and I wrote this chapter before reading her article.
6. *Oxford English Dictionary*, 2d ed., vol. V (Oxford: Clarendon, 1989), 1014.
7. Mardi Jon Horowitz, "Flashbacks: Recurrent Intrusive Images After the Use of LSD," *American Journal of Psychiatry* 126, no. 4 (1969).
8. Jim Goodwin, "The Etiology of Combat-Related Post-Traumatic Stress Disorders," in *Post-Traumatic Stress Disorders of the Vietnam Veteran*, ed. Tom Williams (Cincinnati: Disabled American Veterans, 1980) 17. Signaling the acceptance of the term by the psychiatric mainstream was its inclusion as a symptom of PTSD in the *DSM III-R*: American Psychiatric Association, *Diagnostic and Statistical Manual of Mental Disorders*, 3d ed.-revised (Washington, D.C.: American Psychiatric Association, 1987), 250.

Note that the word *flashback* was predated by the expression *to flash back*. The *OED* defines this on p. 1013 as "to jump back, as when a flame in a Bunsen burner retreats down the tube and burns at the air-inlet," and dates this usage to 1902. However, Gerald Karam points out, in a personal correspondence, that *to flash back* was used to describe not a physical but a psychological event as early as 1872, in George Eliot's novel *Middlemarch*: "To be a poet is to have a soul . . . in which knowledge passes instantaneously into feeling, and feeling flashes back as a new organ of knowledge"; quoted in Robert Andrews, *The Columbia Dictionary of Quotations* (New York: Columbia University Press, 1993), 697. The much older word *flash* seems to have migrated extensively between physical and mental realms, a process that accelerated with the industrial revolution, and the sudden cultural penetration of engines and, later, cinema. Note also the etymological connection between the words *flashback* and *holocaust*; one of the earliest meanings of flash was "a sudden breaking forth of fire" (*OED*, 1013); *holocaust* derives from the Greek word for burnt whole.

9. Paul Virilio pursues this line of thinking as well, in *War and Cinema*.

10. Sigmund Freud, *Moses and Monotheism*, trans. and ed. James Strachey (London: Hogarth, 1964), 75–76, vol. XXIII of *The Standard Edition of the Complete Psychological Works of Sigmund Freud*.

11. For an overview of the psychiatric discourse on flashbacks, see Fred H. Frankel, "The Concept of Flashbacks in Historical Perspective," *International Journal of Clinical and Experimental Hypnosis* 42, no. 4 (1994): 321–34.

12. Quoted in Pierre Janet, *The Major Symptoms of Hysteria*, 2d ed. (New York: Macmillan, 1920), 25–26.

13. Ibid., 33–35.

14. The case of Irène is discussed in van der Kolk and van der Hart, "Intrusive Past," 162. Freud also noted, "The repressed retains its upward surge, its effort to force its way to consciousness . . . if at any time in recent experience impressions or experiences occur which resemble the repressed so closely that they are able to awaken it"; *Moses*, 95.

15. Abram Kardiner, *The Traumatic Neuroses of War* (New York: Paul B. Hoeber-Harper & Brothers, 1941), 37, 82.

16. Mardi Jon Horowitz, *Image Formation and Psychotherapy* (New York: Jason Aronson, 1983), 8.

17 . Henry Krystal and William G. Niederland, "Clinical Observations on the Survivor Syndrome," in Krystal, *Massive Psychic Trauma*, 329.

18. Thomas A. Mellman and Glenn C. Davis, "Combat-Related Flashbacks in Posttraumatic Stress Disorder: Phenomenology and Similarity to Panic Attacks," *Journal of Clinical Psychiatry* 46, no. 9 (1985): 380.

19. Freud, *Pleasure*, 13.

20. Caruth, *Trauma*, 5.

21. On the early history of flashbacks, see Turim, *Flashbacks*, 21–59. On standardization and differentiation in classical Hollywood cinema, see David Bordwell, Janet Staiger, and Kristin Thompson, *The Classical Hollywood Cinema: Film*

Style and Mode of Production to 1960 (New York: Columbia University Press, 1985), 96–97.

22. Turim, *Flashbacks*, 28.

23. Modifications included the adaptation to sound, and the absorption of a degree of modernism in film noir flashbacks, which one could argue was a response to the traumas of World War II combat, urbanization, the atomic bomb, and the like.

24. This notion of classical flashback genres is my own, though it is derived from information in Turim's second chapter. These are theoretical, not historical genres. That is, they represent my own and Turim's conceptions, not the period conceptions of the film industry or audience.

25. Turim discusses this flashback from *The Birth of a Nation* on pp. 40–43. This analysis is my own, however. The fade-out was an early type of marking, later replaced by dissolves and the like. Note also that the one-second length of this flashback seems quite short by later standards, but is actually a standard length for "tableau"-style flashbacks of the silent period.

26. Turim, *Flashbacks*, 61–101.

27. Turim discusses the flashback in *La Maternelle* on pp. 78–79.

28. *Hiroshima* was not the first film to begin a flashback with a graphic match, but it may have been the first to use the graphic match as an analogue of post-traumatic memory triggering. Note also the intriguing presence of the bed in both the *Hiroshima* scene and Janet's case study of Irène.

29. Turim discusses the flashbacks in *Hiroshima* on pp. 210–16.

30. Freud, *Pleasure*, 12–13.

31. Turim, *Flashbacks*, 16–17.

32. See Chapter 1, note 8.

33. Casablanca is the name given to a bar in which the two characters in *Hiroshima, mon amour* continue to excavate and struggle over the woman's memories. Resnais and Duras, too, seem to identify the classical discourse of memory in cinema with *Casablanca*.

34. The meaning of the recorder music is revealed during the flashback; Sophie's daughter plays a recorder in the cattle car on the way to Auschwitz. Note that the deportation of Sophie's two children, the immediate murder and cremation of her daughter, and hence the choice highlighted by the title are based on a glaring historical inaccuracy. The children of political deportees like Sophie were not deported, to my knowledge. The only children who were deported to camps, as far as I am aware, were Jews and Gypsies.

35. In this sense, the protagonist of *Sophie's Choice* is not only Stingo, but also the American coming-of-age story itself, which comes of age by confronting its European parentage.

36. There is a certain self-consciousness associated with the flashbacks in *Sophie's Choice*. This, however, is not the modernist, posttraumatic self-consciousness with which I have been concerned, which encourages in the spectator a critical awareness of the problem of narrating trauma. It is, rather, the

self-consciousness of nostalgia, which encourages pleasure in the return to a cherished narrative tradition.
Note also that the flashback's assumption of Stingo's formal point of view is supported by Sophie's direct address, which literally aligns the spectator with Stingo's desire for her, and for her memories.

37. Elie Wiesel, *A Jew Today*, trans. Marion Wiesel (New York: Random House, 1978), 15–16.

38. Lawrence Langer, *Holocaust Testimonies: The Ruins of Memory* (New Haven: Yale University Press, 1991), 95.

39. Susan Fromberg Schaeffer, *Anya* (New York: Macmillan, 1974), 301.

40. For an example of crosscutting in Wallant's novel, see his Chapter 25. Wallant uses the word *cinematographic* to describe his literary talent in his essay, "The Artist's Eyesight," in *Teacher's Notebook in English* (New York: Harcourt, Brace & World School Department, 1963), 3.

41. Wallant, *Pawnbroker*, 242.

42. Wallant, "Artist's Eyesight," 4, emphasis in the original.

43. Rosenblum and Karen, *When the Shooting Stops . . .*, 141, 152.

44. See p. 32.

45. "I began with the basis that for Sol the past is not past, it is much more present than what is going on at the moment around him. . . . Then, knowing the way my own memory works, when it is something that I do not want to remember I will fight it and fight it; but it keeps intruding itself in larger and larger bursts, and if it is important enough it finally breaks through and takes over completely, and then recedes in the same way." Sidney Lumet, "Keep Them on the Hook," *Films and Filming* 11, no. 1 (1964): 19–20.

46. Ernest Becker, *Angel in Armor: A Post-Freudian Perspective on the Nature of Man* (New York: George Braziller, 1969), 77–78.

47. The spectator is tutored in this way. The film's first images show a dream-like pre-Holocaust picnic enjoyed by Sol and his family, then a cut to Sol waking up in his New York suburban back yard. The first flashback occurs shortly thereafter, when Sol's sister reminds him of the coming twenty-fifth anniversary of their deportation. It is a split-second shot of Sol's wife from the dream. The overall unintelligibility of this initial flashback, as opposed to the one analyzed at length here, is slightly mitigated by its redundant content.

48. I base this statement about the film's effectiveness not only on a perusal of published sources, but also on numerous conversations with people, mostly Jews, who saw the film in its first theatrical run. They almost uniformly recall the film as highly disturbing, often seeming to reexperience that disturbance while pinpointing the flashbacks as the thing they remember most clearly about the film.

49. Rosenblum and Karen, *When the Shooting Stops . . .*, 142–45; Lumet, "Keep Them on the Hook," 20. I am referring to the *Pawnbroker* flashback that takes place on a train.

50. Lumet, 20.

51. Vance Oakley Packard, *The Hidden Persuaders* (New York: D. McKay, 1957). The impact of the Packard book is described in Wilson Bryan Key, *The Clam-Plate Orgy, and Other Subliminals the Media Use to Manipulate Your Behavior* (Englewood Cliffs, N.J.: Prentice Hall, 1980), 132.

52. Caruth writes of *Hiroshima, mon amour*, "The return of the flashback as an interruption—as something with a disrupting force or impact—suggests that it cannot be thought simply as a representation." Caruth, *Unclaimed Experience*, 115, note 6. If the split-second flashbacks in *The Pawnbroker* both increase and decrease spectator identification with the fiction, what is the relationship between these two functions, one might ask? I would suggest that the shock of the flashbacks acts like a revolving door through which the spectator can repeatedly exit and reenter the fictional world. Ultimately, though, I would characterize *The Pawnbroker* as a realist film with modernist tendencies; as such, it may provide an exit, but works hard to cycle the spectator immediately back into the fiction through this revolving door.

53. This is not to say that *The Pawnbroker* subverts the male gaze of classical cinema that Laura Mulvey critiqued in her influential article, "Visual Pleasure and Narrative Cinema," *Movies and Methods*, ed. Bill Nichols, vol. 2 (Berkeley: University of California Press, 1985), 303–15. Rather, the film assumes the classical male gaze as the norm, and then demonstrates its breakdown in posttraumatic memory. According to this logic, the flashbacks in *The Pawnbroker* constitute a kind of visual castration, and the female characters Mabel and Ruth become objects of exchange in this phallic discourse. Two additional elements of the flashback scene reinforce this argument: the broken glass as another possible castration symbol, and the replacement of Sol's phallic power by that of his wife's rapist.

This argument is consistent with Kaja Silverman's argument about *The Best Years of our Lives* in her essay, "Historical Trauma and Male Subjectivity," in *Psychoanalysis and Cinema*, ed. E. Ann Kaplan (New York: Routledge, 1990), 110–27. Silverman argues that the "dominant fiction" of classical cinema is a cultural stimulus barrier, binding the incoming energy of history and converting it into narrative. She argues that *The Best Years of our Lives* is one of a number of postwar films in which aspects of classical film practice break down under the pressure of overwhelming historical energy, which is to say, trauma. She, too, identifies this breakdown with castration. This question of the relationship between cinematic discourses of trauma and castration will return in the chapter on István Szabó.

See also Judith Doneson, "The Jew as a Female Figure in Holocaust Film," *Shoah: A Review of Holocaust Studies and Commemorations* 1, no. 1 (1978): 11–13, 18.

54. The naming of the assistant *Jesus* is consistent with an overall Christian motif in the film that is common in Jewish-themed Holocaust films and that many critics have found disturbing.

55. Both *The Pawnbroker* and *Hiroshima* are existential narratives asking whether it is possible for two individuals from separate worlds of pain—or,

perhaps by extension, any two individuals—to understand one another, and to enter into a relationship that is better than the worlds from which they came. In fact, both films have been criticized for seeming to equate and universalize particular historical traumas. These criticisms, however, focus only on the films' historical content in the narrowest sense, failing to take into account their more broadly formal historical consciousness. The ways in which the juxtaposed memories are represented are starkly opposed in each film. Contrast, for example, the fragmentation of shot/reverse shot in *The Pawnbroker*'s flashbacks with the use of a classical shot/reverse shot structure in the film's opening title sequence depicting Sol's morning drive into Harlem. Shots of Sol looking out his car window are intercut with shots of the ghetto streets. The formal directness with which the film constructs an epistemology of Harlem could not be more directly opposed to the formal fragmentation with which it constructs an epistemology of the Holocaust.

56. Hitchcock experimented with posttraumatic flashbacks as well, in *Spellbound* (1945) and *Marnie* (1964).

57. The female protagonist of *Hiroshima* is certainly troubled by memory, but she does not display symptoms of PTSD, as Sol does. The accuracy of *The Pawnbroker*'s portrait of PTSD resulted largely from Wallant's novel, which is said to have been influenced in part by his friendship with a Holocaust survivor. See David Galloway, *Edward Lewis Wallant* (Boston: Twayne-G. K. Hall, 1979), 156. As pointed out to me by the psychologist Lionel Joseph, this accuracy may have also been influenced by the prior publication of two relatively popular books dealing with the psychological effects of concentration camps, both by psychiatrists who were themselves Jewish survivors of the camps: Viktor Frankl's *From Death-Camp to Existentialism: A Psychiatrist's Path to a New Therapy*, trans. Ilse Lasch (Boston: Beacon, 1959); and Bruno Bettelheim's *The Informed Heart: Autonomy in a Mass Age* (Glencoe, Ill.: The Free Press, 1960).

58. *The Pawnbroker* was, however, one of the first mass-distributed American fiction films to visualize the camps. I am aware of only three previous such films that did so: *The Young Lions* (1958), with a brief scene at the end dramatizing the liberation of a camp; *Judgment at Nuremberg* (1961), which showed archival footage of the liberated camps; and a brief scene in a largely forgotten B film, *Operation Eichmann* (1961), about Eichmann's capture by Israeli agents in 1960. This meager history can be contrasted with that of Eastern European cinema; one can begin by mentioning the Polish fiction film *The Last Stage* (1948), which is set almost entirely in Auschwitz, and which is discussed in Chapter 6.

59. *The Pawnbroker* was produced by Ely Landau's production company and distributed by Allied Artists. Some of the film's financing history is recounted by one of the film's producers, Roger Lewis, in his article, "On the Producer," in *Movie People: At Work in the Business of Film*, ed. Fred Baker (New York: Douglas, 1972), 14–22.

It may not be surprising that it was European films like *La Maternelle* and *Hiroshima* that originated the posttraumatic flashback. What may be surprising is that it was an American film that demonstrated both the most systematic elaboration of the posttraumatic flashback and its application to the memory of an essentially European catastrophe. Contrast *The Pawnbroker* with, for example, a critically acclaimed Polish Holocaust film of the same period, *The Passenger* (1962), which used a different form of flashback to address less the psychology than the politics of memory. Perhaps *The Pawnbroker* is symptomatic of an American cultural tendency toward psychiatric explanations, as against a European, and especially socialist, tendency toward ideological explanations.

60. Some examples of later American films containing posttraumatic flashbacks are *Straw Dogs* (1971), which used them to represent a woman's memory of being raped; *Foxfire* (1982), which used them for a memory of Vietnam combat; and *Alan & Naomi* (1992), which used them once again for Holocaust memory. The acceptance of posttraumatic flashbacks into mainstream cinema is perhaps demonstrated most clearly by their attribution—in a scene of pure kitsch—to the canine hero of the family film *Benji* (1974).

CHAPTER 5. ISTVÁN SZABÓ AND POSTTRAUMATIC AUTOBIOGRAPHY

1. *The Garden of the Finzi-Continis* is based on an autobiographical novel by Giorgio Bassani; *Europa, Europa* is based on an autobiography by Solomon Perel. Some other examples: *Diamonds in the Night* (Czechoslovakia, 1964), based on a novel by Arnost Lustig; *Landscape After Battle* (Poland, 1970), based on stories by Tadeusz Borowski; and *The Truce* (Italy, 1998), based on an autobiography by Primo Levi.

2. Some autobiographical films dealing with the Holocaust (including documentaries) that I have come across are *Lang ist der Veg* (1948, co-written and with an uncredited co-directing credit by Israel Becker), *The Two of Us* (France, 1966, Claude Berri), *Reminiscences of a Journey to Lithuania* (United States, 1971, Jonas Mekas), *Les Violons du bal* (France, 1973, Michel Drach), *1942* (France, 1975, Simone Boruchowicz), *The Fire* (Netherlands, 1981, Hedy Honigmann), *Return to Poland* (United Staes, 1981, Marian Marzynski), *The Distance to Nearby* (Netherlands, 1982, Barbara Meter), *Sarah* (Australia, 1982, Yoram Gross), *The Revolt of Job* (Hungary, 1983, Imre Gyöngyössy and Barna Kabay), *Martha and Me* (France/Germany, 1990, Jirí Weiss), *Diamonds in the Snow* (United States, 1994, Mira Reym Binford), and *A Kenyéreslány Balladája/The Ballad of the Bread Girl* (Hungary, 1995, János Herskó). Significant also are two Israeli films written by and starring the Holocaust refugee Gilah Almagor: *The Summer of Aviya* (1988) and *Under the Domim Tree* (1994). It is unclear to me whether *The Cellar* (Israel, 1963) is autobiographical; see Avisar, "Personal Fears and National Nightmares" 143. For information on some of these films, see the *Jewish Film Directory* (Westport, Conn.: Greenwood, 1992). For information on *Lang ist der Veg*, see Konigsberg, *"Our Children,"* 8–11.

3. Insdorf, *Indelible Shadows*, 152–56; Avisar, *Screening the Holocaust*, 35–38.

4. Avisar, *Screening the Holocaust*, 36–37.

5. Quoted in William Friedberg, "Nazi Concentration Camp Reactivated for Film," *New York Times*, 20 February 1949, sec. 2: 5.

6. Ibid.

Lanzmann rejected the omniscience of the high-angle shot a priori. He has said, "I remember I wanted to show the village of Chelmno and the cameraman told me there is only one way: by helicopter, to shoot from the sky. I said, 'Never. There were no helicopters for the Jews when they were locked in the church or in the castle.' This would have been a crime—a moral and artistic crime. What is the meaning of seeing things from the sky? This is a point of view of God, which is not mine. I remember that Jean-Paul Sartre wrote . . . that there was no point of view in [François] Mauriac's novels. At the end he says that Mauriac had, precisely, the point of view of God, because it was nowhere. And he offered, 'God is not an artist, Monsieur Mauriac non plus!' "

This strikes me as being, in effect, a rather eloquent argument for the restricted point of view in posttraumatic cinema. Claude Lanzmann, "Seminar with Claude Lanzmann: 11 April 1990," *Yale French Studies* 79 (1991): 94.

7. A problematic side effect of my criticism of *The Last Stage* for denying trauma, and of my attempt to displace it somewhat within the canon of Holocaust films in order to make room for Szabó's posttraumatic films, is that it also displaces a feminist film for a masculinist one. As productive as Szabó's posttraumatic discourse might be, for the most part his films display, as I will argue below, a classically male point of view. *The Last Stage*, on the other hand, for all its denial of trauma, is a remarkable document in which socialism, realism, feminism, and the memory of the Holocaust coincide, and deserves a separate analysis using a more sympathetic method.

8. Elie Wiesel, *A Jew Today*, trans. Marion Wiesel (New York: Random House, 1978), 15.

9. Lawrence Weschler develops an analysis of Holocaust themes in Polanski's films in his article, "Artist in Exile," *The New Yorker*, 5 December 1994, 88–106. Polanski's discouragement of an autobiographical reading of his films is mentioned on p. 90.

10. Roman Polanski, *Roman* (New York: William Morrow, 1984), 23. The "cul-de-sac" passage from Polanski's autobiography is explicitly dramatized as an event in Wladyslaw Szpilman's life in *The Pianist*. This could be viewed as evidence of Polanski's general tendency to slip autobiographical material into his films.

11. The information on Szabó comes from David Paul, "Szabó," in *Five Filmmakers*, ed. Daniel J. Goulding (Bloomington: Indiana University Press, 1994), 157. Information on the Holocaust in Hungary comes from Randolph L. Braham, *The Politics of Genocide: The Holocaust in Hungary* (New York: Columbia University Press, 1981), 1143–44.

12. Tom Tugend, in an article on Szabó's latest film, *Sunshine*, writes, "It

might have been fascinating to delve deeper into the life of Szabó . . . But Szabó would have none of it. After reluctantly acknowledging that he was hidden by nuns during the Holocaust, he declares firmly, 'I am not happy talking about myself.' " "Szabó's Challenges of History," *The Jerusalem Post Internet Edition*, 11 July 2000, <http://www.jpost.com/Editions/20006/29/Culture/Culture News.8949.html>.

13. Gyula Gazdag was assistant director for *Love Film*, and played the role of Öcsi in *25 Fireman Street*. I interviewed him in Los Angeles during the fall of 1994.

14. Ibid.

15. Ibid.

16. Ibid.

17. On autobiography in *Meeting Venus*, see Janet Maslin, " 'Meeting Venus' Sings of Politics," *New York Times*, 10 November 1991, sec. 2, 17–18.

18. Szabó's role as artistic producer for the Hungarian film *The Book of Esther* (1990) demonstrates his historical ambivalence toward the representation of the Holocaust. The film—written and directed by Krisztina Deák, and featuring Bálint—tells the story of a Hungarian Jewish Holocaust survivor who returns to Budapest after the war in search of her missing daughter. Szabó's involvement with the film exemplifies the productive marginalization of the Holocaust within his career, while the film's conclusion with the mother's suicide seems to sum up his attitude, until recently, toward explicitly representing the Holocaust: a suicidal enterprise, best left to others. Szabó is not credited for *The Book of Esther*, but his involvement is mentioned in Paul "Szabó," 159.

19. Insdorf, *Indelible Shadows*, 168–72. The prominence of *Mephisto* in this book is indicative of the imprecision of its selection of films. *Mephisto* is arguably not about the Holocaust at all, but, rather, fascism.

20. Braham, *Politics of Geocide*, 1–4.

21. Ibid., 16–20, 28.

22. Ibid., 28–32, 122–27, 153–56, 194–95.

23. Zsuzsanna Ozsvath, "Can Words Kill? Anti-Semitic Texts and Their Impact on the Hungarian Jewish Catastrophe," in *The Holocaust in Hungary: Fifty Years Later*, ed. Randolph L. Braham and Attila Pok (New York: Columbia University Press, 1997), 79–116.

24. This period is discussed in detail in Braham, *Politics of Genocide,* 362–685.

25. Ibid., 732–39.

26. Ibid., 829–43.

27. Randolph L. Braham, "Hungary," in *The World Reacts to the Holocaust*, ed. David S. Wyman (Baltimore: Johns Hopkins University Press, 1996), 207–19.

28. According to Gyula Gazdag, János Herskó is a crucial figure in the history of Jewish memory in Hungarian film. He was a mentor to Szabó, serving as head of the studio in which Szabó made his first three features. A poster for *Dialogue* appears in the background of a scene in Szabó's first feature. Gazdag says Herskó attracted several Jewish filmmakers to his studio and mentored

them. He emigrated to Sweden in 1970, reportedly attributing his decision to Hungarian anti-Judaism. In 1992, he appeared in the film *Zentropa*, playing a German Jewish refugee returning to Germany after the Second World War. His wife tells him she wants to go to Palestine; he replies, "But we're Germans," and she replies, "But we're Jews." In 1995, Herskó returned to Hungary to make the autobiographical documentary *A Kenyéreslány Balladája/The Ballad of the Bread Girl*. The film consists entirely of shots of Hersko revisiting the places he was sent as a Jewish slave laborer during the war, standing in front of the camera, and testifying.

29. I asked Szabó about this scene in an interview on 7 July 1997, in Budapest. He explained that the mother's remark was her way of simplifying the issue for Takó, because he is so young. Szabó gave no indication of agreeing with my argument about the role of Holocaust autobiography in his films. For me, the evidence for this argument lies in the films themselves and the historical record. If I am confident about the methodological risk of interpreting the films against the author's stated intentions, however, I am ambivalent about the ethical risk of "outing" the author's work, particularly since, being the American child of a Hungarian Holocaust survivor, I am essentially an outsider to the Jewish community in Hungary, and to its ethical constraints.

30. I am not arguing here that Szabó has mentally repressed his own memories, which I have no reason to believe. I have neither the evidence to make such an argument nor the desire to do so. The repression that I am discussing takes place only at the level of the filmic texts.

An additional symptom of Jewish discourse in the film appears in a fantasy sequence in which people paste homemade signs to the outside of a trolley car. These signs contain photographs and descriptions of lost loved ones who are being sought. According to Zsuzsanna Ozsvath, in personal correspondence, Jews did post such signs in postwar Budapest. The only posted name I can make out in the scene is Steiner, a typically Jewish name.

Note another detail of the repressed autobiography: the Jewish father who hides is transformed, in Takó's fantasy, into the partisan father who hides Jews. This is consistent with Freud's discussions of reversal in dreams in *The Interpretation of Dreams*, trans. and ed. James Strachey (London: Hogarth, 1955), passim, *The Standard Edition of the Complete Psychological Works of Sigmund Freud*, vols. IV and V.

The repressed autobiography in *Father* suggests that the father's victimization as a Jew and his death by heart attack were not coincidental, and that the stress of victimization or the lack of medicine in hiding contributed to his death, as is suggested more forcefully in *25 Fireman Street*. This is not a question that we should ask of Szabó, who has a right to his privacy, but rather one that the narrative seems to be asking of itself.

31. Gusztáv Kosztolányi, "Jewish Life in Hungary, Part One," *Central Europe Review* 2, no. 4 (2000), <http://www.ce-review.org/00/4/csardas4.html>.

32. See my discussion of historical trauma and symbolic castration in relation to Kaja Silverman's work: Chapter 5, note 53.

33. Freud's story about his father having his cap knocked off by an anti-Jew also seems to suggest an element of castration anxiety. See Freud's *The Psychopathology of Everyday Life*, trans. and ed. James Strachey (London: Hogarth, 1966), 219–20, vol. VI of *The Standard Edition of the Complete Psychological Works of Sigmund Freud*.

34. Another way in which *Father* subverts the repression of its Holocaust material is by failing to do a better job of repressing that material than it does. While the film could be said to have a classical narrative structure in many senses, especially in terms of the resolutions of the personal and generational crises, it departs from the classical model in the following sense. A more classical narrative would have done a better job of smoothing over the symptoms of repression, covering over the gaps in the father's backstory, and resolving the enigmas. I take the film's failure to do this not as sloppiness, but rather as indicative of a modernist tendency to allow the inevitable contradictions that structure the text to remain on its surface.

Corresponding to *Father*'s insistent pointing to the repressed Holocaust autobiography it contains is a statement by Szabó that seems to be in marked contrast to his repeated denials: "Every filmmaker has only one message, because he has only one life; and in this one life, there is only one important experience." See Paul, "Szabó," 199.

35. Bözsi's husband is identified as a non-Jew, since Jews were excluded from the army at the time. In reality, such roundups were carried out by the Hungarian Arrow Cross, not by Germans. The historically inaccurate identification of perpetrators as German in several instances throughout the Szabó trilogy is typical of postwar Hungarian discourse on the Occupation.

36. Maurice Halbwachs, "The Social Frameworks of Memory," in *On Collective Memory*, trans. Lewis A. Coser (Chicago: University of Chicago Press, 1992), 37–189. When Halbwachs protested after his Jewish parents-in-law were deported during the Occupation, he was sent to Buchenwald, where he died in 1945.

37. Miklos Radnóti, *Under Gemini, A Prose Memoir and Selected Poetry*, trans. Kenneth and Zita McRobbie and Jascha Kessler (Athens: Ohio University Press, 1985). Radnóti pays tribute to Proust in a poem entitled "A la Recherche."

38. Another influence on *Love Film* is *The Long Voyage*, Jorge Semprun's 1963 autobiographical novel, which also influenced Resnais, in which flashbacks are triggered by a train voyage, but Semprun's train is a deportation train to Auschwitz. Semprun was not a Jew, but Auschwitz provides an indirect link to the Hungarian Jewish Holocaust.

One wonders why train voyages seem to have so much artistic appeal as catalysts of memory. Perhaps the moving images one glimpses through the frames of train windows resemble nothing so much as cinematic flashbacks.

39. The detail of this traditional Hungarian coat suggests a condemnation of Hungarian, not just German, anti-Judaism.

40. See Walker, "Traumatic Paradox." One wonders whether the fact that Szabó was only six years old when he experienced the Holocaust may have heightened the presence of this paradox in his trilogy. Early childhood memories seem to be both more indelible and more distorted than adult memories.

CHAPTER 6. POSTMODERNISM, THE SECOND GENERATION, AND CROSS-CULTURAL POSTTRAUMATIC CINEMA

1. Hal Foster, "Postmodernism: A Preface," in *The Anti-Aesthetic: Essays on Postmodern Culture*, ed. Hal Foster (Port Townsend, Wash.: Bay Press, 1983), xi–xii.

2. Fredric Jameson, "Postmodernism and Consumer Society," *The Anti-Aesthetic*, 116–17.

3. The $23 million figure is cited in Gary Weissman, "A Fantasy of Witnessing," *Media, Culture, and Society* 17 (1995): 297.

4. Ellen S. Fine, "The Absent Memory: The Act of Writing in Post-Holocaust French Literature," in *Writing and the Holocaust*, ed. Berel Lang (New York: Holmes & Meier, 1988), 41–57. I have paraphrased a passage from Elie Wiesel's novel *The Fifth Son*, trans. Marion Wiesel (New York: Warner, 1985), 180: "I suffer from an Event I did not even experience," quoted in the Fine article. Absent memory can, in turn, be thought of as an especially intense manifestation of collective memory, as defined by Maurice Halbwachs.

5. Jameson, "Postmodernism," 125.

6. Ibid., 113–14.

7. I identify *Schindler's List* at least partly with the victims' discourse while acknowledging the paradoxical fact that the film's hero is not a victim but a rescuer.

8. Whereas it is conceivable that Baz Luhrmann considers his film *Moulin Rouge* to be postmodern, it is inconceivable that Spielberg considers *Schindler's List* to be so. On the other hand, the postmodernism of *Schindler's List* is characteristic of Spielberg's entire oeuvre.

9. See Sara R. Horowitz, "But Is It Good for the Jews? Spielberg's Schindler and the Aesthetics of Atrocity," in *Spielberg's Holocaust*, 123.

10. Bryan Cheyette notes Spielberg's consultation with Wajda in his article "The Uncertain Certainty of *Schindler's List*," in *Spielberg's Holocaust*, 230.

11. Quotations of *Citizen Kane* are discussed in Hansen, "*Schindler's List* is not *Shoah*," 97, 102.

12. Cheyette, "Uncertain Certainty," 230, 235–37.

13. The realism/expressionism debate is surveyed in Irving Howe, "Writing and the Holocaust," in *Writing and the Holocaust*, ed. Berel Lang (New York: Holmes & Meier, 1988), 175–99. This debate is carried out in relation to cinema by Ilan Avisar in Chapters 2 and 3 of *Screening the Holocaust*.

14. Rothberg, *Traumatic Realism*, 231. Yosefa Loshitzky wins the spot-the-style-quotation competition, citing German expressionism, Italian neorealism, Second World War newsreels, and CNN news, in her article "Holocaust Others: Spielberg's *Schindler's List* versus Lanzmann's *Shoah*," in *Spielberg's Holocaust*, 109.

15. The Moses reference is noted in Michael André Bernstein, "The *Schindler's List* Effect," *American Scholar* 63, no. 3 (1994): 430.

16. See Marcia Landy, *Cinematic Uses of the Past* (Minneapolis: University of Minnesota Press, 1996), 255.

17. On postmodern nostalgia, see Jameson, "Postmodernism," 116–17. Of Spielberg's use of black and white, Leon Wieseltier commented, "The film is designed to look like a restored print of itself." "Close Encounters of the Nazi Kind," *The New Republic*, 24 January 1994, 42.

18. Information on digital effects comes from a personal interview with Branko Lustig, one of the film's producers, in May 1995.

19. On postmodern high/low mixing, see Jameson, "Postmodernism," 112.

20. For a discussion of *Schindler's List* and capitalism, see Adam Bresnick's "The Six-Billion-Dollar Man," *Times Literary Supplement*, 18 July 1997, 18. As Bresnick notes, the key to the capitalist link between Schindler and Spielberg is Time-Warner mogul Steve Ross, to whom the film is dedicated.

21. Quoted in J. Hoberman, "*Schindler's List*: Myth, Movie, Memory," *Village Voice*, 29 March 1994, 24. The Schindler/Spielberg theme is discussed in Rothberg, *Traumatic Realism*, 223.

22. Hoberman, "*Schindler's List*," 30.

23. See Chapter 2, note 13.

24. This point is made in Loshitzky, "Holocaust Others," 110, Horowitz, "But Is It Good for the Jews?" 123, and Gertrud Koch in Hoberman, "*Schindler's List*," 25.

25. As such, *Schindler's List* is the polar opposite of *The Last Stage*, with its telos of female socialist collective struggle.

26. Rothberg discusses this scene on pp. 237–38 of his book. This postmodern inside/outside game seems to have had a rather uncanny manifestation at another level. When Spielberg was denied permission to film a train entering Birkenau through its iconic arched guardhouse and the Schindler women being unloaded inside, he worked out an ingenious compromise. He got permission to build a replica of the interior ramp area just outside the guardhouse, and then filmed the train exiting the camp through the real arch into the fake ramp area, thus creating a mirror image of Birkenau. See Weissman, "Fantasy," 298–99.

27. Nadine Fresco, "Remembering the Unknown," *International Review of Psycho-Analysis* 11 (1984): 421.

28. Natan P. F. Kellerman, "Psychopathology in Children of Holocaust Survivors: A Review of the Research Literature," *The Israel Journal of Psychiatry and Related Sciences* 1 (2001): 37. Note, however, that the term *vicarious trauma* was not used until 1990.

29. Nanette C. Auerhahn and Dori Laub, "Intergenerational Memory of the Holocaust," in *International Handbook of Multigenerational Legacies of Trauma*, ed. Yael Danieli (New York: Plenum, 1998), 37.

30. Auerhahn and Laub, "Intergenerational Memory," 38.

31. Fresco, "Remembering," 419.

32. Ibid., 422.

33. Ibid., 420.

34. Ibid., 421.

35. Ibid., 423.

36. All of Akerman's films may be relevant, but especially *Les Rendez-vous d'Anna* (1978) and her installation *D'Est* (1995). Ravett's relevant films are *Half Sister* (1985), *Everything's For You* (1989), *In Memory* (1997), and *The March* (1999). A number of other films have been made about the children of Holocaust survivors; I have only mentioned some I have seen that strike me as particularly posttraumatic.

37. On the monumentalist discourse of history, see Friedrich Nietzsche, *The Use and Abuse of History*, trans. Adrian Collins (Indianapolis: Bobbs-Merrill, 1949), 12–17.

38. Laura U. Marks, *The Skin of the Film: Intercultural Cinema, Embodiment, and the Senses* (Durham: Duke University Press, 2000).

39. Rape as a self-contained category is conspicuous in its absence from the book.

40. See Elisabeth Weis, "Family Portraits," *American Film* 1, no. 2 (1975): 54–59; and Michael Renov, "The Subject in History: The New Autobiography in Film and Video," *Afterimage* 17, no. 1 (1989): 4–7.

41. See Paul Arthur, "The Appearance of History in Recent Avant-Garde Film," *Framework* 3 (1989–90): 39–45; Erika Suderburg, "The Electronic Corpse: Notes for an Alternative Language of History and Amnesia," in *Resolutions: Contemporary Video Practices*, ed. Michael Renov and Erika Suderburg (Minneapolis: University of Minnesota Press, 1996), 102–23; and Marita Sturken, "The Politics of Video Memory: Electronic Erasures and Inscriptions," *Resolutions*, 1–12.

42. Kobena Mercer, "Recoding Narratives of Race and Nation," in *Postmodern After-images*, ed. Peter Brooker and Will Brooker (New York: Arnold/St. Martins, 1997), 140–44.

43. *History and Memory* has been much discussed by scholars, some of whom have noted its relations to trauma and postmodernism. Significant contributions are Chapters 1 and 7 of Nichols, *Blurred Boundaries*; Janet Walker, "Traumatic Paradox"; Glen Masato Mimura, "Antidote for Collective Amnesia? Rea Tajiri's Germinal Image," in *Countervisions: Asian American Film Criticism*, ed. Darrell Y. Hamamoto and Sandra Liu (Philadelphia: Temple University Press, 2000), 150–62; and Chapter 1 of Marks, *The Skin of the Film*. Janice Tanaka has also made two experimental videos dealing with second-generation memory of the Japanese

American internment: *Memories From the Department of Amnesia* (1991) and *Who's Going to Pay for These Donuts Anyway* (1992).

44. Fresco, "Remembering," 421.
45. Van der Kolk and van der Hart, "Intrusive Past," 172.
46. Caruth, *Trauma*, 8.

Works Cited

Abzug, Robert H. *Inside the Vicious Heart: Americans and the Liberation of the Nazi Concentration Camps*. New York: Oxford University Press, 1985.

Adorno, Theodor. "Cultural Criticism and Society." In *Prisms*. Trans. Samuel and Shierry Weber. London: Neville Spearman, 1967.

American Psychiatric Association. *Diagnostic and Statistical Manual of Mental Disorders*. 3d ed.-revised. Washington, D.C.: American Psychiatric Association, 1987.

————. *Diagnostic and Statistical Manual of Mental Disorders*. 4th ed. Washington, D.C.: American Psychiatric Association, 1994.

Arad, Yitzhak, ed. *The Pictorial History of the Holocaust*. New York: Macmillan, 1990.

Arthur, Paul. "The Appearance of History in Recent Avant-Garde Film." *Framework* 3 (1989–90): 39–45.

Auerbach, Erich. *Mimesis: The Representation of Reality in Western Literature*. Princeton: Princeton University Press, 1953.

Auerhahn, Nanette C., and Dori Laub. "Intergenerational Memory of the Holocaust." In *International Handbook of Multigenerational Legacies of Trauma*. Ed. Yael Danieli. New York: Plenum, 1998. 21–41.

Avisar, Ilan. "Personal Fears and National Nightmares: The Holocaust Complex in Israeli Cinema." In *Breaking Crystal: Writing and Memory After Auschwitz*. Ed. Efraim Sicher. Urbana: University of Illinois Press, 1998. 137–59.

————. *Screening the Holocaust: Cinema's Images of the Unimaginable*. Bloomington: University of Indiana Press, 1988.

Avni, Ora. "Narrative Subject, Historic Subject: *Shoah* and *La Place de l'Etoile*." *Poetics Today* 12, no. 3 (1991): 495–516.

Barnouw, Erik. *Documentary: A History of the Non-fiction Film*. 2d rev. ed. New York: Oxford University Press, 1993.

Barthes, Roland. *Writing Degree Zero*. Trans. Annette Lavers and Colin Smith. New York: Hill and Wang, 1968.

Bartov, Omer. *Murder in Our Midst: The Holocaust, Industrial Killing, and Representation*. New York: Oxford University Press, 1996.

Becker, Ernest. *Angel in Armor: A Post-Freudian Perspective on the Nature of Man*. New York: George Braziller, 1969.

Benjamin, Walter. "On Some Motifs in Baudelaire." In *Illuminations*. Trans. Harry Zohn. New York: Harcourt, Brace, & World, 1968. 157–202.

————. "The Work of Art in the Age of Mechanical Reproduction." *Film Theory and Criticism*. Ed. Gerald Mast and Marshall Cohen. New York: Oxford University Press, 1979. 848–70.

Berger, James. "Trauma and Literary Theory." *Contemporary Literature* 38, no. 3 (1997): 569–82.

Bernstein, Michael André. "The *Schindler's List* Effect." *American Scholar* 63, no. 3 (1994): 429–32.

Bersani, Leo, and Ulysse Dutoit. *Arts of Impoverishment: Beckett, Rothko, Resnais*. Cambridge, Mass.: Harvard University Press, 1993.

Bettelheim, Bruno. *The Informed Heart: Autonomy in a Mass Age*. Glencoe, Ill.: The Free Press, 1960.

Blanchot, Maurice. "N'oubliez pas!" *La Quinzaine litteraire* 459 (1986).

Bloch, Marc. *The Historians' Craft*. Trans. Peter Putnam. New York: Vintage, 1953.

Bordwell, David. *Making Meaning: Inference and Rhetoric in the Interpretation of Cinema*. Cambridge, Mass.: Harvard University Press, 1989.

Bordwell, David, Janet Staiger, and Kristin Thompson. *The Classical Hollywood Cinema: Film Style and Mode of Production to 1960*. New York: Columbia University Press, 1985.

Braham, Randolph L. "Hungary." In *The World Reacts to the Holocaust*. Ed. David S. Wyman. Baltimore: Johns Hopkins University Press, 1996. 207–23.

————. *The Politics of Genocide: The Holocaust in Hungary*. New York: Columbia University Press, 1981.

Bresnick, Adam. "The Six-Billion-Dollar Man." *Times Literary Supplement*, 18 July 1997, 18–19.

Burton, Julianne. "Democratizing Documentary: Modes of Address in the New Latin American Cinema, 1958–1972." In *The Social Documentary in Latin America*. Ed. Julianne Burton. Pittsburgh: University of Pittsburgh Press, 1990. 49–84.

Caruth, Cathy. *Unclaimed Experience: Trauma, Narrative, and History*. Baltimore: Johns Hopkins University Press, 1996.

Caruth, Cathy, ed. *Trauma: Explorations in Memory*. Baltimore: Johns Hopkins University Press, 1995.

Cayrol, Jean. *Foreign Bodies*. Trans. Richard Howard. New York: G. P. Putnam's Sons, 1960.

————. *Je vivrai l'amour des autres*. Paris: Seuil, 1947–50.

————. *Miroir de la rédemption*. Neuchâtel: Éditions de la Baconnière, 1944.

————. *Poèmes de la nuit et du brouillard*. Paris: Seghers, 1946.

Cheyette, Bryan. "The Uncertain Certainty of *Schindler's List*." In *Spielberg's Holocaust: Critical Perspectives on "Schindler's List"*. Ed. Yosefa Loshitzky. Bloomington: Indiana University Press, 1996. 226–38.

Colombat, André Pierre. *The Holocaust in French Film*. Metuchen, N.J.: Scarecrow, 1993.

Danieli, Yael. "Therapists' Difficulties in Treating Survivors of the Nazi Holocaust and Their Children." Ph.D. diss. New York University, 1981.

Danieli, Yael, ed. *International Handbook of Multigenerational Legacies of Trauma.* New York: Plenum, 1998.

Davies, Mark I., and David M. Clark. "Predictors of Analogue Post-Traumatic Intrusive Cognitions." *Behavioral and Cognitive Psychology* 26 (1998): 303–14.

Dawidowicz, Lucy S. "Visualizing the Warsaw Ghetto." *Shoah: A Review of Holocaust Studies and Commemorations* 1, no. 1 (1978): 5+.

Doneson, Judith. "The Jew as a Female Figure in Holocaust Film." *Shoah: A Review of Holocaust Studies and Commemorations* 1, no. 1 (1978): 11–13, 18.

Duras, Marguerite. *The War: A Memoir.* Trans. Barbara Bray. New York: Pantheon, 1986.

Edelheit, Abraham J., and Hershel Edelheit, eds. *History of the Holocaust: A Handbook and Dictionary.* Boulder: Westview, 1994.

Elsaesser, Thomas. "Postmodernism as Mourning Work." *Screen* 42, no. 2 (2001): 193–201.

———. "Subject Positions, Speaking Positions: From *Holocaust, Our Hitler,* and *Heimat* to *Shoah* and *Schindler's List.*" In *The Persistence of History: Cinema, Television, and the Modernist Event.* Ed. Vivian Sobchack. New York: Routledge, 1996. 145–83.

Felman, Shoshana. "The Return of the Voice: Claude Lanzmann's *Shoah.*" In *Testimony: Crises of Witnessing in Literature, Psychoanalysis, and History.* By Shoshana Felman and Dori Laub. New York: Routledge, 1992. 204–83.

Felman, Shoshana, and Dori Laub. *Testimony: Crises of Witnessing in Literature, Psychoanalysis, and History.* New York: Routledge, 1992.

Fine, Ellen S. "The Absent Memory: The Act of Writing in Post-Holocaust French Literature." In *Writing and the Holocaust.* Ed. Berel Lang. New York: Holmes & Meier, 1988. 41–57.

Foster, Hal. "Postmodernism: A Preface." In *The Anti-Aesthetic: Essays on Postmodern Culture.* Ed. Hal Foster. Port Townsend, Wash.: Bay Press, 1983. ix-xvi.

Francés-Rousseau, Pierre. *Intact aux yeux du monde.* Paris: Hachette, 1987.

Frankel, Fred H. "The Concept of Flashbacks in Historical Perspective." *International Journal of Clinical and Experimental Hypnosis* 42, no. 4 (1994): 321–34.

Frankl, Viktor. *From Death Camp to Existentialism: A Psychiatrist's Path to a New Therapy.* Trans. Ilse Lasch. Boston: Beacon, 1959.

Fresco, Nadine. "Remembering the Unknown." *International Review of Psycho-Analysis* 11 (1984): 417–27.

Freud, Sigmund. *Beyond the Pleasure Principle.* Trans. and ed. James Strachey. London: Hogarth, 1955. Vol. XVIII, *The Standard Edition of the Complete Psychological Works of Sigmund Freud.*

———. *The Interpretation of Dreams.* Trans. and ed. James Strachey. London: Hogarth, 1955. Vols. IV and V, *The Standard Edition of the Complete Psychological Works of Sigmund Freud.*

———. *Moses and Monotheism.* Trans. and ed. James Strachey. London: Hogarth, 1964. Vol. XXIII, *The Standard Edition of the Complete Psychological Works of Sigmund Freud.*

————. *The Psychopathology of Everyday Life*. Trans. and ed. James Strachey. London: Hogarth, 1966. Vol. VI, *The Standard Edition of the Complete Psychological Works of Sigmund Freud*.

————. *Totem and Taboo*. Trans. and ed. James Strachey. London: Hogarth, 1950. Vol. XIII, *The Standard Edition of the Complete Psychological Works of Sigmund Freud*.

Freyer, Ellen. "Chronicle of a Summer—Ten Years After." In *The Documentary Tradition: From Nanook to Woodstock*. Ed. Lewis Jacobs. New York: Hopkinson and Blake, 1971. 437–43.

Friedberg, William. "Nazi Concentration Camp Reactivated For Film." *New York Times*, 20 February 1949, sec. 2: 5.

Friedlander, Saul. *Memory, History, and the Extermination of the Jews of Europe*. Bloomington: Indiana University Press, 1993.

Friedlander, Saul, ed. *Probing the Limits of Representation: Nazism and the "Final Solution."* Cambridge, Mass.: Harvard University Press, 1992.

Galloway, David. *Edward Lewis Wallant*. Boston: Twayne-G. K. Hall, 1979.

Gannon, J. Patrick. "The Traumatic Commercial Film Experience: An Extension of Laboratory Findings on Stress in a Naturalistic Setting." Ph.D. diss. California School of Professional Psychology, 1979.

Genette, Gerard. *Narrative Discourse: An Essay in Method*. Trans. Jane E. Lewin. Ithaca: Cornell University Press, 1980.

Goodwin, Jim. "The Etiology of Combat-Related Post-Traumatic Stress Disorders." In *Post-Traumatic Stress Disorders of the Vietnam Veteran*. Ed. Tom Williams. Cincinnati: Disabled American Veterans, 1980.

Greene, Naomi. *Landscapes of Loss: The National Past in Postwar French Cinema*. Princeton: Princeton University Press, 1999.

Gutman, Israel, ed. *Encyclopedia of the Holocaust*. New York: Macmillan, 1990.

Halbwachs, Maurice. "The Social Frameworks of Memory." In *On Collective Memory*. Trans. Lewis A. Coser. Chicago: University of Chicago Press, 1992. 37–189.

Hallam, Julia, and Margaret Marshment. *Realism and Popular Cinema*. Manchester: Manchester University Press, 2000.

Hansen, Miriam Bratu. "*Schindler's List* is not *Shoah*: The Second Commandment, Popular Modernism, and Public Memory." *Critical Inquiry* 22, no. 2 (1996): 292–312. Reprinted in *Spielberg's Holocaust: Critical Perspectives on Schindler's List*. Ed. Yosefa Loshitzky. Bloomington: Indiana University Press, 1996. 77–103.

Hartman, Geoffrey H. "Holocaust Testimony, Art, and Trauma." In *The Longest Shadow: In the Aftermath of the Holocaust*. Bloomington: Indiana University Press, 1996. 151–72.

————. "On Traumatic Knowledge and Literary Studies." *New Literary History* 26, no. 3 (1995): 537–63.

Higgins, Lynn A. *New Novel, New Wave, New Politics: Fiction and the Representation of History in Postwar France*. Lincoln: University of Nebraska Press, 1996.

Hilberg, Raul. *The Destruction of the European Jews.* New York: Holmes & Meier, 1985.

Hoberman, J. "*Schindler's List*: Myth, Movie, Memory." *Village Voice,* 29 March 1994, 24–31.

———. " 'Shoah': Witness to Annihilation." *Village Voice,* 29 October, 1985, 46.

Horowitz, Mardi J. "Flashbacks: Recurrent Intrusive Images After the Use of LSD." *American Journal of Psychiatry* 126, no. 4 (1969): 565–69.

———. *Image Formation and Psychotherapy.* New York: Jason Aronson, 1983.

———. "Psychic Trauma: Return of Images After a Stress Film." *Archives of General Psychiatry* 20 (1969): 552–59.

Horowitz, Mardi, and Nancy Wilner. "Stress Films, Emotion, and Cognitive Response." *Archives of General Psychiatry* 30 (1976): 1339–44.

Horowitz, Sara R. "But Is It Good for the Jews? Spielberg's Schindler and the Aesthetics of Atrocity." In *Spielberg's Holocaust: Critical Perspectives on "Schindler's List."* Ed. Yosefa Loshitzky. Bloomington: Indiana University Press, 1996. 119–39.

Howe, Irving. "Writing and the Holocaust." In *Writing and the Holocaust.* Ed. Berel Lang. New York: Holmes & Meier, 1988. 175–99.

Hughes, Robert. "*Hiroshima, mon amour*: A Composite Interview with Alain Resnais." In *Film: Book 2; Films of War and Peace.* Ed. Robert Hughes. New York: Grove, 1962. 49–64.

Huyssen, Andreas. "The Politics of Identification: *Holocaust* and West Germany." *New German Critique* 19 (1980): 117–36.

Insdorf, Annette. *Indelible Shadows: Film and the Holocaust.* New York: Cambridge University Press, 1989.

Jameson, Fredric. "Postmodernism and Consumer Society." In *The Anti-Aesthetic: Essays on Postmodern Culture.* Ed. Hal Foster. Port Townsend, Wash.: Bay Press, 1983. 111–25.

Janet, Pierre. *The Major Symptoms of Hysteria.* 2d ed. New York: Macmillan, 1920.

Jewish Film Directory. Westport, Conn.: Greenwood, 1992.

Kaplan, E. Ann. "Melodrama, Cinema, and Trauma." *Screen* 42, no. 2 (2001): 201–5.

Kardiner, Abram. *The Traumatic Neuroses of War.* New York: Paul B. Hoeber-Harper & Brothers, 1941.

Kellerman, Natan P. F. "Psychopathology in Children of Holocaust Survivors: A Review of the Research Literature." *The Israel Journal of Psychiatry and Related Sciences* 1 (2001): 36–46.

Key, Wilson Bryan. *The Clam-Plate Orgy, and Other Subliminals the Media Use to Manipulate Your Behavior.* Englewood Cliffs, N.J.: Prentice Hall, 1980.

Kirmayer, Laurence J. "Landscapes of Memory: Trauma, Narrative, and Dissociation." In *Tense Past: Cultural Essays in Trauma and Memory.* Ed. Paul Antze and Michael Lambek. New York: Routledge, 1996. 173–98.

Knapp, Bettina. *French Novelists Speak Out.* Troy, N.Y.: Whitson, 1976.

Koch, Gertrud. "The Aesthetic Transformation of the Image of the Unimaginable." *October* 48 (1989): 15–24.

———. "The Angel of Forgetfulness and the Black Box of Facticity: Trauma and Memory in Claude Lanzmann's Film *Shoah*." Trans. Ora Wiskind. *History and Memory* 3, no. 1 (1991): 119–32.

Konigsberg, Ira. "*Our Children* and the Limits of Cinema: Early Jewish Responses to the Holocaust." *Film Quarterly* 52, no. 1 (1998): 7–19.

Kosztolányi, Gusztav. "Jewish Life in Hungary, Part One." *Central Europe Review* 2, no. 4 (2000) <*http://www.ce-review.org/00/4/csardas4.html*>.

Krantz, Charles K. "Alain Resnais' *Nuit et Brouillard*: A Historical and Cultural Analysis." *Holocaust Studies Annual* 3 (1985): 107–20.

Kreidl, John Francis. *Alain Resnais*. Boston: Twayne, 1977.

Kristeva, Julia. "The Pain of Sorrow in the Modern World: The Works of Marguerite Duras." *PMLA* 102, no. 2 (1987): 138–52.

Krystal, Henry, ed. *Massive Psychic Trauma*. New York: International Universities Press, 1968.

Krystal, Henry, and William G. Niederland. "Clinical Observations on the Survivor Syndrome." In *Massive Psychic Trauma*. Ed. Henry Krystal. New York: International Universities Press, 1968. 327–48.

LaCapra, Dominick. *History and Memory After Auschwitz*. Ithaca: Cornell University Press, 1998.

———. "Lanzmann's *Shoah*: 'Here There Is No Why.' " *Critical Inquiry* 23, no. 2 (1997): 245–50. Reprinted in LaCapra, *History and Memory After Auschwitz*, 95–138.

———. *Representing the Holocaust: History, Theory, Trauma*. Ithaca: Cornell University Press, 1994.

Landy, Marcia. *Cinematic Uses of the Past*. Minneapolis: University of Minnesota Press, 1996.

Lang, Berel. "The Representation of Limits." In *Probing the Limits of Representation: Nazism and the "Final Solution."* Ed. Saul Friedlander. Cambridge, Mass.: Harvard University Press, 1992. 300–317.

Langer, Lawrence. *Admitting the Holocaust: Collected Essays*. New York: Oxford University Press, 1995.

———. *Holocaust Testimonies: The Ruins of Memory*. New Haven: Yale University Press, 1991.

Lanzmann, Claude. "From the Holocaust to the *Holocaust*." *Telos* 42 (1979–80): 141.

———. "Les Non-lieux de la mémoire." In *Au sujet de "Shoah": Le Film de Claude Lanzmann*. Ed. Michel Deguy. Paris: Belin, 1990.

———. "Seminar With Claude Lanzmann: 11 April 1990." *Yale French Studies* 79 (1991): 82–99.

———. *Shoah: The Complete Text of the Acclaimed Holocaust Film*. New York: Da Capo, 1995.

————. "Why Spielberg Has Distorted the Truth." *Guardian Weekly*, 3 April, 1994, 14.

Laplanche, Jean, and J. B. Pontalis. *The Language of Psycho-analysis*. Trans. Donald Nicholson Smith. New York: W. W. Norton, 1973.

Lazarus, R. S., et al. "A Laboratory Study of Psychological Stress Produced by a Motion Picture Film." *Psychological Monographs* 76 (1962).

Lewis, Roger. "On the Producer." In *Movie People: At Work in the Business of Film*. Ed. Fred Baker. New York: Douglas, 1972. 11–22.

Lewy, Guenter. *The Nazi Persecution of the Gypsies*. New York: Oxford University Press, 2000.

Leyda, Jay. *Films Beget Films*. New York: Hill and Wang, 1964.

Loshitzky, Yosefa. "Holocaust Others: Spielberg's *Schindler's List* versus Lanzmann's *Shoah*." In *Spielberg's Holocaust: Critical Perspectives on "Schindler's List*." Ed. Yosefa Loshitzky. Bloomington: Indiana University Press, 1996. 104–18.

Losson, Nicolas. "Notes on the Images of the Camps." Trans. Annette Michelson. *October* 90 (1999): 25–35.

Louvish, Simon. "Spielberg's Apocalypse." *Sight & Sound* 4, no. 3 (1994): 12–15.

Lumet, Sidney. "Keep Them on the Hook." *Films and Filming* 11, no. 1 (1964): 19–20.

MacCann, Lisa, and Laurie Anne Pearlman, "Vicarious Traumatization: A Framework for Understanding the Psychological Effects of Working with Victims." *Journal of Traumatic Stress* 3, no. 1 (1990): 131–49.

Marks, Laura U. *The Skin of the Film: Intercultural Cinema, Embodiment, and the Senses*. Durham: Duke University Press, 2000.

Maslin, Janet. " 'Meeting Venus' Sings of Politics." *New York Times*, 10 November 1991, sec. 2, 17–18.

Mehlman, Jeffrey. *Legacies of Anti-Semitism in France*. Minneapolis: University of Minnesota Press, 1983.

Mellman, Thomas A., and Glenn C. Davis. "Combat-Related Flashbacks in Post-traumatic Stress Disorder: Phenomenology and Similarity to Panic Attacks." *Journal of Clinical Psychiatry* 46, no. 9 (1985): 379–32.

Mercer, Kobena. "Recoding Narratives of Race and Nation." In *Postmodern Afterimages*. Ed. Peter Brooker and Will Brooker. New York: Arnold/St. Martins, 1997. 129–45.

Merritt, Russell L. "Mr. Griffith, *The Painted Lady*, and the Distractive Frame." *Image* [Rochester] 19, no. 4 (1976): 26–30.

Metz, Christian. *The Imaginary Signifier: Psychoanalysis and the Cinema*. Trans. Celia Britton, Annwyl Williams, Ben Brewster, and Alfred Guzzetti. Bloomington: Indiana University Press, 1975–82.

Mimura, Glen Masato. "Antidote for Collective Amnesia? Rea Tajiri's Germinal Image." In *Countervisions: Asian American Film Criticism*. Ed. Darrell Y. Hamamoto and Sandra Liu. Philadelphia: Temple University Press, 2000. 150–62.

Monaco, James. *Alain Resnais*. New York: Oxford University Press, 1979.

Mulvey, Laura. "Visual Pleasure and Narrative Cinema." In *Movies and Methods*. Ed. Bill Nichols. Vol. 2. Berkeley: University of California Press, 1985. 303–15.

Münsterberg, Hugo. *The Film: A Psychological Study*. New York: Dover, 1970 [1916].

Nichols, Bill. *Blurred Boundaries: Questions of Meaning in Contemporary Culture*. Bloomington: Indiana University Press, 1994.

———. *Representing Reality: Issues and Concepts in Documentary*. Bloomington: Indiana University Press, 1991.

Niederland, William G. "An Interpretation of the Psychological Stresses and Defenses in Concentration Camp Life and the Late Aftereffects." In *Massive Psychic Trauma*. Ed. Henry Krystal. New York: International Universities Press, 1968. 60–70.

Nietzsche, Friedrich. *On the Genealogy of Morals*. Trans. Walter Kaufmann and R. J. Hollingdale. New York: Vintage, 1989.

———. *The Use and Abuse of History*. Trans. Adrian Collins. Indianapolis: Bobbs-Merrill, 1949.

Ozsvath, Zsuzsanna. "Can Words Kill? Anti-Semitic Texts and Their Impact on the Hungarian Jewish Catastrophe." In *The Holocaust in Hungary: Fifty Years Later*. Ed. Randolph L. Braham and Attila Pok. New York: Columbia University Press, 1997. 79–116.

Packard, Vance Oakley. *The Hidden Persuaders*. New York: D. McKay, 1957.

Paul, David. "Szabó." In *Five Filmmakers*. Ed. Daniel J. Goulding. Bloomington: Indiana University Press, 1994. 156–208.

Plantinga, Carl R. *Rhetoric and Representation in Nonfiction Film*. New York: Cambridge University Press, 1997.

Polanski, Roman. *Roman*. New York: William Morrow, 1984.

Prédal, René. *Alain Resnais*. Paris: Minard, 1968.

Proust, Marcel. *Remembrance of Things Past*. Trans. C. K. Scott Moncrieff, Terence Kilmartin, and Andreas Mayor. New York: Vintage, 1981.

Prouty, Richard. "The Well-Furnished Interior of the Masses: Kirsanoff's *Menilmontant* and the Streets of Paris." *Cinema Journal* 36, no. 1 (1996): 3–17.

Rabinowitz, Paula. *They Must Be Represented: The Politics of Documentary*. New York: Verso, 1994.

Radnóti, Miklos. *Under Gemini, A Prose Memoir and Selected Poetry*. Trans. Kenneth and Zita McRobbie and Jascha Kessler. Athens: Ohio University Press, 1985.

Radstone, Susannah. "Trauma and Screen Studies: Opening the Debate." *Screen* 42, no. 2 (2001): 188–93.

Raskin, Richard. *Nuit et Brouillard by Alain Resnais: On the Making, Reception, and Functions of a Major Documentary Film*. Aarhus, Denmark: Aarhus University Press, 1987.

Rauch, Angelika. "Post-Traumatic Hermeneutics: Melancholia in the Wake of Trauma." *Diacritics* 28, no. 4 (1998): 111–20.

Renov, Michael. "The Subject in History: The New Autobiography in Film and Video." *Afterimage* 17, no. 1 (1989): 4–7.

Robbe-Grillet, Alain. "Alain Robbe-Grillet." In *Three Decades of the French New Novel.* Ed. Lois Oppenheim. Urbana: University of Illinois Press, 1986.

Rosenblum, Ralph, and Robert Karen. *When the Shooting Stops . . . The Cutting Begins.* New York: Viking, 1979.

Rothberg, Michael. *Traumatic Realism: The Demands of Holocaust Representation.* Minneapolis: University of Minnesota Press, 2000.

Rousso, Henry. *The Vichy Syndrome: History and Memory in France Since 1944.* Cambridge, Mass.: Harvard University Press, 1991.

Santner, Eric. "History Beyond the Pleasure Principle: Some Thoughts on the Representation of Trauma." In *Probing the Limits of Representation: Nazism and the "Final Solution."* Ed. Saul Friedlander. Cambridge, Mass.: Harvard University Press, 1992, 143–54.

———. *Stranded Objects: Mourning, Memory, and Film in Post-war Germany.* Ithaca: Cornell University Press, 1990.

Scarry, Elaine. *The Body in Pain: The Making and Unmaking of the World.* New York: Oxford University Press, 1985.

Schaeffer, Susan Fromberg. *Anya.* New York: Macmillan, 1974.

Semprun, Jorge. *The Long Voyage.* Trans. Richard Seaver. New York: Grove, 1964.

Short, K.R.M., and Stephan Dolezel. *Hitler's Fall: The Newsreel Witness.* New York: Croon Helm, 1988.

Silverman, Kaja. "Historical Trauma and Male Subjectivity." In *Psychoanalysis and Cinema.* Ed. E. Ann Kaplan. New York: Routledge, 1990. 110–27. Reprinted in *Male Subjectivity at the Margins.* By Kaja Silverman. New York: Routledge, 1992.

Sobchack, Vivian. "Inscribing Ethical Space: Ten Propositions on Death, Representation, and Documentary." *Quarterly Review of Film Studies* 9, no. 4 (1984): 283–300.

Sontag, Susan. *On Photography.* New York: Anchor, 1990.

Spiegelman, Art. *Maus: A Survivor's Tale.* New York: Pantheon, 1986.

———. *Maus: A Survivor's Tale II: And Here My Troubles Began.* New York: Pantheon, 1991.

Stam, Robert, Robert Burgoyne, and Sandy Flitterman-Lewis, eds. *New Vocabularies in Film Semiotics.* New York: Routledge, 1992.

Sturken, Marita. "The Politics of Video Memory: Electronic Erasures and Inscriptions." In *Resolutions: Contemporary Video Practices.* Ed. Michael Renov and Erika Suderburg. Minneapolis: University of Minnesota Press, 1996. 1–12.

Suderburg, Erika. "The Electronic Corpse: Notes for an Alternative Language of History and Amnesia." In *Resolutions: Contemporary Video Practices.* Ed. Michael Renov and Erika Suderburg. Minneapolis: University of Minnesota Press, 1996. 102–23.

Truffaut, François. "Rencontre avec Alain Resnais." *Arts et Spectacles*, 22 Febru-ary, 1956, 5. Reprinted in *Nuit et Brouillard by Alain Resnais: On the Making, Reception, and Functions of a Major Documentary Film*. Ed. Richard Raskin. Aarhus, Denmark: Aarhus University Press, 1987. 138.

Tugend, Tom. "Szabó's Challenges of History." *The Jerusalem Post Internet Edition*, 11 July 2000, *http://www.jpost.com/Editions/20006/29/Culture/Culture News.8949.html* >.

Turim, Maureen. *Flashbacks in Film: Memory and History*. New York: Routledge, 1989.

———. "The Trauma of History: Flashbacks Upon Flashbacks." *Screen* 42, no. 2 (2001): 205–10.

Van der Kolk, Bessel, and Onno van der Hart. "The Intrusive Past: The Flexi-bility of Memory and the Engraving of Trauma." In *Trauma: Explorations in Memory*. Ed. Cathy Caruth. Baltimore: Johns Hopkins University Press, 1995.

Virilio, Paul. *War and Cinema*. Trans. Patrick Camiller. New York: Verso, 1989.

Walker, Janet. "The Traumatic Paradox: Documentary Films, Historical Fictions and Cataclysmic Past Events." *Signs* 22, no. 4 (1997): 803–25.

Wallant, Edward Lewis. *The Pawnbroker*. New York: Harcourt Brace Jovanovich, 1961.

———. "The Artist's Eyesight." In *Teacher's Notebook in English*. New York: Har-court, Brace & World School Department, 1963.

Weinberg, David. "France." In *The World Reacts to the Holocaust*. Ed. David S. Wyman. Baltimore: Johns Hopkins University Press, 1996. 3–44.

Weis, Elisabeth. "Family Portraits." *American Film* 1, no. 2 (1975): 54–59.

Weissman, Gary. "A Fantasy of Witnessing." *Media, Culture, and Society* 17 (1995): 293–307.

Weschler, Lawrence. "Artist in Exile." *The New Yorker*, 5 December 1994, 88–106.

White, Hayden. *The Content of the Form: Narrative Discourse and Historical Repre-sentation*. Baltimore: John Hopkins University Press, 1987.

———. "Historical Emplotment and the Problem of Truth." In *Probing the Limits of Representation: Nazism and the "Final Solution."* Ed. Saul Friedlander. Cam-bridge, Mass.: Harvard University Press, 1992. 37–53.

Wiesel, Elie. *The Fifth Son*. Trans. Marion Wiesel. New York: Warner, 1985.

———. *A Jew Today*. Trans. Marion Wiesel. New York: Random House, 1978.

———. *Night*. Trans. Stella Rodway. New York: Bantam, 1986.

———. "Trivializing the Holocaust: Semi-Fact and Semi-Fiction." *New York Times*, 16 April 1978, sec. 2: 1+.

Wieseltier, Leon. "Close Encounters of the Nazi Kind." *The New Republic*, 24 Jan-uary 1994, 42.

Wieviorka, Anne. "On Testimony." In *Holocaust Remembrance: The Shapes of Mem-ory*. Ed. Geoffrey H. Hartman. Cambridge, Mass.: Blackwell, 1994. 23–32.

Williams, Linda. "Mirrors Without Memories: Truth, History, and the New Doc-umentary." *Film Quarterly* 46, no. 3 (1993): 9–21.

Wollen, Peter. *Signs and Meaning in the Cinema*. 3d ed. Bloomington: Indiana University Press, 1972.

Woolf, Virginia. *To the Lighthouse*. New York: Harcourt, Brace & World, 1927.

Wormser, Olga, and Henri Michel, eds. *Tragédie de la déportation 1940–1945: Témoignages de survivants des camps de concentration allemands*. Paris: Hachette, 1955.

Young, James. *Writing and Rewriting the Holocaust: Narrative and the Consequences of Interpretation*. Bloomington: Indiana University Press, 1988.

Index

Index 207